1956

CAGLIOSTRO

HOUDON'S BUST OF CAGLIOSTRO

CARDINAL DE ROHAN

(*From an old French print*)

SERAPHINIA FELICHIANI,
COMTESSE DE CAGLIOSTRO.

(*From a very rare French print*)

ADAMWEISHAVPT.

(After Mansinger)

THEVENEAU DE MORANDE

PHILIP JAMES DE LOUTHERBOURG

Count Cagliostro

Savant or scoundrel? The true role

of this splendid, tragic figure

CAGLIOSTRO

by

W. R. H. Trowbridge

UNIVERSITY BOOKS   *New Hyde Park, New York*

MANUFACTURED IN THE UNITED STATES OF AMERICA

CONTENTS

INTRODUCTION

by JOHN C. WILSON

Few names are more important in the history of psychical phenomena than that of Cagliostro. He figures as one of the great pioneers in every serious account of hypnotism and telepathy, magic and alchemy, precognition and spiritualism, psychic healing and modern mysticism. Yet the simplest facts about his life and his teachings remain bitterly disputed now, two hundred years after he was born.

Almost his only defenders are occult writers who, in reaction against his detractors, make exaggerated claims for him, but who correctly see his great role as a pioneer in psychical phenomena and revere him as a martyr at the hands of monarchical and papal tyranny. Most of the written records, however, regard Cagliostro as a charlatan and an impostor, perpetuating the historian Carlyle's attack upon him as the "Prince of Quacks." Most of us, I confess, would find it hard to choose between Madame Blavatsky's wild claims that he was still living in her father's house thirty years after his death and the latest editions of the *Encyclopedia Britannica* and *Columbia Encyclopedia,* which still attribute to him the patently false biographical details which were invented for him by his monarchical and papal persecutors.

The great value of this book, W. R. H. Trowbridge's CAGLIOSTRO, is that it gives us a solid foundation of fact; for anyone free to see the truth without prejudice, Trowbridge destroys for all time the frameup against Cagliostro. Trowbridge's book is perhaps even more important because Trowbridge himself is quite unsympathetic toward occultism and psychical phenomena. It is clear that he thinks that the Egyptian rite of Freemasonry, to which Cagliostro devoted

Introduction

his life and for which the Inquisition destroyed him, is nothing but mumbo-jumbo, so that he finds it hard to understand, except as a kind of aberration. But Trowbridge the historian, the indefatigable digger in the French archives, has made it impossible for any conscientious foe of Cagliostro to repeat the old calumnies.

Cagliostro first appears in recorded history at the age of 28 in 1776 in London. He dies at the age of 47 in 1795 in the hands of the Holy Roman Inquisition. His public life is thus only 19 years. A considerable number of these, too, are in impenetrable obscurity. It is quite true that Cagliostro seemed to delight in clothing in mystery everything connected with his life. Trowbridge's account, however, makes it very plain to us that the mystery was primarily not a matter of affectation, but a matter of life and death. To put it quite simply, Cagliostro was a secret revolutionary and his head was at stake if the kings and the cardinals knew what his life work really was. To the end, he could never safely explain the source of the great wealth in which he lived and which he expended so generously. After nine dreadful months in the Bastille, thanks to the animus of Marie Antoinette against his friend and protector Cardinal Rohan, Cagliostro had to explain to the French Parliament, which sat as the Court, how he lived:

"But your manner of living is expensive; you give away much, and accept of nothing in return; you pay everybody; how do you contrive to get money?"

Under the real circumstances, his answer could not but sound like mystification and bombast. He answered: "What difference does it make whether I am the son of a monarch or a beggar, or by what means I procure the money I want, as long as I regard religion and the laws and pay everyone his due? I have always taken a pleasure in refusing to gratify the public curiosity on this score. Nevertheless I will condescend to tell you that which I have never revealed to anyone before. The principal resource I have to boast of is that as soon as I set foot in any country I find there a banker who supplies me with everything I want. For instance, M. Sarazin,

Introduction

of Bâle, would give me up his whole fortune were I to ask it. So would M. Sancotar at Lyons."

This is the closest that Cagliostro came to admitting the source of his wealth. The bankers he named were close friends and one, the Swiss Sarazin, was particularly devoted to Cagliostro, whose psychic healing had succeeded in making him and his wife parents late in life. But the main point is that these were the bankers of European Freemasonry and it was as the paymasters of the movement that they supplied Cagliostro with unlimited funds.

There does remain to this day the mystery of Cagliostro's origins. I think that any fair-minded reader will agree that Trowbridge knocks into a cocked hat the long-standing story, first circulated by Marie Antoinette's agents and the Inquisition, then endlessly repeated by historians of great reputation like Carlyle and Funck-Brentano, of the low birth of Cagliostro as one Giuseppe Balsamo, a Sicilian criminal and adventurer.* Trowbridge has, however, no authenticated story to take its place. Certainly there are no documents to be found to prove Cagliostro's own story, which he never told until 1786, and then only because he was in the Bastille about to go on trial before the French Parliament and could not hope to go free without answering the presumably simple question of what his real name was, where he was born, and where he grew up. Cagliostro was acquitted. But the French Parliament roared with laughter at his story of his origins. It became one of the hilarious jokes of the age and one of the main factors in convincing people that he was a charlatan and an adventurer. No wonder! Like all great myths, it begins with the statement that he has never been able to find out who his real parents are. His childhood years are spent in the city of Medina in Arabia, waited upon by servants and a governor, who is an adept. They go to Mecca, and to Malta, where the Grand Master of the Knights of Malta

---

*Trowbridge's proof has not, however, prevented later biographers (Trowbridge originally wrote in 1910) from repeating the discredited Balsamo story. Frank King (1929) and Michael Harrison (1942) repeat it, utterly without proof.

Introduction

provides them with sumptuous living quarters and where his governor now appears in a clerical dress with the insignia of the Order of Malta. And so on.

Only after the reader has completed this book will he understand that, if you want to hazard a hypothesis, there is no serious alternative to accepting the biography which Cagliostro supplied to the French Parliament. There is an indirect indication which I find of particular interest. We know well enough Cagliostro's source of wealth once he became a leader of the Freemasons of France and Germany. Yet he begins his public life at the age of 28 in London, where he first joins the Freemasons, but is already living as a nobleman in high style, with his beautiful wife covered with jewels. It is a time in London when foreign noblemen are fair game for thieves and scoundrels, and lawyers and bailiffs. It cost the Count and Countess Cagliostro a great deal of money to live and to extricate themselves. Where did these funds come from? The discredited story that they were really the Sicilian thieves named Balsamo, and what they could not steal was provided by selling Madame Cagliostro's favors, becomes quite ridiculous when one adds up the sums Trowbridge shows they spent in London. How little it cost to buy the favors of beautiful women in London and elsewhere at this time, we know from Boswell and (a little later) from Byron. In the end, we are left with the fantastic but really more plausible statement of Cagliostro that these were the last of the funds supplied him by the Grand Master of the Order of Malta.

Trowbridge's book, let us remember once more, is written by a conscientious historian who knows little or nothing about psychical phenomena. Trowbridge does not grasp the inner connection in the 18th century between occultism and Freemasonry; it was the philosophy of those who opened themselves to all knowledge without regard to church and state, and who therefore opposed the absolute monarchies and papal tyranny of the time. Too often, Trowbridge seems to think that Cagliostro's vanity drove him to exhibitions of occult powers and fails to understand that all this was like a

Introduction

secret password, and that as excitement about Cagliostro's séances spread through each new country that he visited, it brought to his side the Freemasons of that country and those who would be Freemasons.

It is enough, and more than enough, that Trowbridge has dug in the unpublished materials of the French archives and has overthrown the 150 year old story which identified Cagliostro with the Sicilian thief, Balsamo. It is manifest that Trowbridge did so with no ulterior ideological motives in mind. He is neither a fellow occultist or fellow Mason. He does share Cagliostro's hatred of absolute monarchies and papal tyranny, but he abhors the secret revolutionary weapons that Cagliostro employed against them. All this makes Trowbridge's testimony for Cagliostro the more valuable.

It would be pleasant to be able to advise the reader where he could supplement Trowbridge's work with a rounded picture of the history of Freemasonry and occultism in Cagliostro's time. Unfortunately, the larger story is no less obscure, complicated and controversial than the story of Cagliostro. The one scholar to whom I can refer the reader at all is Arthur Edward Waite, whose studies in the history of occultism and Freemasonry in the 17th and 18th centuries remain the best. The reader who wants to understand the origins of Freemasonry, and its temporary but profound connection with occultism in the 18th century, can best do so in two large works of Waite: *The Secret Tradition in Freemasonry* (1911) and *A New Encyclopaedia of Freemasonry* (2 vols., 1930) .

It is abundantly clear from these works why Cagliostro was triumphant in European Freemasonry, but not among the English Freemasons. In England Freemasonry remained within the limits of Christianity and monarchism. England was no longer an absolute monarchy and had broken with Rome. Whatever needs were filled by English Masonry, they were not those of the European Freemasonry of the time. Two great needs sought expression through European Freemasonry. Both were abhorred by the absolute state and therefore were compelled to seek secret pathways.

Introduction

One need was a broader and more variegated spiritual path than that of the absolute church. The principal forms that this took are summed up unsympathetically but accurately by Waite:

"The occult movements, sometimes tinged with Mysticism, which originated in Germany at the close of the sixteenth century and thence passed into England, found their final field in France at the period in question. There Rosicrucians reappeared; there Anton Mesmer restored and made public an important elementary process of psychic practice; there the Marquis de Puységur discovered clairvoyance; there Martines de Pasqually instructed his disciples in a most remarkable variant of ceremonial magic; there the illustrious Saint-Martin, *le philosophe inconnu,* developed his metaphysics of spiritual rëintegration; there the central doctrine of inward life took possession of some great minds within the fold of the Gallican church; there alchemy flourished; there both spiritual and political princes sought after an elixir of life; there also rose up a line of magnificent impostors who posed as initiates of occult sciences, as possessors of the Great Secret and Grand Magisterium; and there in consequence the Higher Mysteries — real or alleged — of Emblematic Masonry took root and grew and flourished, developing an hundred splendors of romantic legends, of sonorous names and titles. In a word, the quixotic side of all metaphysical invention concentrated its forces at Paris and Lyons, gathering under the shadow of the Square and Compasses — a natural centre to which they all gravitated, from which they all worked" *(Encyclopaedia,* Vol. II, pp. 202-203).

In this atmosphere combining occultism and Freemasonry, Cagliostro had his great successes, in contrast to England. Waite says elsewhere:

"The Egyptian Rite, which Cagliostro had invented or acquired . . . was unsuited to the frigid imaginations and meagre wit of the laidly Georgian epoch in England. In the principality of Courland, at Strasbourg, Bordeaux and Lyons he attained, however, an immense if transient triumph. But his crowning ambition was 'to inaugurate a Mother-Lodge at

Introduction

Paris, to which Masonry should be subordinated entirely,' and for this purpose he proclaimed himself the bearer of the Mysteries of Isis and Anubis from the Far East. He spared no pains: all his devices and inventions were shaped with some reference ultimately to this end. His career has been represented as one of untinctured imposture, but it is precisely one of those cases in which an unbiased judgment was at all times difficult to give, and new considerations have arisen which deserve a serious hearing, as we shall see.

"Much of the testimony against him was made public by the Roman Inquisition, a source from which the sense of historical justice might demand an appeal with reason. In any case, he intoxicated Paris and Strasbourg; he had an illustrious cardinal of the period for his humble admirer; and — to serve only as an instance of things said and reported — there is the fabulous affirmation that Louis XVI once notified that anyone who molested Cagliostro should be held guilty of treason. There were other rumors, and none of them can be taken seriously; but over his Egyptian Freemasonry even Cagliostro was serious, while as regards the mendacity of his claims they were not more glaring and were assuredly far more attractive than those which had been made previously in respect of every system and every bunch of Degrees, from the time when Anderson first forged credentials for the Craft itself in his Book of Constitutions" *(Encyclopaedia,* Vol. 1, pp. 90-91) .

The second great need served by European Freemasonry was the need for freedom of political thought and action. As the reader will see, when the Holy Roman Inquisition condemns Cagliostro, it was this political role of Freemasonry that most concerned the papal authority. The first Papal Bull against Freemansonry, that of Pope Clement XII, dated April 28, 1738, is concerned because men of various religions and sects join secretly together in a Masonic lodge. The second Bull, that of Pope Benedict XIV, dated May 18, 1751, considers Freemasonry a challenge to the authority of both Church and State. To some, the libertarian role of Freemasonry in this period has been obscured by the presence of

Introduction

royal dukes and other great aristocrats in the leadership of the Freemasons. Thus in 1771 the Duc de Chartres, who was subsequently Duc de Lyons, became Grand Master. But this Duke was Philippe Egalité, typical of the anti-absolutist nobility who sympathized with the first stages of the French Revolution. Behind their protective backs, financed by Swiss and German bankers, Cagliostro and his associates did the spadework of the coming revolution. I should warn the reader whom I have referred to Waite's works on Freemasonry that for this revolutionary role that it played he has no sympathy and little understanding. That is why he respects Trowbridge's findings in favor of Cagliostro, and conscientiously reports them, but cannot quite accept them. Today, after the Moscow trials, after the "big lies" of Hitler and Stalin, we can understand better than the relatively peaceful nineteenth century the bold lies made out of whole cloth launched against Cagliostro by absolutist church and state. Where there is smoke there is fire, says the eternal Philistine, ever fearful and respectful of constituted law and order. But we have learned that the smoke of Cagliostro and the hell-fire of his enemies belong to two different worlds. Nor has the Philistine been misled only by monarchical and papal lies. Beyond this, there was and remains the Philistine hatred of occultism and psychical research. This hatred has its continued reason for being. The National Council of the Churches of Christ in the United States neither has nor desires the instruments of the Inquisition, but is quite equally opposed to psychical research which, after all the polite things have been said, cannot be reconciled with any particular revealed religion.

The poor, martyred Cagliostro remains the abhorred enemy of church and state. That is why, except for the unusually conscientious historian, and his minority of readers, Cagliostro continues to get such a bad press.

NOTE

A. E. Waite's Criticisms of Trowbridge's Cagliostro

"... Until a few years since it was accepted implicitly that Count Cagliostro was Guiseppe Balsamo, a Sicilian rogue born at Palermo, who perambulated Europe, and even visited London in the course of his career. However, in the year 1910 Trowbridge succeeded in casting a certain doubt on the identification by an elaborate and interesting study of the evidence at large. This is no place in which to attempt a criticism of his findings, and I register only at its value the personal conclusion that his argument against the identity is not altogether satisfactory, so that the question remains open, with nothing whatever attaching to it for the purpose of the present work. It will be sufficient to say that in place of antecedents that are known on the Balsamo hypothesis, Trowbridge produces Cagliostro in London, accompanied by his wife, in the summer of 1776, having liberal means for the moment, but with a cloud of darkness behind them in respect of their past, especially that of the Count. On the whole I consider that Trowbridge in the part of an intelligent and engaging apologist does much better service to his subject by the independent light which he casts upon his later history. It is not that he has discovered any new and unlooked-for facts, but he encourages us to regard the Magus under a fresh and more favorable aspect.

"While the work mentioned is a real contribution to our knowledge, it is open in accessory matters to serious correction. The author is not a Freemason and — among many

Note

other points — he does not seem to realize the absurdity of a periodical called *Courier de L'Europe,* when it spoke ... of the Count's Initiation in London by an alleged Espérance Lodge together with his wife. Whether such a Lodge existed at the period I do not know; that, if so, it was affiliated with the *Rite of the Strict Observance* I do not believe; but there neither was then nor is now any warranted Lodge in England which would have received a woman, and the *Strict Observance* was about the last Masonic Obedience against which the accusation could be brought.

"From other sources Trowbridge derived errors of fact in respect of Louis Claude de Saint-Martin, and I question whether he consulted any authority posterior to Matter. He can have never seen *Des Erreurs et de la Vérité,* the first work of the French mystic, two volumes octavo — respectively pp. 230 and 236 — or he could scarcely describe it as 'a strange little book.' He can neither have read nor seen Saint-Martin's later writings, or he could not have affirmed that Liberty, Equality and Fraternity were the sacred triad of the mystic. He could know nothing of his life and his attitude towards external secret societies, or he would not have reproduced the old fable that Saint-Martin established a Masonic Rite, above all a *Rite of Swedenborg,* about whom he has left a very definite statement of opinion. He would not in fine have called him the founder of the Martinists: this is another fiction, which has been exploded long ago. Similar exception must be taken to every Rosicrucian reference which occurs in the memoir. The members of this Fraternity did not revolutionize belief in the supernatural; their first manifesto did not claim to have been found in the tomb of Christian Rosenkreutz; the so-called doctrine of Elementary Spirits was the least part of their concern, the Abbé de Villars being responsible in the *Comte de Gabalis* for its great popularity, he writing a century and a half later and deriving from Paracelsus; they did not regard the Philosopher's Stone as signifying contentment; and their impostures, real or alleged, in no sense led up to the Masonic Convention at Wilhelmsbad, which was called by the Grand Master of the *Strict*

Note

Observance. At that period they were working under a Masonic aegis and their Secret Rituals are in my possession. Lastly, in respect of Alchemy, if Trowbridge in his brief review and in his casual references had made a starting-point in the collections of Byzantine, Syrian and Arabian alchemists published by Berthelot, he would have given us a more informed account, and his allusion to Geber would have appeared in another form. The fact that there was a mystical as well as a physical school in Alchemy might still have escaped him, but this is an involved subject" (*Encyclopaedia of Freemasonry*, Vol. I, pp. 91-93).

PREFACE

THOUGH much has been written about Cagliostro, most of it is confined to articles in encyclopedias and magazines, or to descriptive paragraphs in works dealing with magic, freemasonry and the period in which he lived.[1]   This material may be described as a footnote which has been raised to the dignity of a page of history.   It is based on contemporary records inspired by envy, hatred and contempt in an age notoriously passionate, revengeful and unscrupulous. It is, moreover, extremely superficial, being merely a repetition of information obtained second-hand by compilers apparently too ignorant or too lazy to make their own investigations.   Even M. Funck-Brentano, whose brilliant historical monographs have earned him a deservedly high reputation, is not to be relied upon. In the sequel [2] to his entertaining account of the affair of the Diamond Necklace, the brief chapter he devotes to Cagliostro contains so many inaccuracies as to suggest that, like the majority of his predecessors, he was content to impart his information without previously taking the trouble to examine the sources from which it was derived.

It has been said that every book on Cagliostro

[1] Prior to the present volume no complete biography of Cagliostro has been published in English.

[2] *La Mort de la Reine : Les suites de l'affaire du collier*. Translated into English under the title of *Cagliostro and Company*.

Preface

must be a book *against* him. With this opinion I totally disagree. In choosing Cagliostro as the subject of an historical memoir I was guided at first, I admit, by the belief that he was the arch-impostor he is popularly supposed to be. With his mystery, magic, and highly sensational career he seemed just the sort of picturesque personality I was in search of. The moment, however, I began to make my researches I was astonished to find how little foundation there was in point of *fact* for the popular conception. The deeper I went into the subject—how deep this has been the reader may gather from the Bibliography, which contains but a portion of the material I have sifted—the more convinced I became of the fallacy of this conception. Under such circumstances there seemed but two alternatives open to me : either to abandon the subject altogether as unsuited for the purpose I had in view, or to follow the line of least resistance and, dishonestly adhering to the old method, which from custom had almost become *de rigueur*, help to perpetuate an impression I believed to be unfounded and unjust.

On reflection I have adopted neither course. Irritation caused by the ignorance and carelessness of the so-called " authorities " awoke a fresh and unexpected interest in their victim ; and I decided to stick to the subject I had chosen and treat it for the first time honestly. As Baron de Gleichen says in his *Souvenirs*, " Enough ill has been said of Cagliostro. I intend to speak well of him, because I think this is always preferable providing one can, and at least I shall not bore the reader by repeating what he has already heard."

Preface

Such a statement made in connection with such a character as Cagliostro is popularly supposed to be will, no doubt, expose me to the charge of having "whitewashed" him. This, however, I emphatically deny. "Whitewashing," as I understand this term, is a plausible attempt to portray base or detestable characters as worthy of esteem by palliating their vices and attributing noble motives to their crimes. This manner of treating historical figures is certainly not one of which I can be accused, as those who may have read previous biographical books of mine will admit. Whatever sympathy for Cagliostro my researches may have evoked it has always been exceeded by contempt of those who, combining an unreasoning prejudice with a slovenly system of compilation, have repeated the old charges against him with parrot-like stupidity. The object of this book is not so much an attempt to vindicate Cagliostro as to correct and revise, if possible, what I believe to be a false judgment of history.

W. R. H. TROWBRIDGE

London, August 1910.

BIBLIOGRAPHY

THE books and documents relating to Cagliostro are very numerous. Their value, however, is so questionable that in making a critical choice it is extremely difficult to avoid including many that are worthless.

In the French Archives:

A *dossier* entitled *Documents à l'aide desquels la police de Paris a cherché à établir, lors du procès du Collier, que Cagliostro n'était autre qu'un aventurier nommé Joseph Balsamo, qui avait déjà séjourné à Paris en 1772*:

Lettre adressée par un anonyme au commissaire Fontaine, remise de Palerme, le 2 Nov., 1786.

Plainte adressée à M. de Sartine par J. Balsamo contre sa femme.

Ordre de M. de Sartine au commissaire Fontaine de dresser procès-verbal de la capture de la dame Balsamo, 23 Janvier, 1773.

Procès-verbal de capture de la dame Balsamo, 1 Fevrier, 1773.

Interrogatoire de la dame Balsamo, 20 Fevrier, 1773.

Rapport au Ministre.

The above have also been printed in full in Emile Campardon's *Marie Antoinette et le Procès du Collier*.

The following documents are unprinted:

Procès-verbal de capture des sieur et dame Cagliostro.

Procès-verbal de perquisition fait par le commissaire Chesnon le 23 Aôut, 1785, chez le sieur Cagliostro.

Interrogatoire de Cagliostro le 30 Janvier, 1786.

Bibliography

In the French Archives (*continued*):

Minute des confrontations des témoins de Cagliostro.

Procès-verbal de la remise faite à Cagliostro, lors de sa mise en liberté, des effets saisis à son domicile le jour de sa mise en état d'arrestation.

Journal du libraire Hardy.

Copie d'une lettre écrite de Londres par un officier français remise á Paris le 19 Juillet 1786.

Lettre au peuple français.

Published Works:

Vie de Joseph Balsamo, connu sous le nom de Comte Cagliostro; extraite de la procédure instruite contre lui à Rome, en 1790, traduite d'après l'original italien, imprimé à la Chambre Apostolique.

Courier de l'Europe, gazette anglo-française, September, October, November, 1786; also Gazette de Hollande, Gazette d' Utrecht, Gazette de Leyde, Gazette de Florence, Courier du Bas-Rhin, Journal de Berlin, Public Advertizer, Feuille Villageoise, and Moniteur Universel.

Cagliostro démasqué à Varsovie en 1780.

Nachricht von des berüchtigten Cagliostro aufenthalte in Mitau, im jahre 1779 (Countess Elisa von der Recke).

Lettres sur la Suisse en 1781 (J. B. de Laborde).

Geschichten, geheime und räthselhafte Menschen (F. Bulau); or the French translation by William Duckett *Personnages Énigmatiques*.

Souvenirs de Baron de Gleichen.

Souvenirs de la Marquise de Créquy.

Correspondance littéraire (Grimm).

Mémoires récréatifs, scientifiques, et anecdotiques du physicien—aéronaute G. E. Roberson.

Mémoires authentiques de Comte Cagliostro (spurious, by the Marquis de Luchet).

Mémoires de Brissot, Abbé Georgel, Baronne d'Oberkirch, Madame du Hausset, Grosley, Bachaumont, Métra, Casanova, Comte Beugnot, and Baron de Besenval.

Réflexions de P. J. J. N. Motus

Cagliostro: La Franc-Maçonnerie et l'Occultisme au XVIIIe siècle (Henri d'Alméras).

Bibliography

Othodoxie Maçonnique (Ragon).

La Franc-Maçonne, ou Révélations des Mystères des Francs-Maçons.

Annales de l'origine du Grand Orient en France.

Acta Latomorum (Thory).

Mémoires pour servir à l'histoire du Jacobinisme (Abbé Barruel).

Histoire du Merveilleux (Figuier).

Histoire de la Franc-Maçonnerie (Clavel).

Histoire philosophique de la Maçonnerie (Kauffmann et Cherpin).

Les Sectes et les sociétés secrètes (Comte Le Couteulx de Canteleu).

Schlosser's History of the Eighteenth Century.

Histoire de la Révolution Française : Les Révolutionnaires Mystiques (Louis Blanc).

Histoire de France : XVIIIᵉ siècle (Henri Martin).

Histoire de France : L'Affaire du Collier (Michelet).

Recueil de toutes les pièces (31) qui ont paru dans l'affaire de M. le Cardinal de Rohan.

Marie Antoinette et le Procès du Collier (Emile Campardon).

L'Affaire du Collier (Funck-Brentano).

The Diamond Necklace (Henry Vizetelly).

Marie Antoinette et le Procès du Collier (Chaix d'Est-Ange).

La Dernière Pièce du fameux Collier.

Mémoire du Sieur Sacchi.

Lettre de Labarthe à l'archéologue Seguier.

Lettre d'un Garde du Roi (Manuel).

Lettres du Comte de Mirabeau à . . . sur Cagliostro et Lavater.

Requête au Parlement par le Comte de Cagliostro.

Mémoire pour le Comte de Cagliostro, demandeur, contre M. Chesnon le fils et le sieur de Launay.

Lettre au Peuple Anglais par le Comte de Cagliostro.

Theveneau de Morande (Paul Robiquet).

Liber Memorialis de Caleostro dum esset Roboretti.

Alessandro di Cagliostro. Impostor or Martyr ? (Charles Sotheran).

Count Cagliostro (Critical and Miscellaneous Essays ; Carlyle).

Vieux papiers, vieilles maisons (G. Lenôtre).

Italiänische Reise (Goethe).

CAGLIOSTRO

PART I

CHAPTER I

THE POWER OF PREJUDICE

I

THE mention of Cagliostro always suggests the
marvellous, the mysterious, the unknown. There is
something cabalistic in the very sound of the name
that, considering the occult phenomena performed by
the strange personality who assumed it, is curiously
appropriate. As an *incognito* it is, perhaps, the most
suitable ever invented. The name fits the man like
a glove; and, recalling the mystery in which his
career was wrapped, one involuntarily wonders if it has
ever been cleared up. In a word, what was Cagliostro
really? Charlatan, adventurer, swindler, whose impostures were finally exposed by the ever-memorable
Necklace Affair in which he was implicated? Or
"friend of humanity," as he claimed, whose benefac-
tions excited the enmity of the envious, who took
advantage of his misfortunes to calumniate and ruin
him? Knave, or martyr—which?

This question is more easily answered by saying
what Cagliostro was *not* than what he *was*. It has
been stated by competent judges—and all who have

studied the subject will agree with them—that there is, perhaps, no other equally celebrated figure in modern history whose character is so baffling to the biographer. Documents and books relating to him abound, but they possess little or no value. The most interesting are frequently the most unreliable. The fact that material so questionable should provide as many reasons for rejecting its evidence—which is, by the way, almost entirely hostile—as for accepting it, has induced theosophists, spiritualists, occultists, and all who are sympathetically drawn to the mysterious to become his apologists. By these amiable visionaries Cagliostro is regarded as one of the princes of occultism whose mystical touch has revealed the arcana of the spiritual world to the initiated, and illumined the path along which the speculative scientist proceeds on entering the labyrinth of the supernatural. To them the striking contrasts with which his agitated existence was chequered are unimpeachable witnesses in his favour, and they stubbornly refuse to accept the unsatisfactory and contemptuous explanation of his miracles given by those who regard him as an impostor.

Unfortunately, greater weight is attached to police reports than to theosophical eulogies; and something more substantial than the enthusiasm of the occultists is required to support their contention. However, those who take this extravagant (I had almost said ridiculous) view of Cagliostro may obtain what consolation they can from the fact—which cannot be stated too emphatically—that though it is utterly impossible to grant their prophet the halo they would accord him, it is equally impossible to accept the verdict of his enemies.

In reality, it is by the evil that has been said and

The Power of Prejudice

written of him that he is best known. In his own day, with very few exceptions, those whom he charmed or duped—as you will—by acts that in any case should have inspired gratitude rather than contempt observed a profound silence. When the Necklace Affair opened its flood-gates of ridicule and calumny, his former admirers saw him washed away with indifference. To defend him was to risk being compromised along with him ; and, no doubt, as happens in our own times, the pleasure of trailing in the mud one who has fallen was too delightful to be neglected. It is from this epoch—1785—when people were engaged in blighting his character rather than in trying to judge it, that nearly all the material relating to Cagliostro dates. With only such documents, then, to hand as have been inspired by hate, envy, or simply a love of detraction, the difficulty of forming a correct opinion of him is apparent.

The portrait Carlyle has drawn of Cagliostro is the one most familiar to English readers. Now, though Carlyle's judgments have in the main been upheld by the latest historians (who have had the advantage of information to which he was denied access), nevertheless, like everybody else, he made mistakes. In his case, however, these mistakes were inexcusable, for they were due, not to the lack of data, but to the strong prejudices by which he suffered himself to be swayed to the exclusion of that honesty and fairness he deemed so essential to the historian. He approached Cagliostro with a mind already biassed against him. Distasteful at the start, the subject on closer acquaintance became positively repugnant to him. The flagrant mendacity of the documentary evidence—which, discount it as he

3

might, still left the truth in doubt—only served to strengthen his prejudice. It could surely be no innocent victim of injustice who aroused contempt so malevolent, hatred so universal. The mystery in which he masqueraded was alone sufficient to excite suspicion. And yet, whispered the conscience of the historian enraged at the mendacity of the witnesses he consulted, what noble ideals, what lofty aspirations misjudged, misunderstood, exposed to ridicule, pelted with calumny, may not have sought shelter under that mantle of mystery?

"Looking at thy so attractively decorated private theatre, wherein thou actedst and livedst," he exclaims, "what hand but itches to draw aside thy curtain; overhaul thy paste-boards, paint-pots, paper-mantles, stage-lamps; and turning the whole inside out, find *thee* in the middle thereof!"

And suiting the action to the word, he clutches with an indignant hand at that metaphorical curtain; but in the very act of drawing it aside his old ingrained prejudice asserts itself. Bah! what else but a fraud can a Grand Cophta of Egyptian Masonry be? Can a Madame von der Recke, a Baroness d'Oberkirch, whose opinions at least are above suspicion, be other than right? The man is a shameless liar; and if he has been so shamelessly lied about in turn, he has only got what he deserved. And exasperated that such a creature should have been permitted even for a moment to cross the threshold of history, Carlyle dropped the curtain his fingers "itched to draw aside" and proceeded to empty all the vials of his wrath on Cagliostro.

In his brilliant essay, in the *Diamond Necklace*, in the

The Power of Prejudice

French Revolution—wherever he meets him—he brands him as a "King of Liars," a "Prince of Scoundrels," an "Arch-Quack," "Count Front of Brass-Pinchbeckostrum," "Bubby-jock," "a babbling, bubbling Turkey-cock," *et cetera.* But such violence defeats its intention. When on every page the historian's conscience is smitten with doubts that prejudice cannot succeed in stilling, the critical and inquisitive reader comes to the conclusion he knows less about the *real* Cagliostro at the end than he did at the beginning. He has merely seen Carlyle in one of his fine literary rages; it is all very interesting and memorable, but by no means what he wanted. As a matter of fact, in this instance Carlyle's judgment is absolutely at sea; and the modern biographers of Cagliostro do not even refer to it.

Nevertheless, these writers have come pretty much to the same conclusion. M. Henri d'Alméras, whose book on Cagliostro is the best, speaking of the questionable evidence that so incensed Carlyle, declares "the historian, even in handling it with care, finds himself willy-nilly adopting the old prejudice. That is to say, every book written on Cagliostro, even under the pretext of rehabilitating him, can only be a book *against* him." But while holding to the old conventional opinion, he considers that "a rogue so picturesque disarms anger, and deserves to be treated with indulgence." D'Alméras pictures Cagliostro as a sort of clown, which is certainly the most curious view ever taken of the "Front of Brass," and even more unjustifiable than Carlyle's.

"What a good-natured, amusing, original rascal!" he exclaims. "The Figaro of Alchemy, more intelligent than Diafoirus, and more cunning than Scapin. And with what imperturbable serenity did he lie in five or six languages, as well as in a gibberish that had no meaning at all. To lie like that gives one a great superiority over the majority of one's fellow-men. He did not lie because he was afraid to speak the truth, but because, as in the case of many another, falsehood was in him an excessive development of the imagination. He was himself, moreover, the first victim of his lies. By the familiar phenomenon of auto-suggestion, he ended by believing what he said from force of saying it. If he was successful, in a certain sense, he deserved to be."

From all of which it may be gathered that whether Cagliostro is depicted as an Apostle of Light by his friends the occultists, or a rank impostor by his enemies, of whom Carlyle is the most implacable and d'Alméras the most charitably inclined, the real man has been as effectually hidden from view by prejudice as by the mystery in which he wrapped himself. But heavy though the curtain is that conceals him, it is perhaps possible for the hand that "itches" to draw it aside. As a matter of fact, no really honest attempt has ever been made to do so. It is true it is only a fleeting, somewhat nebulous, glimpse that can be obtained of this singular personality. There is, moreover, one condition to be observed. Before this glimpse can be obtained it is essential that some attempt should be made to discover, if possible, *who* Cagliostro was.

The Power of Prejudice

II

Considering that one has only to turn to the biographical dictionaries and encyclopedias to find it definitely asserted that "Count Cagliostro" was the best known of many *aliases* assumed by Giuseppe Balsamo, a Sicilian adventurer born in Palermo in 1743 or 1748, the above statement would appear to be directly contrary to recorded fact. For though biographical dictionaries and encyclopedias are notoriously superficial and frequently misleading, they are perhaps in this instance accurate enough for the purpose of casual inquiry, which is after all what they are compiled for. Indeed, this Balsamo legend is so plausible an explanation of the mystery of Cagliostro's origin that, for lack of any other, it has satisfied all who are entitled to be regarded as authorities. The evidence, however, on which they have based their belief is circumstantial rather than positive.

Now circumstantial evidence, as everybody knows, is not always to be trusted. There are many cases on record of persons having been condemned on the strength of it who were afterwards found to be innocent. In this particular case, moreover, doubts *do* exist, and all "authorities" have admitted the fact. Those prejudiced against Cagliostro have agreed to attach no importance to them, those prejudiced in his favour the greatest. To the occultists they are the rock on which their faith in him is founded. Their opinion, however, may be ruled aside as untenable, for the doubts are entirely of a negative character, and suggest no counter-theory of identity whatever.

Cagliostro

Nevertheless, since they exist they are worth examining—not so much for the purpose of questioning the accuracy of the "authorities" as to show how the Balsamo legend, which plays so important a part in the history of Cagliostro, originated.

It was not till Cardinal Rohan entangled him in the Diamond Necklace Affair that the name of Cagliostro hitherto familiar only to a limited number of people who, as the case might be, had derived benefit or suffered misfortune from a personal experience of his fabulous powers, acquired European notoriety.

The excitement caused by this *cause célèbre*, as is well known, was intense and universal. The arrest of the Cardinal in the Oeil-de-Boeuf at Versailles, in the presence of the Court and a great concourse of people from Paris, as he was about to celebrate mass in the Royal Chapel on Assumption Day, on the charge of having purchased a necklace for 1,600,000 livres for the Queen, who denied all knowledge of the transaction ; the subsequent disappearance of the jewel and the suspicion of intent to swindle the jeweller which attached itself to both Queen and Cardinal ; the further implication of the Countess de Lamotte, with her strangely romantic history ; of Cagliostro, with his mystery and magic ; and of a host of other shady persons—these were elements sensational enough to strike the dullest imagination, fire the wildest curiosity, and rivet the attention of all Europe upon the actors in so unparalleled a drama.

After the Cardinal, whose position as Grand Almoner of France (a sort of French Archbishop of Canterbury, so to speak) made him the protagonist of this drama, the self-styled Count Cagliostro was the

8

The Power of Prejudice

figure in whom the public were most interested. The prodigies he was said to have performed, magnified by rumour, and his strange undecipherable personality gave him an importance out of all proportion to the small part he played in the famous Affair of the Necklace. Speculation as to his origin was naturally rife. But neither the police nor the lawyers could throw any light on his past. The evidence of the Countess de Lamotte, who in open court denounced him as an impostor formerly known as Don Tiscio, a name under which she declared he had fleeced many people in various parts of Spain, was too palpably untrustworthy and ridiculous to be treated seriously. Cagliostro himself did, indeed, attempt to satisfy curiosity, but the fantastic account he gave of his career only served—as perhaps he intended—to deepen its mystery.

The more it was baffled, the keener became the curiosity to discover a secret so cleverly guarded. The "noble traveller," as he described himself with ridiculous pomposity on his examination, confessed that Cagliostro was only one of the several names he had assumed in the course of his life. An *alias*—he had termed it *incognito*—is always suspicious. Coupled, as it was in his case, with alchemical experiments, prognostications, spiritualist séances, and quack medicines, it suggested rascality. From ridicule to calumny is but a step, and for every voice raised in defence of his honesty there were a dozen to decry him.

On the day he was set at liberty—for he had no difficulty in proving his innocence—eight or ten thousand people came *en masse* to offer him their

9

congratulations. The court-yard, the staircase, the very rooms of his house in the Rue St. Claude were filled with them. But this ovation, flattering though it was to his vanity, was intended less as a mark of respect to him than as an insult to the Queen, who was known to regard the verdict as a stigma on her honour, and whose waning popularity the hatred engendered by this scandalous affair had completely obliterated. Banished the following day by the Government, which sought to repair the prestige of the throne by persecuting and calumniating those who might be deemed instrumental in shattering it, Cagliostro lost what little credit the trial had left him. *Who*ever he was, the world had made up its mind *what* he was, and its opinion was wholly unfavourable to the "noble traveller."

From France, which he left on June 21, 1786, Cagliostro went to England. It was here, in the following September, that the assertion was made for the first time by the *Courier de l'Europe*, a French paper published in London, that he was Giuseppe Balsamo. This announcement, made with every assurance of its accuracy, was at once repeated by other journals throughout Europe. It would be interesting, though not particularly important, to know how the *Courier de l'Europe* obtained its information. It is permissible, however, to conjecture that the Anglo-French journal had been informed of the rumour current in Palermo at the time of Cagliostro's imprisonment in the Bastille that he was a native of that city, and on investigating the matter decided there were sufficient grounds for identifying him with Balsamo.

The Power of Prejudice

Be this as it may, it is the manner in which the statement made by the *Courier de l'Europe* appears to be confirmed that gives the whole theory its weight.

On December 2, 1786—dates are important factors in the evidence—Fontaine, the chief of the Paris police, received a very curious anonymous letter from Palermo. The writer began by saying that he had read in the *Gazette de Leyde* of September 25 an article taken from the *Courier de l'Europe* stating that the "famous Cagliostro was called Balsamo," from which he gathered that the Balsamo referred to was the same who in 1773 had caused his wife to be shut up in Sainte Pélagie at Paris for having deserted him, and who had afterwards applied to the courts for her release. To confirm Fontaine in this opinion, he gave him in detail the history of this Balsamo's career, which had been imparted to him on June 2 by the said Balsamo's uncle, Antonio Braconieri, who was firmly convinced that his nephew, of whom he had heard nothing for some years, was none other than Cagliostro. As he learnt this the day after Cagliostro's acquittal and release from the Bastille, the news of which could not have reached Palermo in less than a week, it proves that Braconieri's conviction was formed long before the Press began to maintain it.

In fact the anonymous writer stated that this conviction was prevalent in Palermo as far back as the previous year, when the news arrived there of the arrest of Cagliostro in connection with the Diamond Necklace Affair.

He went on to say that he had personally ridiculed

the report at the time, but having reflected on the grounds that Braconieri had given him for believing it "he had come to the conclusion that Count Cagliostro was Giuseppe Balsamo of Palermo or that Antonio Braconieri, his uncle, was a scoundrel worthy of being the uncle of M. le Comte de Cagliostro." As it was not till November 2 that this somewhat ingenuous person sent anonymously to Fontaine the information he had received on June 2 from Braconieri, his reflections on the veracity of the latter, one suspects, were scarcely complimentary. However, such doubts as he might still have cherished were finally set at rest on October 31, when Antonio Braconieri met him in one of the chief thoroughfares of Palermo and showed him a *Gazette de Florence* which confirmed everything Braconieri had told him more than four months before. Hereupon, the anonymous individual, convinced at last beyond the shadow of a doubt that the "*soi-disant* Count Cagliostro was really Giuseppe Balsamo of Palermo," decided to inform the chief of the Paris police of his discovery.

Such is the history of the proofs in favour of the Balsamo legend. Now to examine the proofs.

As the late M. Émile Campardon was the first to unearth this anonymous letter together with the official report upon it in the National Archives, and as his opinion is the one commonly accepted, it will be sufficient to quote what he has to say on the subject.

" The adventures," he asks, " of Giuseppe Balsamo and those of Alessandro Cagliostro—do they belong to the history of the same career ? Was the individual who had his wife shut up in Sainte Pélagie in 1773 the same who in 1786 protested so vehemently against the imprisonment of his wife? [1]

" Everything goes to prove it. The Countess Cagliostro was born in Rome ; Balsamo's wife was likewise a Roman. The maiden name of both was Feliciani.

" Madame Balsamo was married at fourteen ; the Countess Cagliostro at the time of her marriage was still a child.

" Cagliostro stated at his trial that his wife did not know how to write ; Madame Balsamo at *her* trial also declared she could not write.

" Her husband at any rate could. At the time of his petition against his wife Balsamo signed two documents which are still to be seen in the Archives. By comparing—as Fontaine had done—these two signatures with a letter written whilst in the Bastille by Cagliostro the experts declared the writing of Balsamo and that of Cagliostro to be identically the same.

"Furthermore, according to the statement of Antonio Braconieri, Balsamo had frequently written him under the name of Count Cagliostro. Nor had he invented the name, for Giuseppe Cagliostro of Messina, steward of the Prince of Villafranca, was Braconieri's uncle, and consequently Giuseppe Balsamo's great-uncle.

" If to these probabilities one adds certain minor resemblances—such as Cagliostro's declaration that Cardinal Orsini and the Duke of Alba could vouch for the truth of the account he gave of himself, who were

[1] On hearing that his wife had been arrested as well as himself in connection with the Necklace Affair, Cagliostro manifested the wildest grief.

personages by whom Balsamo was known to have been employed ; the fact that Cagliostro spoke the Sicilian dialect, and that Balsamo had employed magic in his swindling operations—it is scarcely credible that lives and characters so identical could belong to two different beings."

The arguments in favour of this hypothesis are very plausible and apparently as convincing as such circumstantial evidence usually is. It is possible, however, as stated above, to question the accuracy of the conclusion thus reached for the following reasons.

(1) The basis of the supposition that the Countess Cagliostro and Madame Balsamo were the same rests entirely on coincidence.

Granted that both happened to be Romans, that the maiden name of both was Feliciani, that both were married extremely young, and that neither could write. The fact that both were Romans is no argument at all. Though their maiden name was Feliciani, it was a comparatively common one—there were several families of Feliciani in Rome, and for that matter all over Italy. Madame Balsamo's father came from Calabria. Her Christian name was Lorenza. The statement that the Countess Cagliostro was likewise called Lorenza and changed her name to Seraphina, by which she was known, is based entirely on supposition. That both were married very young and that neither knew how to write, scarcely calls for comment. Italian women usually married in early girlhood, and very few, if any, of the class to which Seraphina Cagliostro and Lorenza Balsamo belonged could write.

(2) The testimony of the experts as to the remarkable similarity between the writing of Balsamo and

The Power of Prejudice

Cagliostro requires something more than an official statement to that effect to be convincing. At the time the experts made their report, the French Government were trying to silence the calumnies with which Marie Antoinette was being attacked by making the character of Cagliostro and others connected with the Necklace Affair appear as bad as possible. The Parisian police in the interest of the Monarchy, jumped at the opportunity of identifying the mysterious Cagliostro with the infamous Balsamo. The experts' evidence is, to say the least, questionable.

(3) The fact that Giuseppe Balsamo had an uncle called Giuseppe Cagliostro is the strongest argument in favour of the identification theory. There is no reason to doubt Antonio Braconieri's statement that he had received letters from his nephew signed "Count Cagliostro." However, the writer of the anonymous letter declared that, desiring to prove Braconieri's word as to the existence of Giuseppe Cagliostro of Messina, he discovered that there were *two* families of the name in that city. The prefix Cagli, moreover, is not unusual in Sicilian, Calabrian and Neapolitan names. The selection of it by Cagliostro as an *incognito* may have been accidental, or invented because of its peculiar cabalistic suggestion as suitable for the occult career on which he embarked, or it may have been suggested to him by some one of the name he had met when wandering about southern Italy. As his identification with Balsamo is based principally on coincidence, it is surely equally permissible to employ a coincidence as the basis of one of the many arguments in an attempt at refutation.

(4) As to the minor points of resemblance between

Cagliostro

Cagliostro and Balsamo given as " probabilities " for supposing them identical : in considering that Cagliostro used as references the names of Cardinal Orsini and the Duke of Alba, by whom Balsamo was known to have been employed at one time, the fantastic account he gave of himself at his trial should be remembered. One of the principal reasons for disbelieving him was the fact that these personages were *dead* and so unable to verify or deny his statement. Again, though the Sicilian dialect was undoubtedly Balsamo's mother-tongue, no one could ever make out to what *patois* Cagliostro's extraordinary abracadabra of accent belonged. But nothing can be weaker than to advance their use of magic and alchemy as a reason for identifying them. Magic and alchemy were the common stock-in-trade of every adventurer in Europe in the eighteenth century.

So much for criticism of the " official " proof.

There is, however, another reason for doubting the identity of the two men. It is the most powerful of all, and has hitherto apparently escaped the attention of those who have taken this singular theory of identification for granted.

Nobody that had *known* Balsamo ever *saw* Cagliostro.

The description of Balsamo's features given by Antonio Braconieri resembles that which others have given of Cagliostro's personal appearance *as far as it goes.* Unfortunately, it merely proves that both were short, had dark complexions, and peculiarly bright eyes. As for their noses, Braconieri described Balsamo's as being *écrasé;* it is a much more forcible and unflattering term than has ever been applied to

16

The Power of Prejudice

the by no means uncommon shape of Cagliostro's nasal organ. There were many pictures of Cagliostro scattered over Europe at the time of the Necklace Affair. In Palermo, where the interest taken in him was great, few printsellers' windows, one would imagine, but would have contained his portrait. Braconieri certainly is likely to have seen it; and had the resemblance to Balsamo been undeniable, he would surely have attached the greatest importance to it as a proof of the identity he desired to establish. As a matter of fact, he barely mentions it.

Again, one wonders why nobody who had known Balsamo ever made the least attempt to identify Cagliostro with him either at the time of the trial or when the articles in the *Courier de l'Europe* brought him a second time prominently before the public. Now Balsamo was known to have lived in London in 1771, when his conduct was so suspicious to the police that he deemed it advisable to leave the country. He and his wife accordingly went to Paris, and it was here that, in 1773, the events occurred which brought both prominently under the notice of the authorities. Six years after Balsamo's disappearance from London, Count Cagliostro appeared in that city, and becoming involved with a set of swindlers in a manner that made him appear a fool rather than a knave, spent four months in the King's Bench jail. How is it, one asks, that the London police, who "wanted" Giuseppe Balsamo, utterly failed to recognize him in the notorious Cagliostro?

Now granting that the police, as well as the persons whom Balsamo fleeced in London in 1771, had forgotten him in 1777, and that all who could have recognized him as Cagliostro in 1786, when the *Courier de l'Europe* exposed him, were dead, is it probable that the same coincidences would repeat themselves in Paris? If the Parisian police, who were doing their best to discover traces of Cagliostro's antecedents in 1785 and 1786 had quite *forgotten* the Balsamo who brought the curious action against his wife in 1773, is it at all likely that the various people the Balsamos had known in their two-years' residence in Paris would all have *died* in the meantime? People are always to be found to identify criminals and suspicious characters to whom the attention of the police is prominently drawn. But before the sort of Sherlock Holmes process of identification employed by the *Courier de l'Europe* and the Parisian police, not a soul was ever heard to declare that Cagliostro and Balsamo were the same.

To the reader who, knowing little or nothing of Cagliostro, takes up this book with an unbiassed mind, the above objections to the Balsamo legend may seem proof conclusive of its falsity. This would, however, be to go further than I, who attach much greater importance to these doubts than historians are inclined to do, care to admit. They merely show that it is neither right nor excusable to treat as a conviction what is purely a conjecture.

If this conclusion, wrapping as it does the origin and early life of Cagliostro once more in a veil of mystery, be accepted, it will go far to remove the prejudice which has hitherto made the answer to that other and more important question "What was Cagliostro?" so unsatisfactory.

CHAPTER II

GIUSEPPE BALSAMO

I

THERE could be no better illustration of the perplexities that confront the biographer of Cagliostro at every stage of his mysterious career than the uncertainty that prevails regarding the career of Giuseppe Balsamo himself. For rightly or wrongly, their identity has so long been taken for granted that the history of one has become indissolubly linked to that of the other.

Now, not only is it extremely difficult, when not altogether impossible, to verify the information we have concerning Balsamo, but the very integrity of those from whom the information is derived, is questionable. These tainted sources, so to speak, from which there meanders a confused and maze-like stream of contradictory details and unverifiable episodes, are (1) Balsamo's wife, Lorenza, (2) the Editor of the *Courier de l'Europe*, and (3) the Inquisition-biographer of Cagliostro.

Lorenza's statement is mainly the itinerary of the wanderings of herself and husband about Europe from their marriage to her imprisonment in Paris in 1773. Such *facts* as it purports to give as to the character of their wanderings are very meagre, and coloured so as to depict her in a favourable light. The *dossier* containing the particulars of her arrest is in the Archives of Paris, where it was *discovered* by the French Government in 1786, and where it is still to be seen. Query : considering the suspicious circumstances that led to its discovery, is the *dossier* a forgery ?

Opposed to the evidence of the *Courier de l'Europe* are the character, secret motives, and avowed enmity of the Editor.

As to the life of Balsamo,[1] published anonymously in Rome in 1791, under the auspices of the Inquisition, into whose power Cagliostro had fallen, the tone of hostility in which it is written, excessive even from an ultra-Catholic point of view, its lack of precision, and the absence of dates which makes it impossible to verify its statements, have caused critics of every shade of opinion, to consider it partially, if not wholly, unauthenticated.

It purports to be the confession of Cagliostro, extracted either by torture or the fear of torture, during his trial by the Inquisition. That Cagliostro did indeed "confess" is quite likely. But what sort of value could such a confession possibly have? The manner in which the Inquisition conducted its trials has rendered its verdicts suspect the world over. His condemnation was decided on from the very start, as the charge on which he was arrested proves—as will be shown in due course—and to escape torture, perhaps also in the hope of acquittal, Cagliostro was ready enough to oblige his terrible judges and "confess" whatever they wished.

---

[1] This book is now very rare. The French version is the more available. It is entitled : *Vie de Joseph Balsamo connu sous le nom de Comte Cagliostro, extraite de la procédure instruite contre lui à Rome en 1790; traduite d'après l'original italien, imprimé à la Chambre Apostolique.*

Giuseppe Balsamo

It is, moreover, a question whether the adventures related in the *Vie de Joseph Balsamo* are those of one or of several persons. As it is quite inconceivable that the Cagliostro of the Necklace Affair could ever have been the very ordinary adventurer here depicted, it has been suggested—and there is much to support the view— that Giuseppe Balsamo, as known to history, is a sort of composite individual manufactured out of all the rogues of whom the Inquisition-writer had any knowledge.

One thing, however, may be confidently asserted : whether the exploits of Giuseppe Balsamo were partially or wholly his, imaginary or real, they are at any rate typical of the adventurer of the age.

Like Cagliostro, he boasted a noble origin, and never failed on the various occasions of changing his name to give himself a title. There is, however, no reason to suppose that he was in any way related to, or even aware of the existence of the aristocratic family of the same name who derived *their* title from the little town of Balsamo near Monza in the Milanese. As a matter of fact the name was a fairly common one in Italy, and the Balsamos of Palermo were of no consequence whatever. Nothing is known of Giuseppe's father, beyond the fact that he was a petty tradesman who became bankrupt, and died at the age of forty-five, a few months after the birth of his son. Pietro Balsamo was *thought* to be of mixed Jewish and Moorish extraction, which would account for his obscurity and the slight esteem in which his name was held in Palermo, where the Levantines were the scum of the population.

Such scant consideration as the family may have enjoyed was due entirely to Giuseppe's mother, who though of humble birth was of good, honest Sicilian stock. Through her he could at least claim to have had a great-grandfather, one Matteo Martello, whom it has been supposed Cagliostro had in mind when in his fantastic account of himself at the time of the Necklace Affair he claimed to be descended from Charles Martel, the founder of the Carlovingian dynasty. This Matteo Martello had two daughters, the youngest of whom Vincenza married Giuseppe Cagliostro of Messina, whose name and relationship to Giuseppe Balsamo is the chief argument in the attempt to prove the identity of the latter with Cagliostro. Vincenza's elder sister married Giuseppe Braconieri and had three children, Felice, Matteo, and Antonio Braconieri. The former was Giuseppe's mother. He had also a sister older than himself, Maria, who became the wife of Giovanni Capitummino. On the death of her husband she returned with her children to live with her mother, all of whom Goethe met when in Palermo in 1787.

The poverty in which Pietro Balsamo died obliged his widow to appeal to her brother for assistance. Fortunately they were in a position and willing to come to her relief. Matteo, the elder, was chief clerk in the post-office at Palermo ; while Antonio was book-keeper in the firm of J. F. Aubert & Co. Both brothers, as well as their sister, appear to have been deeply religious, and it is not unlikely that the severity and repression to which Giuseppe was continually subjected may have fostered the spirit of rebellion, already latent in him, which was to turn him into the blackguard he became.

It manifested itself at an early age. From the

Giuseppe Balsamo

Seminary of San Rocco, where he received his first
schooling, he ran away several times. As the rod,
which appears to have played an important part in the
curriculum of the seminary, failed to produce the beneficial results that are supposed to ensue from its frequent application, his uncles, anxious to get rid of so
troublesome a charge, decided to confide the difficult
task of coaxing or licking him into shape to the Benfratelli of Cartegirone. Giuseppe was accordingly en-
rolled as a novice in this brotherhood, whose existence
was consecrated to the healing of the sick, and placed
under the supervision of the Convent-Apothecary.
He was at the time thirteen.

According to the Inquisition-biographer, it was in
the laboratory of the convent that Cagliostro learnt
"the principles of chemistry and medicine" which he
afterwards practised with such astonishing results. If
so, he must have been gifted with remarkable aptitude,
which both his conduct and brief sojourn at Cartegirone
belie. For whatever hopes his mother and uncles may
have founded on the effect of this pious environment
were soon dispelled. He had not been long in the
convent before he manifested his utter distaste for the
life of a Brother of Mercy. Naturally insubordinate
and bold he determined to escape; but as experience
had taught him at the Seminary of San Rocco that
running away merely resulted in being thrashed and
sent back, and as he had neither the means nor the
desire to go anywhere save home to Palermo, he
cunningly cast about in his mind to obtain his release
from the Brothers themselves. This was not easy to
accomplish, but in spite of the severe punishment his
wilfully idle and refractory conduct entailed he was

persistent and finally succeeded in wearing out the
patience of the long-suffering monks.

From the manner in which he attained his object
Carlyle detects in him a "touch of grim humour—or
deep world-irony, as the Germans call it—the surest
sign, as is often said, of a character naturally great."
It was a universal custom in all religious associations
that one of their number during meals should read
aloud to the others passages from the Lives of the
Saints.   This dull and unpopular task having one day
been allotted to Giuseppe—probably as a punishment
—he straightway proceeded, careless of the consequences, to read out whatever came into his head,
substituting for the names of the Saints those of the
most notable courtezans of Palermo.   The effect of
this daring sacrilege was dire and immediate.   With
fist and foot the scandalized monks instantly fell upon
the boy and having belaboured him, as the saying is,
within an inch of his life, indignantly packed him back
to Palermo as hopelessly incorrigible and utterly unworthy of ever becoming a Benfratello.

No fatted calf, needless to say, was killed to celebrate the return of the prodigal.   But Giuseppe having
gained his object, took whatever chastisement he received from his mother and uncles philosophically, and
left them to swallow their mortification as best they
could.   However, sorely tried though they were, they
did not even now wash their hands of him.   Somehow
—just how it would be difficult to say—one forms a
vague idea he was never without a plausible excuse for
his conduct.   Adventurers, even the lowest, more or
less understand the art of pleasing ; and many little
things seem to indicate that with all his viciousness his

disposition was not unattractive. On the contrary there is much in the character of his early villainies to suggest his powers of persuasion were considerable.

Thus, after his expulsion from Cartegirone the Inquisition-biographer tells us that he took lessons in drawing for which, no doubt, he must have given some proof of talent and inclination. Far, however, from showing any disposition to conform to the wishes of his uncles, who for his mother's sake, if not for his own, continued to take an interest in him, the boy rapidly went from bad to worse. As neither reproof nor restraint produced any effect on his headstrong and rebellious nature he appears to have been permitted to run wild, perhaps because he had reached an age when it was no longer possible to control his actions. Nor were the acquaintances he formed of the sort to counteract a natural tendency to viciousness. He was soon hand in glove with all the worst characters of the town.

" There was no fight or street brawl," says the indignant Inquisition-biographer, " in which he was not involved, no theft of which he was not suspected. The band of young desperadoes to which he belonged frequently came into collision with the night-watch, whose prisoners, if any, they would attempt to set free. Even the murder of a canon was attributed to him by the gossips of the town."

In a word Giuseppe Balsamo became a veritable " Apache" destined seemingly sooner or later for the galleys or the gallows. Such a character, it goes without saying, could not fail to attract the notice of the police. He more than once saw the inside of the Palermo jail; but from lack of sufficient proof, or from the nature of the charge against him, or owing to the intercession of his estimable uncles, as often as he was arrested he was let off again.

Even his drawing-lessons, while they lasted, were perverted to the most ignoble ends. To obtain the money he needed he began, like all thieves, with petty thefts from his relations. One of his uncles was his first victim. In a similar way he derived profit from a love-affair between his sister and a cousin. As their parents put obstacles in the way of their meeting Giuseppe offered to act as go-between. In a rash moment they accepted his aid, and he profited by the occasion to substitute forged letters in the place of those he undertook to deliver, by means of which he got possession of the presents the unsuspecting lovers were induced to exchange. Encouraged by the skill he displayed in imitating hand-writing and copying signatures—which seems to have been the extent of his talent for drawing—he turned it to account in other and more profitable ways. Somehow—perhaps by hints dropped by himself in the right quarter—his proficiency in this respect, and his readiness to give others the benefit of it for a consideration, got known. From forging tickets to the theatre for his companions, he was employed to forge leave-of-absence passes for monks, and even to forge a will in favour of a certain Marquis Maurigi, by which a religious institution was defrauded of a large legacy.

There is another version of this affair which the Inquisition-writer has naturally ignored, and from which it would appear that it was the marquis who was defrauded of the legacy by the religious institution. But be this trifling detail as it may, the fact remains that the forgery was so successfully effected that it was not discovered till several years later, when some attempt was made to bring Balsamo to justice, which the impossibility of ascertaining whether he was alive or dead, rendered abortive.

Such sums of money, however, as he obtained in this way must of necessity have been small. It could only have been in copper that his " Apache " friends and the monks paid him for the theatre-tickets and convent-passes he forged for them. Nor was the notary by whom he was employed to forge the will, and who, we are told, was a relation, likely to be much more liberal. In Palermo then, as to-day, scores of just such youths as Giuseppe Balsamo were to be found ready to perform any villainy for a fifty centime piece. He accordingly sought other means of procuring the money he needed and as none, thanks to his compatriots' notorious credulity, was likely to prove so remunerative as an appeal to their love of the marvellous, he had recourse to what was known as " sorcery."

It is to the questionable significance attached to this word that the prejudice against Cagliostro, whose wonders were attributed to magic, has been very largely due. For it is only of comparatively recent date that " sorcery " so-called has ceased to be anathema, owing to the belated investigations of science, which is always, and perhaps with reason, suspicious of occult phenomena, by which the indubitable existence of certain powers—as yet only partially explained—active in some, passive in others, and perhaps latent in all human beings, has been revealed. And even still, so great is the force of tradition, many judging from the frauds frequently perpetrated by persons claiming to possess these secret powers, regard with suspicion, if not with downright contempt, all that is popularly designated as sorcery, magic, or witchcraft.

But this is not the place to discuss the methods by which those who work miracles obtain their results. Suffice it to say, there has been from time immemorial a belief in the ability of certain persons to control the forces of nature. Nowhere is this belief stronger than in Sicily. There the "sorcerer" is as common as the priest; not a village but boasts some sibyl, seer, or wonder-worker. That all are not equally efficient, goes without saying. Some possess remarkable powers, which they themselves would probably be unable to explain. Others, like Giuseppe Balsamo, are only able to deceive very simple or foolish people easy to deceive.

From the single instance cited of Giuseppe's skill in this direction one infers his magical gifts were of the crystal-gazing, sand-divination kind—the ordinary kind with which everybody is more or less familiar, if only by name. According to the Inquisition-biographer, "one day whilst he and his companions were idling away the time together the conversation having turned upon a certain girl whom they all knew, one of the number wondered what she was doing at that moment, whereupon Giuseppe immediately offered to gratify him. Marking a square on the ground he made some passes with his hands above it, after which the figure of the girl was seen in the square playing at *tressette* with three of her friends." So great was the effect of this exhibition of clairvoyance, thought-transference, hypnotic suggestion, what you will, upon the amazed Apaches that they went at once to look for the girl and "found her in the same attitude playing the very game and with the very persons that Balsamo had shown them."

The fact that such phenomena are of quite common occurrence and to be witnessed any day in large cities and summer-resorts on payment of fees, varying according to the renown of the performer, has robbed them if not of their attraction at least of their wonder. One has come to take them for granted. Whatever may be the scientific explanation of such occult—the word must serve for want of a better—power as Giuseppe possessed, he himself, we may be sure, would only have been able to account for it as "sorcery." He was not likely to be a whit less superstitious than the people with whom he associated. Indeed, his faith in the efficacy of the magic properties attributed by vulgar superstition to sacred things would appear to have been greater than his faith in his own supernatural powers.

It is reported of him on one occasion that "under pretext of curing his sister, who he said was possessed of a devil, he obtained from a priest in the country a little cotton dipped in holy oil," to which, doubtless, he attached great importance as the means of successfully performing some wonder he had no confidence in his own powers to effect. Such cryptic attributes as he had been endowed with must have been very slight, or undeveloped, for there is no reference whatever to the marvellous in the swindles of his subsequent history in which one would expect him to have employed it. Very probably whatever magnetic, hypnotic, or telepathic faculty he possessed was first discovered by the apothecary under whom he was placed in the laboratory at Cartegirone, who, like all of his kind, no doubt, experimented in alchemy and kindred sciences. If so, he certainly did not stay long enough with the Benfratelli to turn his mysterious talent to account or to obtain more than the merest glimpse of the "sorcery," of which, though banned by the Church, the monasteries were the secret nursery.

Be this as it may, needless to say those who had witnessed Giuseppe's strange phenomenon required no further proof of his marvellous power, which rapidly noised abroad and exaggerated by rumour gave the young "sorcerer" a reputation he only wanted an opportunity of exploiting for all it was worth. How long he waited for this opportunity is not stated, but he was still in his teens when it eventually turned up in the person of a "certain ninny of a goldsmith named Marano," whose superstition, avarice, and gullibility made him an easy dupe.

One day in conversation with this man, who had been previously nursed to the proper pitch of cupidity, as one nurses a constituency before an election, Giuseppe informed him under pledge of the strictest secrecy that he knew of a certain cave not far from Palermo, in which a great treasure was buried. According to a superstition prevalent in Sicily, where belief in such treasure was common, it was supposed to be guarded by demons, and as it would be necessary to hire a priest to exorcize them, Giuseppe offered to take Marano to the spot and assist him in lifting the hidden wealth for the consideration of "sixty ounces of gold." [1]

Whatever objection Marano might have had to

[1] About £30.

part with such a sum was overcome by the thought of gaining probably a hundred times as much. He accordingly paid the money and set out one night with Giuseppe, the priest, and another man who was in the secret. On arriving at the cave, preparatory to the ceremony of exorcism, the priest proceeded to evoke the demons, which was done with due solemnity by means of magic circles and symbols drawn upon the ground, incantations in Latin, *et cetera*. Suddenly hideous noises were heard, there was a flash and splutter of blue fire, and the air was filled with sulphur. Marano, who was waiting in the greatest terror for the materialization of the powers of darkness, in which he firmly believed, and who, he had been told, on such occasions sometimes got beyond the control of the exorcist, was commanded to dig where he stood. But scarcely had his spade struck the ground when the demons themselves appeared with shrieks and yells—some goat-herds hired for the occasion, as horrible as paint, burnt cork, and Marano's terrified imagination could paint them—and fell upon the wretched man. Whereupon Giuseppe and his confederates took to their heels, leaving their dupe in a fit on the ground.

Fool that he was, it did not take the goldsmith on recovering his senses long to discover that he had been victimized. Indifferent to the ridicule to which he exposed himself he lost no time in bringing an action against Giuseppe for the recovery of the money of which he had been defrauded, swearing at the same time to have the life of the swindler as well. Under such circumstances Palermo was no longer a safe place for the sorcerer, and taking time by the forelock he fled.

II

At this stage in Balsamo's career even the Inquisition-biographer ceases to vouch for the accuracy of what he relates.

"Henceforth," he confesses, "we are obliged to accept Cagliostro's own assertions"—wrung from him in the torture chamber of the Castle of St. Angelo, be it remembered—"without the means of verifying them, as no further trace of his doings is to be found elsewhere."

Considering that accuracy, to which no importance has been attached in all previous books on Cagliostro, is the main object of this, after such a statement the continuation of Balsamo's history would appear to be superfluous. Apart, however, from their romantic interest, Balsamo's subsequent adventures are really an aid to accuracy. For the character of the man as revealed by them will be found to be so dissimilar to Cagliostro's as to serve more forcibly than any argument to prove how slight are the grounds for identifying the two.

By relating what befell Balsamo on fleeing from Palermo one may judge, from the very start, of the sort of faith to be placed in his Inquisition-biographer. In Cagliostro's own account of his life—which will be duly reported in its proper place—his statements in regard to the "noble Althotas," that remarkable magician by whom he avowed he was brought up, were regarded as absolutely ridiculous. Nevertheless for the sole purpose apparently of proving Cagliostro's identity with Balsamo the Inquisition-biographer drags this individual whose very existence is open to doubt into the life of the latter, and unblushingly plunges the two into those fabulous and ludicrous adventures, of which the description caused so much mirth at the time of the Necklace Affair.

Thus the imaginative Inquisition-biographer declares it was at Messina, whither he went on leaving Palermo, that Balsamo met the "noble Althotas," whose power "to dematerialize himself" was, to judge from the last occasion on which he was reported to have been seen in the flesh at Malta, only another way of saying that he was clever in evading the police. But as Balsamo after having "overrun the whole earth" with Althotas emerges once more into something like reality at Naples, in the company of the renegade priest who had assisted in the fleecing of Marano, it is not unreasonable to suppose that this city and not Messina was his immediate destination on leaving Palermo.

He did not stay long, however, at Naples. Owing either to a quarrel with the priest over their ill-gotten funds, or to a hint from the police whose suspicions his conduct aroused, he went to Rome. The statement that on his arrival he presented a letter of introduction from the Grand Master of the Knights of Malta—one of his adventures with Althotas—to the Baron de Bretteville, the envoy from Malta to the Holy See, by whom in turn he was introduced to Cardinals York and Orsini, is scarcely worth refuting. For if the Palermo Apache ever entered the salon of a Roman noble it could of course only have been via the *escalier de service*.

The Inquisition-biographer, however, quickly reduces him to a situation much more in keeping with his character and condition. "Not long," he says, "after his arrival in Rome, Balsamo was sentenced to three days in jail for quarrelling with one of the waiters at the sign of the Sun, where he lodged." On his release, he was, as is highly probable forced to live by his wits, and instead of consorting with Cardinals and diplomatists turned his attention to drawing. But as his talent in this respect appears to have been as limited as his knowledge of the occult, it is not surprising that the revenue he derived from the sketches he copied, or from old prints, freshened up and passed off as originals, was precarious.

Love, however, is the great consoler of poverty. About this time Balsamo conceived a violent passion for Lorenza Feliciani, the fourteen-year-old daughter of a "smelter of copper" who lived in an alley close to the Church of the Trinita de' Pellegrini—one of the poorest quarters of Rome. Marriage followed the love-making, and Lorenza, in spite of her tender years, in due course became his wife. This event—which is one of the few authenticated ones in Balsamo's career—took place in "April 1769 in the Church of San Salvatore in Campo."

As the sale of her husband's pen-and-ink sketches, which in Lorenza's estimation at least were "superb," was not remunerative at the best of times, the young couple made their home at first with the bride's parents. And now for perhaps the only time in his life a decent and comfortable existence was open to Balsamo. He had a young and, according to all accounts, a beautiful wife, whom he loved and by whom he was loved ; he

Giuseppe Balsamo

had a home, and the chance of adopting his father-in-law's more lucrative, if less congenial, trade—of settling down, in a word, and turning over a new leaf. But he was a born blackguard and under the circumstances it is not surprising that he should have had the *nostalgie de la boue*. In other words his Apache nature asserted itself, and he had no sooner married than he proceeded with revolting cynicism to turn his wife's charms to account.

But Lorenza, being at this stage of her career as innocent as she was ignorant, very naturally objected to his odious proposal. By dint, however, of persuasion and argument he finally succeeded in indoctrinating her with his views, to the great indignation of her parents, who, scandalized by such conduct, after frequent altercations finally turned the couple out of the house. Whereupon Lorenza decided to abandon any remaining scruples she had and assist her husband to the best of her ability.

Among the acquaintances they made in this way were two Sicilians of the worst character, Ottavio Nicastro, who finished on the gallows, and a self-styled Marquis Agliata. The latter being an accomplished forger was not long in discovering a similar talent in the husband of Lorenza, by whose charms he had been smitten. He accordingly proposed to take him into partnership, a proposition which Balsamo was ready enough to accept. Nicastro, however, feeling himself slighted by the close intimacy between the two, from which he was excluded, informed the police of their doings; but as he was foolish enough to quarrel with them beforehand, they suspected his intention, and defeated it by a hurried flight.

Cagliostro

If Lorenza is to be believed, their intention was to go to Germany, and it was perhaps with this end in view that Agliata had, as the Inquisition-biographer asserts, previously forged the brevet of a Prussian colonelcy for Balsamo. At any rate, once out of the Papal States they proceeded very leisurely, swindling right and left as they went. At Loretto they obtained "fifty sequins" from the governor of the town by means of a forged letter of introduction from Cardinal Orsini. In this way they got as far as Bergamo, where the crafty Agliata decided to adopt different tactics. He accordingly gave out that he was a recruiting agent of the King of Prussia; but by some chance the suspicions of the authorities were aroused, whereupon Agliata, having somehow got wind of the fact, without more ado decamped, leaving the Balsamos to shift for themselves. Scarcely had he gone when the *sbirri* arrived to arrest him. Not finding him, they seized the Balsamos as his accomplices; they, however, succeeded in clearing themselves, and on being released were ordered to leave the town. As Agliata had gone off with all the money, they were obliged to sell their effects to obey this injunction; and not daring to return to Rome, they proceeded to Milan, where they arrived almost destitute.

Beggary was now their only means of existence, but even beggary may be profitable providing one knows *how* to beg. According to the Countess de Lamotte, who spoke from experience, there was "only one way of asking alms, and that was in a carriage." In fine, "to get on" as a beggar, as in every profession, requires ability. It is the kind of ability with which Balsamo was abundantly gifted. Aware that the pilgrims he saw wandering about Italy from shrine to shrine subsisted on wayside charity, he conceived the ingenious expedient of imitating them. As the objective of this expiatory vagabondage he selected St. James of Compostella, one of the most popular shrines at the time in Christendom, and consequently one to which a pilgrimage might most easily be exploited.

So setting out from Milan, staff in hand, mumbling paternosters, fumbling their beads, begging their way from village to village, from presbytery to presbytery, and constantly on the alert for any chance of improving their condition, the couple took the road to Spain. Of this tour along the Riviera to Barcelona, where the "pilgrimage" ended, Lorenza, on being arrested three years later in Paris, gave an account which the Inquisition-biographer has embellished, and which in one particular at least has been verified by no less a person than Casanova.

As it happened, this prince of adventurers—who in obedience to a time-honoured convention is never mentioned in print, by English writers *bien entendu*, without condemnation, though in private conversation people wax eloquent enough over him—was himself wandering about the South of France at the time. Arriving in Aix-en-Provence in 1770, he actually stopped in the same inn as the Balsamos, who excited his curiosity by their lavish distribution of alms to the poor of the town. Being a man who never missed a single opportunity of improving any acquaintance that chance might throw in his way, he called upon the couple, and recorded his impression in those fascinating Memoirs of his, of which the authenticity is now fully established and, what is more to the point, of which all the details have been verified.[1]

"I found the female pilgrim," he says, "seated in a chair looking like a person exhausted with fatigue, and interesting by reason of her youth and beauty, singularly heightened by a touch of melancholy and by a crucifix of yellow metal six inches long which she held in her hand. Her companion, who was arranging shells on his coat of black baize, made no movement—he appeared to intimate by the looks he cast at his wife I was to attend to her alone."

From the manner in which Lorenza conducted herself on this occasion she appears to have had remarkable aptitude for acting the rôle her husband had given her.

"We are going on foot," she said in answer to Casanova's questions, "living on charity the better to obtain the mercy of God, whom I have so often offended. Though I ask only a sou in charity, people always give me pieces of silver and gold "—a hint Casanova did not take—"so that arriving at a town we have to distribute to the poor all that remains to us, in order not to commit the sin of losing confidence in the Eternal Providence."

Whatever doubts Casanova may have had as to her veracity, the Inquisition-biographer most certainly had none. He declares that the " silver and gold " of which she and her husband were so lavish at Aix was

---

[1] To infer from this, however, as many writers have done, that Casanova's evidence proves Cagliostro and Balsamo to be the same is absurd. He never met the *Cagliostros* in his life. In stating that they were the Balsamos whom he had met in 1770 he merely *repeats* what he had read in the papers. His Memoirs were not written till many years later.

a shameful *quid pro quo* obtained from some officers at Antibes whom she had fascinated.

Unfortunately there is no Casanova at Antibes to verify him or to follow them to London via Barcelona, Madrid, and Lisbon. Lorenza is very explicit as to where they went on leaving Aix, and as to the time they remained in the various places they visited. The Inquisition-biographer, *faute de mieux*, is obliged to confirm her itinerary, but he has his revenge by either denying everything else she says, or by putting the worst construction upon it. At all events, between them one gets the impression that the pilgrims, for some reason or other, abandoned their pilgrimage before reaching the shrine of St. James of Compostella; that Lorenza was probably more truthful than she meant to be when she says they left Lisbon "because the climate was too hot for her"; and that however great the quantity of "silver and gold" she was possessed of at Aix, she and her husband had divested themselves of most of it by the time they reached London.

As to the character of their adventures by the way, it bears too close a resemblance to those already related to be worth describing.

III

The Editor of the *Courier de l'Europe*—which journal, as previously stated, was published in London —is the authority for the information concerning the Balsamos in England. He ferreted out or concocted this information *fourteen years* later; and, as quite apart from his motives, no one of the people he refers to as having known the Balsamos in 1772 came forward to corroborate what he said or to identify them with the Cagliostros, it is impossible to verify his evidence. From the fact, however, that it was commonly accepted at the time, and is still regarded as substantially trustworthy, *entirely because Cagliostro absolutely denied any knowledge of the Balsamos*, the reader may judge at once of the bitterness of the prejudice against Cagliostro as well as of the value to be attached to such "proof."

According to the *Courier de l'Europe*, Balsamo and his wife arrived in London from Lisbon in 1771, and after living for a while in Leadenhall Street moved to New Compton Street, Soho. They were, we are told, in extreme poverty, which Lorenza—to whom vice had long ceased to be repugnant—endeavoured to alleviate by the most despicable expedients. As she had but indifferent success, Balsamo, having quarrelled with a painter and decorator by name of Pergolezzi, by whom he had for a few days been employed, assisted her in the infamous rôle of blackmailer.

Their most profitable victim appears to have been "a Quaker," who, in spite of the rigorous standard of morality prescribed by the sect to which he belonged, occasionally deigned to make some secret concession to the weakness of human nature. Decoyed by Lorenza, this individual was discovered by her husband in so compromising a situation that nothing short of the payment of one hundred pounds could mollify Balsamo's feigned indignation and avert the disgrace with which he threatened the erring and terrified disciple of William Penn.

Their ill-gotten gains, however, did not last long;

and while Lorenza promenaded the streets in the vain quest for others victims, Balsamo was once more obliged to have recourse to his artistic talents. But Fortune remained hostile, and even went out of her way to vent her spite on the couple. For a certain Dr. Moses Benamore, described as "the envoy of the King of Barbary," was induced to purchase some of Balsamo's drawings, payment of which the artist was obliged to seek in the courts. The case, however, was decided against him, and since, after paying the costs to which he was condemned, he was unable to pay his rent, his landlord promptly had him arrested for debt.

To extricate him from this predicament, Lorenza adopted tactics which, according to the Inquisition-biographer, had proved effective under similar circumstances in Barcelona. Instead of endeavouring to excite admiration in the streets, she now sought to stir the compassion of the devout. Every day she was to be seen on her knees in some church or other, with a weather-eye open for some gullible dupe whilst she piously mumbled her prayers. In this way she managed to attract the attention of the charitable Sir Edward Hales, or as she calls him "Sir Dehels," who not only procured Balsamo's release from jail, but on the strength of his pen-and-ink sketches employed him to decorate the ceilings of some rooms at his country-seat near Canterbury—a task for which he had not the least qualification. Four months later, after ruining his ceilings, "Sir Dehels" caught his rascally *protégé* making love to his daughter, whereupon the Balsamos deemed it advisable to seek another country to exploit.

41

IV

Fortune, like Nature, is non-moral. If proof of so palpable a fact where required no more suitable example could be cited than the good luck that came to the Balsamos at the very moment they least deserved it.

Leaving England as poor as when they entered it, they found whilst crossing the Channel between Dover and Calais, if not exactly a fortune, what was to prove no mean equivalent in the person of a certain M. Duplessis de la Radotte. This gentleman, formerly an official in India, had on its evacuation by the French found an equally lucrative post in his native country as agent of the Marquis de Prie. Very susceptible to beauty, as Lorenza was quick to detect, he no sooner beheld her on the deck of the Dover packet than he sought her acquaintance. Lorenza, one imagines, must have been not only particularly attractive and skilled by considerable practice in the art of attraction, but a very good sailor ; for in the short space of the Channel crossing she so far succeeded in captivating Duplessis that on reaching Calais he offered her a seat in his carriage to Paris. Needless to say, it was not the sort of offer she was likely to refuse ; and while her husband trotted behind on horseback she turned her opportunity to such account that Duplessis was induced to invite both the husband and wife to be his guests in Paris.

But to cut a long story short : as the result of the acceptance of this invitation Duplessis after a time quarrelled with Balsamo and persuaded Lorenza to leave her husband and live under his "protection." This was not at all to Balsamo's taste, and he appealed to the courts for redress. He won his case, and Lorenza, according to the law in such matters, was arrested and imprisoned in Sainte Pélagie, the most famous—or infamous—penitentiary for women in France during the eighteenth century.

This event occurred in 1773, if the *dossier* discovered in the French Archives in 1783, which contains the statement Lorenza made at the time, is to be regarded as authentic. That *none* of the numerous people referred to in the *dossier* with whom the Balsamos were very closely connected should have come forward during the Necklace Affair and identified Cagliostro, lays the genuineness of this celebrated document open to doubt. Is it likely that *all* these people had died in the fourteen years that elapsed? If not, why did not those who still lived attempt to satisfy the boundless curiosity that the mysterious Cagliostro excited? He could not have changed out of all recognition during this period, for according to Goethe, in Palermo those who remembered Balsamo discovered, or thought they discovered, a likeness to him in the published portraits of Cagliostro. In any case, however much Cagliostro's appearance may have changed, his wife's most certainly had not. At thirty the Countess Cagliostro possessed the freshness of a girl of twenty. Had she been Lorenza Balsamo, she would have been very quickly recognized.

But from these doubts which shake one's faith, not only in the *dossier* to which so much importance has been attached, but in the Balsamo legend itself, let us return to the still more unauthenticated doings of our adventurers.

It was not long before Balsamo repented of his vengeance. On his intercession his wife was released, and shortly afterwards, to avoid arrest on his own score, the couple disappeared. The Inquisition-biographer states vaguely that they went to "Brussels and Germany." But it is not a matter of any importance. A few months later, however, Giuseppe Balsamo most unquestionably reappeared in his native city, where he astonished all his kindred, to whom alone he made himself known, by the splendour in which he returned.

Somewhere in the interval between his flight from Paris and his arrival in Palermo he had metamorphosed himself into a Marchese Pellegrini, and by the aid of Lorenza picked up a prince. Never before had they been so flush. The Marchese Pellegrini had his carriage and valet, one "Laroca," a Neapolitan barber, who afterwards started business on his own account as an adventurer. The "Marchesa" had her prince and his purse, and what was to prove of even greater value, his influence to draw upon. For a while, indeed, so great was his luck, Balsamo even had thoughts of settling down and living on the fortune Lorenza had plucked from her prince. He actually hired a house on the outskirts of Palermo with this intention. But he counted without Marano, that "ninny of a goldsmith," from whose vengeance he had fled years before. For Marano was still living, and no sooner did he become aware that the boy who had made such a fool of him in the old treasure-digging business was once more in Palermo than he had him seized and clapt into prison.

The matter, no doubt, must have had very serious consequences for the Marchese Pellegrini had it not been for the powerful interest of Lorenza's prince. As this episode in Balsamo's career is one of the very few concerning which the information is authentic, it is worth while describing.

" The manner of his escape," says Goethe, who was told what he relates by eye-witnesses, " deserves to be described. The son of one of the first Sicilian princes and great landed proprietors, who had, more-over, filled important posts at the Neapolitan Court, was a person that united with a strong body and ungovernable temper all the tyrannical caprice which the rich and great, without cultivation, think themselves entitled to exhibit.

" Donna Lorenza had contrived to gain this man, and on him the fictitious Marchese Pellegrini founded his security. The prince had testified openly that he was the protector of this strange pair, and his fury may be imagined when Giuseppe Balsamo, at the instance of the man he had cheated, was cast into prison. He tried various means to deliver him, and as these would not prosper, he publicly, in the President's ante-chamber, threatened Marano's lawyer with the frightfullest misusage if the suit were not dropped and Balsamo forthwith set at liberty. As the lawyer declined such a proposal he clutched him, beat him, threw him on the floor, trampled him with his feet, and could hardly be restrained from still further outrages, when the President himself came running out at the tumult and commanded peace.

Cagliostro

"This latter, a weak, dependent man, made no attempt to punish the injurer ; Marano and his lawyer grew fainthearted, and Balsamo was let go. There was not so much as a registration in the court books specifying his dismissal, who occasioned it, or how it took place.

"The Marchese Pellegrini," Goethe adds, "quickly thereafter left Palermo, and performed various travels, whereof I could obtain no clear information."

Nor apparently could anybody else, for on leaving Palermo this time the Balsamos vanished as completely as if they had ceased to exist. The *Courier de l'Europe* and the Inquisition-biographer, however, were not to be dismayed by any such trifling gap in the chain of evidence they set themselves to string together. Unable to discover the least trace of Balsamo, they seized upon two or three other swindlers, who may or may not have been the creations of their distracted imagination, and boldly labelled them Balsamo.

Lorenza's honest copper-smelting father and brother are dragged from Rome to join in the swindling operations of herself and husband. The brother is whisked off with them to Malta and Spain, where he is abandoned as an incubus, apparently because he objected to exploit his good looks after the manner of his sister. Then, as it is necessary in some way to account for Cagliostro's occult powers, Balsamo suddenly takes up the study of alchemy, and in the moments he snatches from the preparation of "beauty salves" and "longevity pills," picks an occasional pocket.

But the most bare-faced of all these problematic

Giuseppe Balsamo

Balsamos is the Don Tiscio one, for whose existence "Dr." Sacchi is responsible. Of Sacchi, be it said, nothing is known to his credit. Having some knowledge of surgery, and being in very low water, he appealed for assistance to Cagliostro, who found some work for him in his private hospital at Strasburg. But within a week he was dismissed for misconduct. Hereupon Sacchi published a book, or was said to have done so—for no one apparently but the Countess de Lamotte's counsel in the Necklace Trial ever saw it—in which he denounced Cagliostro as a swindler by name of Don Tiscio who had adorned the pillory in Spain, and suffered other punishments of a kind Sacchi preferred not to mention. Notwithstanding, though no credence was attached to this statement when cited by the Countess de Lamotte, it was raked up again by the *Courier de l'Europe* with the addition that Balsamo now becomes Sacchi's Don Tiscio.

Thus, after having been forger, swindler, blackmailer, *souteneur*, quack, pickpocket—all of the commonest type—Balsamo, on the word of a disreputable Sacchi, supported by a few singular coincidences, is saved without rhyme or reason from the gallows in Cadiz, on which he very probably perished, in order to be brought back to London as Count Cagliostro, a highly accomplished charlatan and past-master in wonder-working. An improbability that even the Inquisition-biographer is unable to pass over in silence.

"How," he exclaims in amazement, "could such a man without either physical or intellectual qualities, devoid of education, connections, or even the appearance of respectability, whose very language was a

47

barbarous dialect—how could he have succeeded as
he did ? "

How, indeed ! The transformation is obviously
so improbable that the puzzled reader will very likely
come to the conclusion that, whoever Cagliostro may
have been, he could certainly never have been Giuseppe
Balsamo.

But enough of speculation ; let us now turn our
belated attention to the man whose career under the
impenetrable *incognito* of Count Cagliostro is the
subject of this book.

PART II

CHAPTER I

CAGLIOSTRO IN LONDON

I

Some time in July 1776—the exact date is unascertainable—two foreigners of unmistakable respectability, to judge by their appearance, if not of distinction, arrived in London and engaged a suite of furnished apartments in Whitcombe Street, Leicester Fields. They called themselves Count and Countess Cagliostro; and their landlady, who lost no time in letting everybody in the house, as well as her neighbours, know she had people of title as lodgers, added that she believed they were Italian, though so far as she could understand from the Count's very broken English they had last come from Portugal. A day or two later she was able to inform her gossips, which no doubt she did with even greater satisfaction, that her foreign lodgers were not only titled but undoubtedly rich, for the Countess had very fine jewels and the Count was engaged in turning one of the rooms he had rented into a laboratory, as he intended to devote himself to the study of physics and chemistry, subjects, it seemed, in which he was keenly interested.

Their first visitor was a Madame Blevary, a lady in reduced circumstances who lodged in the same house. Hearing they had come from Portugal, and being herself a native of that country, she sought their acquaintance in the hope of deriving some personal benefit from it. In this she was not disappointed; for the Countess, who knew no English, required a companion, and as Madame Blevary was conversant with several languages and had the manners of a gentlewoman, she readily obtained the post on the recommendation of the landlady.

Among the acquaintances Madame Blevary informed of her good fortune, which she was no doubt induced to dilate upon, was a certain Vitellini, an ex-Jesuit and professor of languages. Like her, he too had fallen on hard times; but in his case the love of gambling had been his ruin. He was also, as it happened, almost equally devoted to the study of chemistry, on a knowledge of which he particularly piqued himself. No sooner, therefore, did he learn that Count Cagliostro had a similar hobby, and a laboratory into the bargain, than he persuaded Madame Blevary to introduce him to the Count, in the hope that he too might profit by the acquaintance as she had done. As a result of this introduction, Vitellini succeeded in ingratiating himself into the favour of Cagliostro, who employed him in the laboratory as an assistant.

Stinginess was a quality of which neither the Count nor his wife was ever accused. On the contrary, as even those most prejudiced against them have been obliged to admit, they were exceedingly generous. With them, however, generosity was one of those amiable weaknesses that are as pernicious in their effect as a vice. There were few who experienced it but abused it in some way. It was so in this instance.

Vitellini, who was at bottom more of a fool than a knave, in the first flush of excitement over the sudden turn of tide in his fortunes which had long been at the lowest ebb, began to brag to his acquaintances in the gambling-dens and coffee-houses he frequented of his connection with Cagliostro, whom he described as "an extraordinary man, a true adept, whose fortune was immense, and who possessed the secret of transmuting metals."

Such praise naturally excited the curiosity of Vitellini's acquaintances, who in their turn were eager to meet the benevolent foreigner. Thus by the indiscretion of Vitellini, Cagliostro was soon besieged by a crowd of shady people whose intentions were so apparent that he was obliged in the end to refuse to receive them when they called. But this only exasperated them ; and one in particular, Pergolezzi—the painter and decorator by whom the reader will recall Balsamo was for a time employed—"threatened to blast the reputation of the Count by circulating a report throughout London that he was ignorant and necessitous, of obscure birth, and had once before resided in England."[1]

Vitellini, needless to say, perceiving the effect of

[1] Cagliostro, however, ignored this threat, which one can scarcely believe he would have done had he had any reason to fear it. Nor did Pergolezzi put it into effect ; and it was not till ten years later, when Cagliostro returned to London thoroughly discredited, that the Editor of the *Courier de l'Europe* got wind of it in some way and twisted it into his Balsamo theory of accounting for the mysterious Cagliostro. Whether Pergolezzi was living at the time is unknown ; in any case the threat which Cagliostro now ignored contained *no mention of Balsamo.*

his folly, now hastened to put a curb on his tongue lest he too should be shown the door. But as the sequel will prove, discretion came to him too late to benefit him. For Madame Blevary, who also entertained in secret a similar opinion of her patron's wealth and knowledge, was one of those whose cupidity had been excited by Vitellini's gossip. She at least had the advantage of being on the inner side of the Count's door, and she determined while she had the chance to profit by it.

To this effect she bethought herself of "one Scott, a man of ambiguous character, and the pliability of whose principles was such that he was ever ready to convert them to the interest of the present moment." It was accordingly arranged between them that Scott should impersonate a Scotch nobleman, in which guise it was hoped the Cagliostros would be effectually deceived as to his intentions. A severe illness, however, with which she was suddenly seized, and during which the Cagliostros "supplied her with every necessary comfort," prevented Madame Blevary from personally introducing her confederate. Nevertheless she did not abandon the idea she had conceived, and ill though she was, she sent word to Cagliostro that "Lord Scott, of whom she had often spoken to him, had arrived in town and proposed to himself the honour of introduction that afternoon."

Entirely unsuspicious of the treachery of a woman who owed so much to their generosity, the Count and Countess received "Lord Scott" on his arrival. His appearance, it seems, did not exactly tally with such notions as Cagliostro had formed either of the man or his rank. But Scott succeeded in dispelling his dis-

appointment, and swindling him into the bargain, by
way of gentle beginning, out of £12 in Portuguese
money which he undertook to get exchanged for its
English equivalent, afterwards declaring with well-
feigned mortification "he had lost it through a hole
in his pocket."

A Giuseppe Balsamo, one imagines, would have
been the last person in the world to be taken in by such
a story. Cagliostro, however, swallowed it without
hesitation; and begging Scott, who confusedly regretted
he was in no position to make good the loss, to think no
more about it, invited him to come to dinner the next day.

Whether Madame Blevary got a share of these or
subsequent spoils is not known, for at this point she
disappears from the scene altogether. Perhaps she
died of that severe illness in which she received from
the Cagliostros while betraying them so many "proofs
of their generosity and humanity." In any case, her
place was most completely filled by "Lady Scott," who
was at this period presented by Scott to the Cagliostros,
and from whom in an incredibly short time she
managed to borrow on her simple note of hand £200.

II

Owing to the prejudice against Cagliostro, a construction wholly unfavourable to him has been placed
upon the extraordinary series of events that now ensued.
This construction, however, cannot be allowed to pass
unchallenged. For it is based solely on the accusations
of the Editor of the *Courier de l'Europe*, who was the
bitter enemy of Cagliostro. Now though it may be

the custom in France for the accused to be considered guilty till he proves his innocence, the contrary is the custom in England, where fortunately it requires something more than the mere word of a single and professedly hostile witness to condemn a man. The Editor of the *Courier de l'Europe* declared that "upwards of twenty persons" would confirm his statements. None, however, offered to do so. Under such circumstances, as we are reduced to dealing with prejudices, I shall in this particular instance confess to one in favour of an ancient English principle of justice, and give Cagliostro the benefit of the doubt. His word at least is as much entitled to respect as that of the Editor of the *Courier de l'Europe.* There is, moreover, much in his spirited defence even worthy of credence.

Having found him so easy to dupe, the crew by whom he was surrounded naturally devoted their attention to increasing the friendship they had formed with him and his wife. Not a day passed but "Lord" Scott and his lady paid the Count and Countess a visit, and as it was their habit to drop in just before dinner or supper they soon managed to obtain their meals at the expense of the hospitable foreigners.

On one of these occasions the conversation having turned on a lottery in which his guests were interested, Cagliostro was reminded of "a manuscript he had found in the course of his travels which contained many curious cabalistic operations by aid of which the author set forth the possibilities of calculating winning numbers." But since the matter was not one in which he had hitherto taken any particular interest, he was unwilling to express an opinion as to the value of these calculations, "having long contracted the habit of suspending his judgment on subjects he had not investigated." On being urged, however, he consented to consult the manuscript; whereupon, to test its system, Scott "risked a trifle" and won upwards of a hundred pounds.

But whatever opinion Cagliostro may now have formed as to the value to be attached to these "cabalistic operations," he refused to put them to further test. Gambling would appear to have had no attraction for him. Not only, if we are to believe him, did he risk nothing himself, or benefit in any way by the winning numbers he predicted on this occasion, but *never afterwards* is there to be found any allusion to gambling in the records that relate to his career. His aversion, however, which others—notably Mirabeau—have also shared, is not necessarily to be regarded as a virtue. There are many who, without objecting to gambling on moral grounds, are unable to find any pleasure in it.

Apart from all other considerations, Cagliostro had a strong personal motive for his refusal to make a business of predicting winning numbers for Scott. He was too completely absorbed in his alchemical experiments to find an interest in anything else. Of what value was the most perfect betting system in the world compared with the secret of transmuting metals, making diamonds, and prolonging life? To the man who is wrapped up in such things, lotteries and the means of winning them are beneath contempt. He has not only got something more profitable to do than waste his time in calculating lucky numbers, but he is on a plane above the ordinary gambler.

This, however, was a distinction that Scott, who was merely a vulgar sharper, was incapable of either making himself or appreciating when made. After his success in testing the system he believed it to be infallible. To be refused so simple a means of making a fortune was intolerable. In his exasperation he dropped the rôle of Scotch nobleman altogether and appeared in his real character as the common rogue he was, whereupon Cagliostro promptly showed him the door and refused to have any further intercourse with him.

" Lady " Scott, however, a few days later forced herself upon the Countess, and endeavoured to excite her compassion with the relation of a pitiful story, in which she declared that Scott, by whom she had been betrayed, had decamped with the profit arising from the lottery, leaving her and three children entirely destitute. The Countess, touched by this imaginary tale, generously interceded in her behalf with the Count, who sent her "a guinea and a number for the following day." Miss Fry, to give her her real name, no sooner obtained this number than she and Scott risked every penny they could raise upon it. Fortune once more favoured them and they won on this occasion the sum of fifteen hundred guineas.

In the first moment of exultation Miss Fry at once rushed off to the Cagliostros with the whole of her winnings, which she offered to the Count as a token of her gratitude and confidence in him. But Cagliostro was not to be caught in this cunningly laid snare. He received her very coldly and refused to concern himself in her affairs.

"If you will take my advice," he said, "you will go into the country with your three children and live on the interest of your money. If I have obliged you, the only return I desire is that you will never more re-enter my doors."

But Miss Fry was not to be got rid of in this fashion. Dazzled by the golden shower the Count's predictions had caused to rain upon her, she sighed for more numbers, and to obtain them she had recourse to Vitellini, in the hope that as he was still employed by the Count he might succeed in getting them for her. So eager was she to procure them that she gave Vitellini twenty guineas in advance as an earnest of her sincerity and to increase his zeal in the matter.

But though Vitellini was, needless to say, only too eager to oblige her, Cagliostro was not to be persuaded to gratify him. Hereupon, Miss Fry, repenting of her liberality, made a debt of her gift, and had Vitellini, who was unable to repay her, imprisoned. Cagliostro, however, generously came to the rescue, and obtained his release. This action awoke a belated sense of gratitude in the fellow, which he afterwards ineffectually attempted to prove.

But to return to Miss Fry. Having failed to turn Vitellini to account, she determined to approach the Countess and lay her, if possible, under an obligation. After considering various schemes by which this was to be effected, she "purchased of a pawnbroker a diamond necklace for which she paid £94." She then procured a box with two compartments, in one of which she placed the necklace, and in the other some snuff of a rare quality that she knew the Countess liked, and watching for an opportunity of finding her alone, managed to get access to her.

In the hands of a Miss Fry, the Countess, who was the most amiable, pliable, and insignificant of creatures, was like wax. Cleverly turning the conversation so as to suit her purpose, Miss Fry casually produced the box and opening the compartment containing the snuff prevailed upon the Countess to take a pinch. After this it was an easy matter to persuade her to keep the box. Two days later the Countess discovered the necklace. As she had been forbidden to receive any presents from Miss Fry, she at once reported the matter to her husband. He was for returning the necklace at once, but as the Countess, who doubtless had no desire to part with it, suggested that to do so after having had it so long in her possession would appear "indelicate," Cagliostro foolishly consented to let her keep it. As to retain the gift without acknowledging it would have been still more indelicate, Miss Fry was accordingly once more permitted to resume her visits.

Fully alive to the fact that she was only received on sufferance, she was naturally very careful not to jeopardize the position she had recovered with so much difficulty by any indiscretion. She by no means, however, lost sight of the object she had in view. Hearing that the Cagliostros were moving to Suffolk Street, she hired a room in the same house where it was impossible to avoid her. As she had told Cagliostro that she intended to follow his advice and live in the country with her three children—a fiction to which she still adhered—he naturally inquired the reason of her continued residence in London. She gave a lack of the necessary funds as her excuse, and hinted, as he had broached the subject, that he should " extricate her from her embarrassment by giving her numbers for the French lottery."

The Count ignored the hint. But in consideration of the necklace she had given the Countess, and with the hope of being entirely rid of her, he gave her £50 to defray the expense of her journey into the country. This was, however, not at all to Miss Fry's taste. She wanted numbers for the French lottery, and meant to have them too, or know the reason why, as the saying is. Accordingly, the next day she trumped up some fresh story of debts and absconding creditors, and, appealing to the compassion of the Countess, implored her to intercede with the Count to give her the numbers she wanted.

Cagliostro was now thoroughly annoyed. To settle the matter once for all, he told her that " he believed the success of the system was due more to chance than to calculation ; but whether it was effected by the one or the other he was resolved to have no further concern in anything of that nature." The manner in which these words were uttered was too emphatic to permit Miss Fry to continue to cherish the least hope of ever being able to induce Cagliostro to change his mind. Still, even now she refused to accept defeat. The numbers had become to her like morphia to a *morphineuse ;* and precisely as the latter to obtain the drug she craves will resort to the most desperate stratagems, so Miss Fry determined to execute a scheme she had long premeditated by which Cagliostro was to be *compelled* to give her the numbers.

Cagliostro

III

This scheme, described by an ardent defender of Cagliostro against the violent denunciations of the Editor of the *Courier de l'Europe* as "the most diabolic that ever entered into the heart of ingratitude," was nothing more nor less than a sort of muscular blackmail. Taking advantage of his ignorance of English, Cagliostro was to be arrested on a false charge and simultaneously robbed of the precious manuscript by which he predicted the numbers.

To assist in the execution of her plan Miss Fry, who was the life and soul of the conspiracy, had the help of a barrister named Reynolds, "who, notwithstanding his expertness in the pettifogging finesse of the low law, could not preserve himself from an ignominious exhibition in the pillory"; a rough known as Broad; and, of course, Scott.

When everything was arranged, Miss Fry brought an action against Cagliostro to recover £190, the writ for which was served by Reynolds, apparently by bribing the sheriff's officer. Thus armed, he proceeded to Cagliostro's house accompanied by the others, and while he explained to the amazed Count, who had never seen him before, the object of his visit and the authority for what he did, Scott and Broad broke into the laboratory, where they found and took possession of the manuscript and the note-of-hand for the two hundred pounds the Count had lent Miss Fry, who during these highly criminal proceedings had the shrewdness to "wait on the stairs" without. Reynolds then conducted Cagliostro to a sponging-house, from

which he was released the following day by depositing
with Saunders, the sheriff's officer, "jewels worth three or
four hundred pounds."

The conspirators, however, baffled by the release
of Cagliostro, from whom they had obtained nothing
but the note-of-hand and the manuscript, of which they
could make neither head nor tail, at once renewed
their persecution. This time they procured a warrant
for the arrest of both himself and his wife on the
charge of practising *witchcraft*. The fact that it was
possible to obtain a warrant on so ridiculous a charge,
which both those who made it, as well as the official
by whom the warrant was granted, were perfectly aware
would be dismissed with contempt the moment it was
investigated, explains how easy it was, under the
corrupt and chaotic state of the legal system of the
period, to convert the protection of the law into a
persecution. Indeed, unauthenticated though they
are, none of the legal proceedings in which Cagliostro
was now involved are improbable. On the contrary
their probability is so great as almost to guarantee
their credibility.

By a bribe—for it can scarcely be termed bail—
Cagliostro and his wife escaped the inconvenience of
being taken to jail before the investigation of the
charge on which they were apprehended. Seeing
that their victim was not to be terrified, his persecutors tried other tactics. Reynolds was deputed
to persuade him, if possible, to explain the system
by which he predicted the winning numbers.
But Cagliostro indignantly refused to gratify him
when he called, whereupon Scott, who had remained
without the door, his ear glued to the key-hole,

perceiving that the eloquence of Reynolds failed to produce the desired effect, suddenly burst into the room, and "presenting a pistol to the breast of the Count, threatened to discharge it that instant unless he consented to reveal the secrets they demanded."

This species of bluff, however, was equally futile. Cagliostro regarded the bully and his pistol with contemptuous composure—particularly as he did not discharge it. He assured him that nothing was to be accomplished by solicitations or threats, but as he desired to be left in peace he was ready "to think no more of the note-of-hand they had robbed him of, and would even let them have the effects he had deposited with Saunders, the sheriff's officer, on condition the proceedings against him were dropped and the manuscript returned."

Seeing there was no better alternative, Reynolds and Scott decided to accept the proposition, and immediately went with Cagliostro to Saunders' house to settle the matter. But Saunders, realizing that Cagliostro's troubles were due to his gullibility, ignorance of English, and apparent fortune, was tempted to reserve the plucking of so fat a bird for himself. He accordingly advised the Count not to compromise the matter, but to bring in his turn an action for robbery against the crew of sharpers into whose power he had fallen. Cagliostro was easily induced to accept this advice, and with the aid of Saunders procured four warrants for the arrest of Scott, Reynolds, Broad, and Miss Fry. The last, however, aware that the charge against her could not be substantiated, as she had not personally been present at the time of the robbery, made no attempt to escape, and was

taken into custody—from which, as she had fore-
seen, she soon freed herself. As for the other three,
perceiving that the game was up, they took time by
the forelock and disappeared while they had the chance.

But Cagliostro had yet to realize what a vindictive
fury he had to deal with in Miss Fry. The two
actions she had instituted against him had not been
quashed, as she took care daily to let him know in
ways studiously calculated to render the reminder
particularly harassing. Saunders, with whom he had
now become intimate, was "much concerned at this
persecution, and repeatedly advised him to take an
apartment in his house."

Now little as Cagliostro was acquainted with English
customs, he was not so ignorant, as he himself confesses,
as not to understand that such a proposition was
" singular "; but as Saunders had been kind to him,
" kept his carriage," and appeared in every way worthy
of respect, the Count, being desirous of purchasing
tranquillity, without hesitation accepted the invitation.

Because no Englishman would have done so, and
it appears absurd to picture even a foreigner passing
six weeks of his own accord in a sponging-house, the
visit Cagliostro now paid to Saunders is generally
regarded as anything but voluntary. But how much
more absurd is the assertion of the Editor of the
Courier de l'Europe—the *only* other source of information beside Cagliostro in regard to these proceedings—
that the Count was " constrained from *poverty* " to
reside with Saunders! Even if foreigners in distress
would be likely to seek refuge in a sponging-house,
is it at all likely that they would be admitted just
because of their *poverty* ?

Cagliostro

" I occupied," says Cagliostro, "the finest apartment in the house. There was always a seat at my table for a chance comer. I defrayed the expenses of the poor prisoners confined there, and even paid the debts of some, who thus obtained their freedom." Of these, one " Shannon, a chemist," is quoted by him as being ready to testify to the truth of the statement. Be this as it may, after six weeks Cagliostro once more returned to his rooms in Suffolk Street to the "sensible regret of Saunders."

But scarcely had he arrived when he was served for the third time with a writ issued at the instigation of Miss Fry for "a debt of £200." At the instance of Saunders, an Italian merchant named Badioli was induced to be his surety. Saunders, whose interest in his affairs was inspired by the profit he calculated on deriving from them, also recommended him to engage as counsel to defend him a certain Priddle whom Cagliostro had met in the sponging-house. Thus supported, and conscious of innocence, he awaited his trial with comparative composure.

The case came on in due course at the King's Bench, but Priddle, discovering that it was to be tried by Lord Mansfield, whom he dared not face, backed out of it altogether. Left without counsel at the last moment, Cagliostro was driven in desperation to defend his cause himself. As his knowledge of English was very imperfect, he was obliged to have an interpreter, and, none other apparently being available, he employed Vitellini. But as Vitellini, either owing to excitement caused by the responsibility he was suddenly called upon to assume, or to an equally imperfect knowledge of English, could not make himself understood, Lord

Mansfield, to avoid further confusion, and perceiving from the charge of witchcraft that the case was trivial, suggested a compromise and recommended a Mr. Howarth as arbitrator. To this proposal Cagliostro was compelled, and Miss Fry was only too glad, to consent.

The first thing Howarth had to decide was Miss Fry's first claim to £190, which she alleged she had lent the Count. As she had no proof whatever to advance in support of her claim, it was at once set aside. The charge of witchcraft was also with similar expedition dismissed as "frivolous."

In her attempt to substantiate her other claim to £200, Miss Fry and her witness Broad very nearly perjured themselves. They both asserted that the money had been expended "in purchasing sequins" for Cagliostro. Questioned by Howarth as to how he had obtained the sequins, Broad replied that he had "bought them of a merchant whose name he could not recollect." At this Howarth, whose suspicions were naturally aroused by such a reply, observed that "it must have been a very large amount of sequins to represent £200, and he did not believe any merchant would have such a quantity on hand." Broad hereupon declared he had not bought them of one merchant, "but of about *fourscore.*" But on being pressed by Howarth he could not remember the names or places of abode of any of them.

Nor could Miss Fry assist him to disentangle himself. She stated that "a Jew of whose name she was ignorant had brought the sequins to her." After this there was nothing for Howarth to do but dismiss the charge, which he did with "a severe reprimand."

Cagliostro

Miss Fry, however, was not to be beaten without a further effort. She demanded that the necklace should be returned to her, which she declared she had only *lent* to the Countess. To this Cagliostro saw fit to protest, but as Vitellini failed to express his reasons intelligibly, Howarth came to the conclusion that the necklace at least belonged to Miss Fry. He therefore ordered the Count to return it to her, and pay the costs of the arbitration into the bargain.

This decision, however, by no means put an end to the troubles of Cagliostro.

Whether at his own request, or by order of Howarth, he seems to have been given a few days in which to conform to the ruling of the arbitrator. But Badioli, his surety, no sooner learnt the result of the case than, dreading lest Cagliostro should decamp and leave him to pay the costs and compensate Miss Fry, he resolved to release himself from his obligations by surrendering the Count. Keeping his intention a profound secret, he paid a friendly visit to Cagliostro, and at the close carried him off for a drive in the park. "On their way," says an anonymous author of the only contemporary book in defence of Cagliostro, "they alighted at a judge's chambers, where Mr. Badioli said he had business to settle. They then again entered the coach, which in a short time stopped before an edifice of which the Count was ignorant. However, his companion entering, he followed his example ; when Mr. Badioli, making a slight apology, desired him to wait there a few minutes, saying which he left him.

"Minutes and hours elapsed, but no Mr. Badioli appeared. The Count then endeavoured to return through the door at which they had entered, but found himself repulsed, though he was ignorant of the cause. He remained till evening in the greatest agitation of mind, roving from place to place, when he attracted the observation of a foreigner, who having heard his story, and made the necessary inquiries, informed him that he was a prisoner in the King's Bench.

"Two days had elapsed before the Countess was able to obtain any information concerning him."

IV

The conduct of Badioli, who had taken so treacherous an advantage of his ignorance of the English language and law, was to Cagliostro the unkindest cut of all. After such convincing proofs of its hostility, to continue to struggle against adversity seemed no doubt futile. He accepted the situation apathetically. More than a month elapsed before he apparently took steps to procure his release— even then the proceedings which resulted in his liberation from the King's Bench prison do not appear to have been instituted by himself, but by a certain O'Reilly. Now as this good Samaritan was previously unknown to him, there is reason to suppose that he was delegated by the Esperance Lodge of Freemasons, of which the Count was a member, to assist him. For O'Reilly was the proprietor of the "King's Head in Gerard Street where the Esperance Lodge assembled."[1]

[1] Were all the *suppositions* on which the general opinion of Cagliostro is based as reasonable as the present, there would be no cause for complaint on that score.

Cagliostro

Through the instrumentality of O'Reilly, for whose kindness on this occasion Cagliostro was ever after grateful, fresh bail was procured. But as the summer vacation had commenced, Miss Fry had the right—which she was only too glad to avail herself of—to refuse to accept the bail offered till the end of the vacation. O'Reilly, however, was not a Saunders ; his interest in the Count was not mercenary, and being fully conversant with the intricate workings of the law, he applied directly to Lord Mansfield, who at once ordered Miss Fry's attorney to accept the bail.

Considering the evidences Cagliostro had had of this woman's fury, it was not surprising that he should have attributed the extraordinary circumstances that now occurred to her vindictive ingenuity. As he was preparing to leave the King's Bench, "Mr. Crisp, the under-marshal of the prison, informed him that one Aylett had lodged a detainer against him by name of Melisa Cagliostro, otherwise Joseph Balsamo, for a debt of £30." The Count demanded with the utmost surprise the meaning of this new intrigue. Crisp replied that Aylett declared the sum specified was due to him as his fee, with interest added, from "one Joseph Balsamo, by whom he had been employed in the year 1772 to recover a debt of a Dr. Benamore."

It mattered not in the least that Cagliostro protested "he had never seen Aylett, and did not believe Aylett had ever seen him," or that Aylett himself did not appear in person. As the law then stood, Crisp's statement was sufficient to detain the unfortunate Count, whom he in his turn was anxious to bleed while he had the chance. Accordingly, while admitting that without Aylett's consent he was not empowered to accept the bail which Cagliostro eagerly offered him, Crisp was only ready to let him go "if he could deposit in his hand thirty pounds to indemnify him."

To this proposition Cagliostro consented, but as he had not the cash upon him he asked Crisp if he would accept its equivalent in plate, promising to redeem it the next day. His request was granted, and Cagliostro remained in King's Bench while O'Reilly went to the Countess for the plate in question, which consisted of "two soup-ladles, two candlesticks, two salt-cellars, two pepper-castors, six forks, six table-spoons, nine knife-handles with blades, a pair of snuffers and stand, all of silver."

The next day, true to his promise, the Count paid Crisp thirty pounds. Crisp, however, instead of giving back the plate, declared that Aylett had been to him in the meantime, and on learning that he had freed the prisoner was highly exasperated and demanded the plate, which had consequently been given him. As Aylett, on the other hand, when questioned, declared that Crisp "was a liar," "it was impossible," says Cagliostro, "for me to ascertain by whom I was plundered."

Of all the incidents in this series of "injustices," as he termed it, of which he was the victim the most curious is undoubtedly the unexpected advent of Aylett upon the scene in a rôle totally unconnected with the development, so to speak, of the plot of the play. Considering that he was the first person on record to state that Cagliostro was Giuseppe

Balsamo, it is worth while inquiring into his reason for doing so and the value to be attached to it.

Aylett's reputation, to begin with, was such as to render the truth of any statement he might make extremely doubtful, if not to invalidate it altogether. Like Reynolds and Priddle, he was a rascally attorney who had been "convicted of perjury and exposed in the pillory." Granting that he had defended Balsamo in his action against Dr. Benamore, and was sufficiently struck by the resemblance of Cagliostro to his old client as to believe them to be the same person, his conduct on the present occasion was decidedly ambiguous. According to his statement, " happening one day in 1777 to be in Westminster Hall, he perceived a person that he immediately recognized as Balsamo, whom he had not seen since 1772." Instead of accosting him then and there, he decided to find out where he lived ; and after much difficulty learnt that the person he had seen and believed to be Balsamo was in the King's Bench prison and that his name was Cagliostro ; whereupon, *without taking the least step to ascertain whether he was right or not in his surmise*, he laid a detainer against him for the money Balsamo owed him. No record of any kind exists as to what passed between Aylett and Cagliostro when they finally met, or in fact whether they met at all.

That Aylett would, after having received Cagliostro's plate or money from Crisp, have admitted he had made a mistake is, judging from the man's character, not to be credited. But what renders this singular matter still more questionable is the fact that the Editor of the *Courier de l'Europe* nine years later,

Cagliostro in London

when publishing his "incontestable proofs" of the identity of Balsamo with Cagliostro, should have accepted the statement of Aylett and *ignored* that of Dr. Benamore, who was also living at the time and whose position as representative in England for thirty years of the various Barbary States would, to say the least, have given the weight of respectability to his word. Now as there is no doubt at all that the Editor of the *Courier de l'Europe* passionately desired that his proofs should really be "incontestable," there is only one explanation of his conduct in this matter possible : Dr. Benamore must have *refused to make the statement requested of him.*

On the other hand, Cagliostro—and his word, even prejudice must admit, is to be trusted quite as much as that of an Aylett or the Editor of the *Courier de l'Europe*—asserts in the most emphatic language that Dr. Benamore was ready to testify in *his* behalf to a total ignorance of the very name of Balsamo.

As it is impossible to verify either one or the other of these statements, the reader must be left to form his own conclusions.

Having once more regained his liberty, Cagliostro very wisely sought safety from further molestation by taking up his abode with his wife "in O'Reilly's hotel," where he resided during the remainder of his stay in London. On the recommendation of his friend he employed a lawyer by the name of James, through whom he succeeded in recovering the jewels which, it will be remembered, he had deposited with Saunders as bail in the first suit brought against him by Miss Fry. As he could, no doubt, have managed to decamp without returning the necklace or paying the costs of his trial as ordered by the arbitrator—the date named for the settlement was still some weeks off—it is, under the circumstances and considering all that has been said against him, decidedly to his credit that he remained and fulfilled his obligations.

He states—and there is no reason to disbelieve him—that O'Reilly and James, after the final settlement of his case, tried hard to persuade him "to commence an action against Aylett for perjury, another against Crisp for swindling, and one of blackmail against Fry, Scott, Reynolds and Broad." He was, however, not to be beguiled into any such costly and uncertain undertakings.

"The injustices," he says, "I had experienced rendered me unjust to myself, and attributing to the whole nation the faults of a few individuals I determined to leave a place in which I had found neither laws, justice, nor hospitality."

Accordingly, having given O'Reilly, with whom he continued in close communication, a power of attorney to use in case of need, he left for Brussels "with no more than fifty pounds in cash and some jewels."

He afterwards asserted that during the eighteen months he had resided in London he had been defrauded of 3000 guineas.

In this a hostile writer—with sheep-like fidelity to popular prejudice—sees "the native excellence of English talent, when the most accomplished swindler of the swindling eighteenth century was so hobbled, duped, and despoiled by the aid of the masterly fictions of English law."

It is possible, however, to draw another and more

sensible inference from this legal *escroquerie* of which Cagliostro was the dupe, than one based on mere prejudice. As his fame, needless to say, lies not in proved charges of embezzlement, but in the secrets of the crucible and the mysteries of Egyptian Masonry, it is clearly by his adventures in the laboratory and the lodge rather than by those which led him to the King's Bench and the Bastille that he is to be judged. Since it is a question of swindling, it is perhaps just as well to bear in mind the *character* of these accomplished impostures to which so much obloquy has been attached. Accordingly, before attempting to draw aside the figurative curtain which conceals him, as Carlyle's "hand itched" to do, it is essential to examine the fabric, so to speak, of the curtain itself—in other words, to get some idea of what was understood by the Occult in Cagliostro's day.

As I have no intention of entering this labyrinth of perpetual darkness which none but an adept is capable of treading, I shall merely stand on the threshold. There, at any rate, it is light enough for the reader to see as much as is necessary for the present purpose.

CHAPTER II

I

MAN, at once instinctively mistrusting his own power, and inspired by the love of the marvellous which is inherent in human nature, has from the beginning invoked, or invented, as you will, the invisible powers of an inaccessible sphere. History is filled with the phenomena arising from this innate tendency to believe in the supernatural, which while varying in form according to epochs, places, and customs are at bottom identical. Belief in the supernatural is, indeed, the basic principle of primitive man's first conception of community of interest, the germ from which religion, social order, civilization have developed.

In the beginning religion and magic were one. All the priests of Egypt and the East were invested with supernatural and mysterious powers of which they long possessed the monopoly. These powers were precisely the same as those of the mediums of the present day; but the effects they produced no doubt appeared infinitely greater owing to the boundless credulity, simplicity, and ignorance of those who witnessed them.

By degrees, as civilization after civilization perished, knowledge became more diffused. Magic passed from the sanctuary to the street. The Pagan world was

74

Eighteenth Century Occultism

filled with astrologers, sorcerers, sibyls, sooth-sayers, wonder-workers of all descriptions. In the Middle Ages, when Christianity finally superseded Paganism, the supernatural once more took up its abode in religion. Demonology, which had survived all the revolutions of antiquity, and which still exists without much fundamental difference under other forms all over the world, assimilated itself to the dogmas of the Church. The Popes affirmed the popular belief in sorcery, magic and diabolic possession. But the supernatural phenomena associated with the belief in these things were regarded as the work of the devil, in whose existence the Christian world believed as implicitly as in the existence of God ; so while the Church sanctioned this belief as one of the mysteries of religion it waged a merciless war againt all persons suspected of having commerce with demons. From its terrible ban the mystical visionaries alone were exempt. These persons, ascetics all, the sanctity of whose reputations was unquestioned and whose hallucinations were due to hysteria, epilepsy, or neuroticism, were canonized.

Towards the close of the seventeenth century, with the revival of a tolerant and enlightened philosophy, the devil had grown old and accusations of sorcery were rare. But the belief in the supernatural still continued to thrive ; and in the century of universal scepticism, the century of Voltaire and the Encyclopedists, when faith in everything till then venerated was exploded, that in the marvellous alone survived. "The more civilization advances," wrote Voltaire, "the more noise does superstition make."

On the eve of the French Revolution, Mesmer

electrified the world with his animal magnetism.
With this discovery the belief in the supernatural
entered a new and more wonderful phase. The
marvellous had passed from a grossly material to
a purely spiritual plane. The magnetism of Mesmer
was followed by the hypnotism of the Marquis de
Puységur, with its attendant train of table-turning and telepathy, clairvoyance and clairaudience,
spiritualism, theosophy, and Christian science. To-
day the whole system of the hermetic philosophy of the
Egyptians and Hindus has been re-discovered, re-
deciphered, and restored with the most astonishing
results and the most conspicuous success to the
amazement of the world.

Never has the belief in the supernatural been more
flourishing and more invincible than at the present.
Side by side with the positivism of modern science
marches the mysticism of the occult, equally confident
and undaunted, and equally victorious. Not a link
in the chain that connects the phenomena of the
mediums and adepts of to-day with those of the
Chaldaeans has been broken. Madame Blavatsky
and Mrs. Eddy are the latest descendants of Hermes
Trismegistus, who whether regarded as man, god,
or the personification of all the knowledge of his
remote times, is the parent of all the wonder-workers,
scientific as well as unscientific, of the world. The
prodigies of these priestesses of theosophy and
Christian science, which are the last and most
popular manifestations of the marvellous, are no
less significant, and much more wonderful because
more inexplicable, than those of a Ramsay or a Curie.

As to the future of this faith in the supernatural,

one thing may reasonably be taken for granted ; the marvellous will never cease to appeal to the imagination of mankind till the riddle of the universe is solved. To deride it is ridiculous. Occultism is not a menace to progress, but a spur. Its secrets are not to be ridiculed, but to be explained. That is its challenge to modern science, which is at once its offspring and its servant.

The desire to prolong life, the desire to enjoy life, and the desire to look beyond life are inherent in human nature, and man has sought from time immemorial to realize them. To-day it is to science that we look for the realization of the first two of these great desires of which it is the outcome ; while it is only with the third that the marvellous, or what is understood by occultism, is now associated.

Formerly, however, the search for remedies for the irremediable was conducted exclusively in the sphere of the supernatural. The love of life gave rise to the quest for the Fountain of Youth, which still continues under innumerable other forms and names that will occur to every one. The latest, perhaps, is the Menshikov Sour Milk Cure. From the love of ease sprang the search for the "philosopher's stone," which was to create wealth by the transmutation of metals into gold. This quest which long captivated the imagination of men is now entirely abandoned, though its object, needless to say, is more furiously desired than ever. While to the curiosity as to the future we owe the pseudo-sciences of astrology, palmistry, fortune-telling, divination, etc.

Cagliostro

Those who devoted their lives to these things were divided into three classes—alchemists, astrologers, and the motley tribe of quacks and charlatans, who may be summed up for sake of convenience under the name of sorcerers. These divisions, however, were by no means hard and fast. United by a common idea each class dabbled in the affairs of the others. Thus astrologers and sorcerers were often alchemists, and alchemists seldom confined their attention solely to the search for the *elixir vitae* and the philosopher's stone.

As the alchemists, owing to their superior knowledge, and the results they obtained, were more considered than the astrologers and sorcerers, alchemy developed into a science at an early date. The obscurity in which its origin is involved is a sign of its antiquity. Some enthusiasts believe it to be coeval with the creation of man. Vincent de Beauvais was of the opinion that all the antediluvians must have had some knowledge of alchemy, and cites Noah as having been acquainted with the *elixir vitae*, "otherwise he could not have lived to so prodigious an age and begotten children when upwards of five hundred." Others have traced it to the Egyptians, from whom Moses was believed to have learnt it. Martini, on the other hand, affirms that alchemy was practised by the Chinese two thousand five hundred years before the birth of Christ. But though a belief in the transmutation of metals was general in the Roman Empire, the practice of alchemy does not appear to have received much consideration before the eighth century. At this period the discoveries of Gebir, an Arabian alchemist, gave so great a stimulus to the quest of the philosopher's stone and the elixir of life that he is generally regarded as the creator of these picturesque delusions, which for a thousand years had so great a hold on the popular imagination.

Banned and fostered in turn, and often at the same time, by the Church; practised in all classes of society and by all sorts and conditions of people; regarded with admiration and contempt; alchemy has played too vast and important a rôle in the history of humanity to be despised, wild and romantic though this rôle has been. Nothing could be more unjust and absurd than to judge it by the charlatans who exploited it. The alchemists whom history still remembers were in reality the pioneers of civilization, who, venturing ahead of the race befogged in dense forests of ignorance and superstition, cut a road through to the light, along which mankind travelled slowly in their wake. Not only were these fantastic spirits of light the parents of modern science and physics, but they have helped to adorn literature and art. Some idea of their importance may be gathered from the many words in common use that they have given to the language, such as: *crucible, amalgam, alcohol, potash, laudanum, precipitate, saturation, distillation, quintessence, affinity,* etc.

The alchemists often stumbled upon discoveries they did not seek. Science is thus indebted to Gebir for the first suggestion of corrosive sublimate, the red oxide of mercury, nitric acid, and nitrate of silver; to Roger Bacon for the telescope, the magic lantern, and gunpowder; to Van Helmont for the properties of gas; to Paracelsus, the most extraordinary of them all, for laudanum. It is to him also that medicine owes the idea of the clinic. As in chemistry so in other sciences the most important discoveries were made by men who had a marked taste for alchemic theories. Kepler was guided in his investigations by cabalistic considerations.

The search for gold and youth, however, were only one phase of alchemy. It was too closely allied to what was known as "magic" not to be confounded with it. In the popular estimation the alchemists were all magicians. Most, perhaps all, of the so-called occult phenomena so familiar to us to-day were performed by them. Long before such things as animal magnetism, hypnotism, telepathy, ventriloquism, autosuggestion, etc., had a name, the alchemists had discovered them, though they themselves were as unable to explain or account for the wonders they performed as the ignorant world that witnessed them.

Albertus Magnus had the power to delude whole crowds, precisely as Indian necromancers do at the present. Cornelius Agrippa "at the request of Erasmus and other learned men called up from the grave many of the great philosophers of antiquity, among others Cicero, whom he caused to re-deliver his celebrated oration for Roscius." He also showed Lord Surrey, when on the continent, "the resemblance in a glass" of his mistress, the fair Geraldine. "She was represented on a couch weeping for her lover. Lord Surrey made a note of the exact time at which he saw this vision and afterwards ascertained that his mistress was so employed at the very minute." The famous Dr. Dee, whose whole life was devoted to the search for the philosopher's stone, was an accomplished crystal-gazer and spirit-rapper.

Eighteenth Century Occultism

It was, without doubt, the strong and crude element of magic in alchemy that prepared the way for the great change that came over the science at the beginning of the seventeenth century. With the revival of learning that followed the Renaissance, there arose a mysterious sect in Germany known as the Rosicrucians, who were destined to revolutionize the belief in the supernatural. They claimed to derive their name from a certain Christian Rosencreutz who, in a pilgrimage to the Holy Land, had been initiated into the mysteries of the wisdom of the East. The tenets of the Rosicrucians, as well as their existence, were first made known to the world at the beginning of the seventeenth century in an anonymous German work said to have been found in the tomb of Rosencreutz, who had died one hundred and twenty years previously.

The absurd legends concerning him have led many to deny that such a person as Rosencreutz ever existed. Such writers attribute the origin of the society to the theories of Paracelsus and Dr. Dee, who unconsciously became the real though unrecognized founders of the Rosicrucians. Be this as it may, no sooner were their doctrines generally known than all the alchemists and believers in the marvellous hastened to accept them. The influence thus acquired by the "Society of the Rose-Cross" was as beneficial as it was far-reaching. Its character was a sort of Protestant mysticism, and its chief aim the gratuitous healing of the sick. Hitherto alchemy and the belief in the supernatural had been grossly materialistic. The Rosicrucians refined the one and spiritualized the other. They claimed that by strictly conforming to the rules of their philosophy, of which chastity was the most rigorous and important, they could ignore hunger or thirst, enjoy perfect health, and prolong their lives indefinitely. Of the occult knowledge they possessed, that of transmuting metals into gold was stripped of its old significance. The philosopher's stone was no longer to be regarded as merely the means of acquiring riches, but the instrument by which mankind could command the service of the spirits of the invisible world.

They denied that these were the horrible and terrifying demons with which the monks had peopled the unseen, but mild, beautiful, and beneficent sprites, anxious to be of service to men. In the Rosicrucian imagination there existed in each element a race of spirits peculiar to it. Thus the air was inhabited by Sylphs, the water by Undines, the earth by Gnomes, and the fire by Salamanders. It was by them that all that was marvellous was done. In the course of their development the mystical tendencies of the Rosicrucians became more and more pronounced. Thus they finally came to regard the philosopher's stone as signifying contentment, the secret of which was compared in the mystical phraseology they adopted to "a spirit that lived within an emerald and converted everything near it to the highest perfection it was capable of."

In fine, Rosicrucianism may be described as the bridge over which the belief in the supernatural passed from sorcery, witchcraft, and the grossest superstition to the highly spiritualized form in which it is manifested at the present. The transit, however, was not effected without interruption. Towards the beginning of the eighteenth century the bridge, undermined by the mockery and scepticism of the age, collapsed. About fifty years later it was reconstructed by Swedenborg on a new and spiritualistic system. In the meantime, as will be seen, superstition adrift on the ocean of unbelief, clutched credulously at every straw that floated by.

II

The old belief in alchemy as a magical science did not survive the seventeenth century. It is true the credulous and ignorant, deluded by swindlers and impostors, long continued to regard alchemy as supernatural; but the bona-fide alchemists themselves, who were able and intelligent men, had begun to understand the nature of their discoveries. The symbolic interpretation of the philosopher's stone led to a new conception of the uses of the crucible. The alchemists of the eighteenth century, during which the name was still in common use, though its original signification had become obsolete, were really amateur chemists. From pseudo-science modern science was beginning to be evolved.

The great changes, however, that upset the convictions and disintegrated the whole fabric of society of the eighteenth century, were favourable to the increase and spread of superstition. The amazing recrudescence of the belief in the supernatural, which was one of the most conspicuous features of the age, was the direct result of the prevailing infidelity and indifference. Persecuted, banned, anathematized, but never exterminated, it crept from the hiding-places in which it had lurked for centuries, and in the age of unbelief emerged boldly into the light of day. The forms it assumed were many and various.

In 1729 Jansenism—a sort of evangelical movement in the Church of Rome—which in its war with Jesuitism in the previous century had been crushed, but not exterminated, took advantage of the apathy of the time to reassert itself. To do this with success it was necessary to make a powerful appeal to the popular imagination, and as no means are as sure of producing effect as supernatural ones, the world was startled by a series of miracles performed at the grave of Deacon Pâris, a famous martyr in the cause of Jansenism. These miracles, which at first took the form of cures such as at the present day are to be seen at Lourdes, soon acquired fame. All sorts of people, whom the doctors were unable to restore to health, began to flock to the Jansenist Cemetery of St. Médard, where it was discovered that other graves beside that of Deacon Pâris, and finally the whole cemetery shared the healing properties of his ashes. The hitherto simple character of the cures was changed. They were accompanied by extraordinary convulsions, considered more divine than the cures themselves, in which the bones cracked, the body was scorched with fever, or parched with cold, and the invalid fell into a prophetic transport.

The noise of these pathological phenomena attracted immense crowds to the Cemetery of St. Médard, where the spectators, who were drawn out of mere idle curiosity, as well as those who came to be cured, were seized or pretended to be seized with the convulsive frenzy. The popularity of St. Médard induced the Jansenists to attach similar virtues to other cemeteries.

Eighteenth Century Occultism

Convulsions became epidemic ; the contagion spread to the provinces which, jealous of Paris, determined to have their share of the Jansenist deacon's favours. Similar scenes to those at St. Médard were enacted in several towns all over France, notably at Troyes and Corbeil. The miracles now gave rise to scandalous scenes. Women *convulsionnaires* ran through the streets "searching for the prophet Elijah." Some believing they had found him in a handsome priest named Vaillant, a visionary who had persuaded himself that he was the reincarnation of Elijah, testified their adoration for him in a manner that indicated their convulsions were caused by erotic hysteria rather than by the miraculous properties of the bones of Deacon Pâris. Others stretched themselves at full length on the ground of the cemetery, and invited the spectators to beat them and otherwise maltreat them, only declaring themselves satisfied when ten or twelve men fell upon them at once.

The cure of a girl who had a frightful collection of infirmities, "swellings in the legs, hernia, paralysis, fistula, etc.," was the signal for a general St. Vitus' dance, led by the Abbé Bécherand, an ecclesiastic with one foot shorter than the other. "He executed daily on the tomb of the sainted deacon," says Figuier, "with a talent not to be matched, his favourite *pas*, the famous 'carp jump,' which the spectators were never tired of admiring."

But by this time the miracles had become a public scandal, and the government hastened to suppress the "*ballet* de St. Médard" and close the cemetery. The Jansenists to escape ridicule, which would have killed them more surely than the Jesuits, were obliged to

disassociate themselves from the *convulsionnaires*, who
formed themselves into a sect, which existed down to
the Revolution.

To-day medical science has stripped the *convulsionnaires* of St. Médard of the last rag of the
supernatural, but in the eighteenth century only the
sane intelligence of the philosophers divested them of
all claims to wonder. Their fame spread throughout
Europe and helped in its way to emphasize the trend
of public opinion in which the boundless credulity and
ignorance of the many advanced side by side through
the century with the scepticism and enlightenment of
the few.

So strong was the passion for the marvellous that
the least mystification acquired a supernatural significance. In Catholic Germany a curé named Gassner
who exorcised people possessed of devils and cured the
sick by a touch had over a million adherents. In
England, "Dr." Graham with his "celestial bed," his
elixirs of generation, and his mud-baths, acquired
an immense reputation. In Switzerland, Lavater, an
orthodox Lutheran pastor, read character and told the
future by the physiognomy with astonishing success.

At Leipsic, Schröpfer, the proprietor of a café,
flattered credulity so cleverly that belief in his ability
to communicate with the invisible world survived even
his exposure as an impostor. His history is not without
dramatic interest. Gifted with a temperament strongly
inclined to mysticism he became so infatuated with the
study of the supernatural that he abandoned his
profession of *cafétier* as beneath him and turned his
café into a masonic lodge where he evoked the souls
of the dead, damned and saved alike. Some of those

who witnessed these apparitions believing they recognized relations or friends, went mad, a fate that was not long in overtaking Schröpfer himself. Intoxicated by the immense vogue he obtained, he next turned his lodge into a private hotel in which he received only persons of rank, assuming himself that of a colonel in the French army to which he declared he was entitled as " a bastard of the Prince de Conti." Unfortunately at Dresden, whither he had gone to evoke the shade of a King of Poland for the benefit of the Duke of Courland, his imposture was exposed. Schröpfer hereupon returned to Leipsic and after giving a grand supper to some of his most faithful adherents blew out his brains. Nevertheless, this did not prevent many from continuing to believe in his evocations. A report that he had predicted he would himself appear after his death to his followers at a given hour in the Rosenthal at Leipsic, caused a vast concourse of people to assemble in that promenade on the day specified in the expectation of beholding his shade.

Still more remarkable than the credulity that clung to imposture after its exposure, was the credulity that discovered supernatural powers in persons who did not even pretend to possess them. The curiosity that scented the marvellous in the impenetrable mystery in which it pleased the self-styled Count de Saint-Germain to wrap himself, induced him to amuse himself at the expense of the credulous. With the aid of his valet, who entered into the jest, he contrived to wrap his very existence in mystery. He had only to speak of persons who had been dead for centuries to convince people he had known them. Many believed he had witnessed the Crucifixion, merely because by a sigh or a hint he conveyed that impression when the subject was mentioned. No absurdity was too extravagant to relate of him that was not credited. Even his servant was supposed to have moistened his lips at the Fountain of Youth.

As the century advanced the folly increased. Rumours began to be current that agitated the popular mind—rumours of secret societies bound by terrible oaths and consecrated to shady designs, rumours of the impending fulfilment of old and awful prophecies ; rumours of vampires and witches ; of strange coincidences and strange disappearances— rumours in which one may trace the origin of the haunting suspicion to which the Reign of Terror was due. All the superstitions regarding the unseen world had their vogue. In Protestant countries interpreters of the Apocalypse were rife. Everywhere the dead came back to affright the living, led by the "White Lady," Death's messenger to the Hohenzollerns.

In such an atmosphere it was not surprising that the *baquet divinatoire* of Mesmer should have seemed more wonderful than the scientific discoveries of Newton and Lavoisier. Cagliostro had only to appear to be welcomed, only to provide credulity with fresh occult novelties to win a niche in the temple of fame.

III

Occultism, however, like human nature of which it is the mystical replica, has its spiritual as well as its material side, and from the depths of gross superstition is capable of mounting to the heights of pure mysticism. In the boundless credulity of the age, symptom of death though it was, the germ of a new life was latent.

The uneasy and forbidding ghosts of dead faiths that haunted Europe awoke aspirations in ardent and passionate souls which sought their realization in the fantastic reign of dreams. From the chaos of superstition the need to believe gradually emerged. In the process the marvellous became mystical. On the ruins of Rosicrucianism, Emmanuel Swedenborg erected a new supernatural belief.

This man whose influence in the latter half of the eighteenth century, especially in the years immediately preceding the Revolution was more subtle than the philosophers who derided him had any conception, is Occultism's Copernicus; the spiritual Abraham from whom all the Blavatskys and Eddys of the present are descended.

He was born at Stockholm in 1688 and throughout his long life—he died in London in 1772 at the age of eighty-four—Fortune was uniformly and exceptionally kind to him. Possessed of brains, sharpened and cultivated by an excellent education, of an attractive personal appearance and influential friends, he began at an early date to make his mark, as the saying is. At twenty-one he started on the "grand tour," which it was customary in those days for young men of wealth and position to make. But young Swedenborg was not one of those who merely wandered luxuriously about Europe pursuing pleasure. Avid of knowledge he devoted the time others spent in dissipation to Greek, Latin, Hebrew, mathematics, science and philosophy. At the end of five years he returned to

Cagliostro

Sweden with the intention of giving himself up entirely to science. He published a scientific review and gained some reputation as an inventor. At the age of twenty-eight Charles XII appointed him assessor of mines ; and three years later Queen Ulrica raised him to the rank of nobility, by which his name was changed from Swedberg, as his family was originally called, to the more euphonious and aristocratic Swedenborg.

Being of an exceedingly inquiring and philosophical mind and having plenty of leisure he naturally widened the area of his investigations. For many years he sought to find the scientific explanation of the universe. This quest and the intensity with which he pursued it insensibly led him to seek to discover the connection between the soul and the body, the relation of the finite to the infinite. From this stage, to which he had been led no doubt by the force of heredity—his father, a Lutheran bishop and professor of theology believed himself in constant intercourse with angels—it was but a step to the supernatural. The scientist, however, takes a long time in turning into the mystic. Sweden-borg was fifty-seven before the transformation was accomplished.

This event occurred in London in 1745.

" I was dining," he says, " one day very late at my hotel in London, and I ate with great appetite, when at the end of my repast I perceived a sort of fog which obstructed my view, and the floor was covered with hideous reptiles. They disappeared, the darkness was dispersed, and I plainly saw in the midst of a bright light, a man sitting in the corner of the room, who said in a terrible voice, *Do not eat so much !* "

From the character of this vision, " Do not

drink so much" would appear to have been the more sensible advice. Be this as it may, Swedenborg was so frightened that he resolved to do as he had been bidden. His diet henceforth was of the simplest, and it is possible that the sudden change from one extreme to the other at an age when the system has lost its elasticity may not be unconnected with the continuation of his visions.

The next night "the same man, resplendent with light," appeared to him again. This time while Swedenborg gazed upon the spectre, which was perhaps a thought visualized by the intensity of its fascination, it said, "I am God the Lord, the Creator and Redeemer of the world. I have chosen thee to explain the meaning of the Holy Scripture. I will dictate to thee what thou shalt write."

Whatever cause Swedenborg may have assigned to the previous vision, he did not doubt for a moment now that the Most High had actually revealed Himself to him. This conviction was so reassuring that the strange things he beheld in his visions ceased to have any terror for him. If he ever asked himself why he should have been selected by the Almighty above the rest of mankind for so great an honour, the frequency of the divine appearances no doubt speedily satisfied his curiosity, for not a day passed during the rest of his life but God descended from Paradise—or if too busy, "sent an angel or saint in His place"—to converse with this remarkably privileged Swede and explain to him the mysteries of Heaven and Hell.

In the visions of St. Francis and St. Theresa, the Virgin, Jesus and the Almighty appeared according to the Roman Catholic conception of them. The faith of

Swedenborg's heavenly visitor was Lutheran—a faith be it said, to which Swedenborg adhered as devotedly as Saints Francis and Theresa did to theirs—and when he appeared he dressed accordingly, wearing neither the Stigmata nor the Crown of Thorns without which no good Catholic would have recognized him. He spoke a mystical jargon which was often so absurd as to be unintelligible.

The Unseen World, as revealed to Swedenborg was the exact counterpart of the seen. It was inhabited by spirits of both sexes—the good ones dwelt in Heaven and the bad ones in Hell. They had the same occupations as people on the earth. They married and begot children, among other things ; and Swedenborg was present at one of these celestial weddings. They also had " schools for infant angels ; universities for the learned ; and fairs for such as were commercially inclined—particularly for the English and Dutch angels ! " For the spirits of the Unseen had all lived in the seen.

According to Swedenborg, man never dies. The day he experiences what he calls death is the day of his eternal resurrection. Christ was the ruler of both these worlds. He was the one and only God. All human desire would be consummated when the two worlds should become one, as they had been in the beginning, before the Fall. On this day the New Jerusalem would be established on earth. To hasten this event, it was necessary to seek the " lost word " or " primitive innocence." This was Swedenborg's idea of the philosopher's stone, which he declared was to be found in the doctrines he taught. Should any person be tempted to seek it elsewhere, he was advised to go in quest of it in Asia, " among the Tartars " !

Eighteenth Century Occultism

It was some time, however, before he became at home in the spiritual world. Time ceased to have any significance to him. He would lie for days in a trance from which he would awake at night "to wrestle with evil spirits" to the terror of his household. Sometimes his soul would escape altogether from his body and "borne on the wings of the Infinite, journey through Immensity from planet to planet." To these travels, the most marvellous that imagination has ever taken, we owe the *Arcana Cœlestia* and *The New Jerusalem*. These books translated from the Latin in which they had been dictated to him by the Almighty had a prodigious success. In Protestant countries—which he personally canvassed—especially in Sweden and England where he made the most converts, they were regarded as the gospel of a new religion, the Bible of the Church of the New Jerusalem.

" Show me four persons," said Fontenelle, " who swear it is midnight when it is noon, and I will show you ten thousand to believe them."

Firmly convinced that he was in daily intercourse with the Almighty, Swedenborg soon convinced others. For his was the faith which removes mountains. He had, moreover, a majestic appearance and a magnetic personality which rendered ridicule silent in his presence, and inspired the confidence and love of all who came in contact with him. Three extraordinary instances of his power to communicate with the unseen world are cited by his followers. Even Kant, the philosopher, was struck by them, though he confesses that on inquiry he dismissed them as having no foundation but report. Nevertheless there were thousands who did not doubt, least of all Queen Ulrica.

93

Had Swedenborg not related to her the contents of a letter known only to herself and her brother who had been dead for years ?

That the sentimental Lutheranized Gnosticism he preached should have been received with enthusiasm in Protestant Europe is not surprising. The peoples of the North are naturally mystical. Nothing that appears to them in the guise of religion is too fantastic to be refused a hearing. In England the more fantastic the more certain is it of success. Swedenborgianism was to the "illuminized Jerusalemites" of Manchester, where alone they numbered twenty thousand, merely a very delicious *rechauffée* of a diet to which their imagination was specially addicted. The eagerness with which it was accepted in England was due entirely to appetite.

Much more remarkable was the influence of Swedenborg in the Catholic world. Naturally it manifested itself differently in different nations, assuming the character peculiar to each. Thus, whilst in England supernaturalism under the influence of Swedenborg became a religious craze, in France it grafted itself upon philosophy, and in Germany infected the secret societies in which the theories of the French philosophers found active political expression.

The secret of this universal appeal is not far to seek. It was one of the articles of faith with the old Rosicrucians that by them "the triple diadem of the pope should be reduced to dust." The theosophy of Swedenborg *presumed* the liberty, equality, and fraternity of mankind. It was at once the spiritual negation and defiance of the arrogant supremacy of both Church and State. Occultism, which has ever proclaimed the spiritual rebellion of the soul against any kind of tyranny, was in the eighteenth century of necessity revolutionary. Of the forces of disintegration to which the *ancien régime* succumbed, it was the only one that worked systematically towards a definite object.

In the previous century, when the social system that deprived the soul of its liberty seemed irrefragable, the Rosicrucians had resignedly considered contentment to be the philosopher's stone. But now when the whole structure was toppling, it was necessary to interpret afresh, and in terms more in accordance with occult principles, the secret of perfection. To the mystics of the eighteenth century the "philosophical egg" by means of which the tyranny of throne and altar was to be transmuted into the gold of absolute liberty was the Revolution.

And the crass credulity and superstition of the age was the crucible in which they sought it.

IV

Nothing is more curious than to note the manner in which these descendants of the old alchemists, pioneers at one and the same time of modern Occultism and modern Socialism, while engaged in shadowing, so to speak, the unbelief of their century, conspired to put an end to the old *régime*.

In spite of the disasters that dimmed the glory of the last years of Louis XIV's long reign, the immense prestige that France had acquired in *le grand siècle* remained unchallenged. Intellectually the influence of France under his successors was so supreme that the decay of French civilization in the eighteenth century may be regarded as a sort of mirror in which the process of the disintegration of European society generally is reflected. Already as early as 1704, eleven years before the death of Louis XIV, when *authority* still seemed to be everywhere dominant, Leibnitz detected "all the signs of the general Revolution with which Europe is menaced." With the passing of Louis XIV respect, the chief stronghold of feudalism, surrendered to the cynicism of the Regency. In that insane Saturnalia chains were snapped, traditions shattered, old and worn-out conventions trampled under-foot. The Regency was but the Revolution in miniature.

The orgy of licence passed in its turn, as the gloomy and bigoted hypocrisy of which it was the natural reaction, had passed before it. But the calm of the exquisite refinement that took its place was only superficial. Freedom conceived in the revels of the Regency yearned to be born. To assist at this *accouchement* was the aim of all the philosophical midwifery of the age. In 1734 Voltaire, physician-in-ordinary to the century, declared "action to be the chief object of mankind." But as freedom of action is impossible without freedom of thought Vauvenargues next demanded in clarion tones that "God should be freed." The idea of "freeing God" in order to free man was an inspiration, and Vauvenargues' magnificent phrase became the tocsin of the philosophers.

But the chief effect of the Regency upon France, and thus indirectly upon Europe, had been to "free unbelief." Authority, which had feared faith when alive and despised it when dead, crawled into the shell from which the snail of belief had departed and displayed the same predatory and brutal instincts as the intolerant religion in whose iron carapace it dwelt. To dislodge it was the first step towards "freeing God"; and all sorts and conditions of athletes entered the arena to battle with prejudice and injustice. In France, where the contest was destined to be decided, the Bastille or banishment was the punishment that brute authority awarded those who dared to defy it. But to crush the rebellion of intelligence against stupidity was impossible. The efforts of the philosophers were reinforced by sovereigns imbued with the spirit of the century. With Frederick the Great a race of benevolent despots sprang into existence, who dazzled by the refulgence of the philosophical light they so much admired did not perceive till too late that in igniting their torches at its flame they were helping to kindle a conflagration destined to destroy the system that would deprive them of the absolute freedom they enjoyed, and to a limited share of which they were willing to admit the nations they ruled.

Nor for that matter did the philosophers themselves. To them as well as to their princely disciples "to free God" was another name for religious toleration. That was the revolution for which the Encyclopedists worked, and which Frederick the Great and the sovereigns who shared his enlightened opinions desired. Nothing was further from their intention than that it should take the form in which it eventually came. It is impossible to believe that the Revolution which demanded the heads of a Lavoisier and a Bailly would have spared those of a Voltaire or a

Rousseau. Least of all would the stupid mob that
watched the victims doomed to the guillotine " spit
into the basket," as it termed in ferocious jest the fall
of the heads beneath the axe, have made any distinction between the virtuous and innocent Louis XVI
and Joseph II, or the Empress Catherine, had it
been possible to arraign them likewise at the bar of
the Revolutionary Tribunal. The gratitude of the
people is even less to be depended on than that of
princes. But God was not to be " freed " in a day.
Seventy-five years elapsed between Freedom's conception in the Regency and birth in the Revolution.

During this long pregnancy the century which was
to die in child-bed developed an extraordinary appetite
for the supernatural. To the materialistic philosophy
that analyzed and sought to control the process of
decay which by the middle of the century had become
visible, even to one so indifferent to " signs of the
times " as Louis XV, the cult of the supernatural
was an element unworthy of serious consideration.
But though long ignored the time was to come when
it obtained from the torch-bearers of reason a questionable and dangerous patronage. It was on the eve
of the birth of Freedom that " the century of Voltaire,"
as Henri Martin expresses it, " extended its hand to
the occultists of the middle ages."

Between Voltaire and cabalistic evocations, between
the scepticism of the Encyclopedists and the mysticism
of Swedenborg who would believe there could be any
affiliation ? Yet the transition was natural enough.
The philosophers in their abuse of analysis had too
persistently sacrificed sentiment to reason. Imagination, which Louis Blanc has called the intoxication

of intelligence, had begun to doubt everything by
the middle of the century. Reaction was inevitable
The sneers of Voltaire were succeeded by the tears
of Rousseau. The age of sensibility followed the age
of unbelief. This was the hour for which a despised
occultism had waited. It alone had a clear and
definite conception of the Revolution. Patronized by
philosophy, which vacillated between sentiment and
reason, it imbued it finally with its own revolutionary
ideas. The extent of their ascendency may be gauged
by the declaration of Condorcet, " that volcano covered
with snow," as he has been called, " that society must
have as its object the amelioration, physical, intellectual and moral of the most numerous and poorest
class." In his desire to escape from materialism the
philosopher trained in the school of Voltaire had but
taken the road to perfection along which the mystics
were leading France and Europe.

Strange to relate, the leader of the mystical movement in France to which philosophy was destined
to attach itself, was himself the mildest and least
revolutionary of men.

Louis Claude de Saint-Martin might be described
as the reincarnation of St. Francis of Assisi in the
eighteenth century. Had he lived four hundred years
earlier he would have passed his gentle flower-like life
in the seclusion of some cloister, had beatific visions
of the Saviour of the world, communed with the
Virgin and Saints, worked miracles, founded a
monastic order, and at his death been canonized by
the Church, of whose faith he would have been the
champion and of its tenderness the exemplar. Pure
and meditative by nature he had been greatly

influenced when a boy by an ascetic book, *The Art of Knowing Oneself*, that he chanced to read. As his father, to whom he was deeply attached, intended him for the Bar he devoted himself to the study of law, and though he had no taste for the profession passed his examinations. But after practising six months he declared himself incapable of distinguishing in any suit between the claims of the defendant and the plaintiff, and requested to be allowed to exchange the legal profession for the military—not because he had any liking for the career of arms, but in order that he might "have leisure to continue the study of religion and philosophy."

To oblige his father the Duc de Choiseul, then Prime Minister, gave him a lieutenancy in the Regiment de Foix, then in garrison at Bordeaux. Here he met one of those strange characters so common in this century, who, either charlatans of genius or dreamers by temperament, supplied with arms from the arsenal of the supernatural boldly asserted the supremacy of the occult and attacked science and philosophy alike. This particular individual was called Martinez Pasqualis, but as like so many of his kind he enveloped himself in mystery it is impossible to discover who or what he was, or where he came from. He was supposed to be a Christianized Jew from one of the Portuguese colonies in the East, which would account perhaps for his skill in the practice of the occult. At any rate, the strange secrecy he maintained in regard to himself was sufficient in the eighteenth century to credit him with supernatural powers.

When Saint-Martin met him in Bordeaux he had

for ten years held a sort of school of theurgy. At Avignon, Toulouse, and other Southern cities his pupils or disciples formed themselves into a sect, known as Martinists after their master, for the practice of his doctrines, which though but vaguely understood were attractive from the hopes they held out of communicating with the invisible world. Saint-Martin was the first to grasp their meaning. He joined the Martinists, whose existence till then was scarcely known, and became their chief when the dissensions to which the private life of Pasqualis had given rise were healed by his sudden and singular departure for Haiti, where he died of yellow fever shortly after his arrival.

Drawn from obscurity by the personal charm and high social position of its new leader, Martinism rapidly attracted attention. In a strange little book, *Des Erreurs et de la Vérité par un philosophe inconnu*, Saint-Martin endeavoured to detach himself and his adherents from the magic in which Pasqualis—who practised it openly—had involved this sect. But though he gave up the quest of supernatural phenomena as unnecessary to an acquaintance with the unseen, and wandered deeper and deeper into pure mysticism, he never wholly succeeded in escaping from the grosser influence of his first initiation in the occult. From the fact, however, that he called himself the "Robinson Crusoe of spiritualism," some idea may be gained of the distance that separated him from those who also claimed connection with the invisible world. He did not count on being understood. Of one of his books he said, " it is too far from ordinary human ideas to be successful. I have often felt in writing it as if I were playing valses on my violin in the cemetery of Montmartre, where for all the magic of my bow, the dead will neither hear nor dance."

Nevertheless, though philosophy failed to follow him to the remote regions of speculation to which he withdrew, it grasped enough of his meaning to apply it. And the Revolution, which before its arrival he had regarded as the "lost word" by which the regeneration of mankind was to be effected, and when it actually came as "the miniature of the last judgment," adopted his sacred ternary "Liberty, Equality, and Fraternity"—the Father, Son and Holy Ghost of Martinism—as its device. Saint-Martin was one of the few who strove to inaugurate it whom it did not devour. He passed through it unmolested, dying as he had lived gently. His only regret in passing from the visible to the invisible was that he had left "the mystery of numbers unsolved."

V

The influence of Saint-Martin, however, was passive rather than active. Though philosophy confusedly and unconsciously imbibed the Socialistic theories of mysticism, the French being at once a practical and an excitable people were not to be kindled by speculations of the intellect, however daring, original, and attractive they might be. The palpable prodigies of Mesmer appealed more powerfully to them than the vague abstractions of Saint-Martin.

It was in Germany that revolutionary mysticism

found its motive power. Whilst Saint-Martin, proclaiming in occult language that "all men were kings," sought to efface himself at the feet of sovereigns, Adam Weishaupt was shaking their thrones. It would be impossible to find two men more unlike. Weishaupt was the very antithesis of Saint-Martin. He was not a mystic at all, and furthermore always professed the greatest contempt for "supernatural tricks." But consumed with an implacable hatred of despotism and with a genius for conspiracy he perceived in the widespread attraction and revolutionary tendency of the supernatural the engine of destruction he required.

Born of Catholic parents at Ingolstadt in Bavaria, Weishaupt had been sent as a boy to the Jesuit seminary in that town, but conceiving a great dislike for the method of instruction employed there he left it for the university. On the temporary abolition of the Order of the Jesuits, having taken his degree, he was appointed to the professorship of jurisprudence till then held by a Jesuit. Though deprived of their functions the members of the suppressed Order still remained in the country, and posing as martyrs continued to exercise in secret their malign influence as powerfully as ever. Weishaupt naturally found in them bitter enemies ; and to fight them conceived the idea of founding a secret society, which the great popularity he enjoyed among the students enabled him to realize.

Perceiving the immense success that Gassner was having at this time by his cures, and fully alive to the powerful hold the passion for the supernatural had obtained on the popular imagination, he decided to give his society a mystic character as a means of recruiting followers. As Weishaupt's object was to convert them into blind instruments of his supreme will, he modelled his organization after that of the Jesuits, adopting in particular their system of espionage, their practice of passive obedience, and their maxim that the end justifies the means. From mysticism he borrowed the name of the society : Illuminés. From freemasonry, the classes and grades into which they were subdivided, the purpose of which was to measure the progress of the adept in assimilating the doctrine of the absolute equality of man and to excite his imagination by making him hope for the communication of some wonderful mystic secret when he reached the highest grade. Those who enjoyed the confidence of Weishaupt were known as *areopagites*. To them alone was he visible, and as he deemed that too many precautions could not be observed in concealing the existence of a society sworn to the abolition of the Christian religion and the overthrow of the established social system, he and his accomplices adopted names by which alone they were known to the others.

Comprised at first of a few students at the University of Ingolstadt, the Illuminés gradually increased their numbers and sought recruits in other places, special attention being given to the enlistment of young men of wealth and position. In this way, the real objects of Illuminism being artfully concealed, the society extended within the course of four or five years all over Germany. Its adepts even had a hand in affairs of State and gained the ear of many of those petty and picturesque sovereigns of the Empire who, catching the fever of philosophy from Frederick the Great and Joseph II, amused themselves in trying to

blend despotism, philanthropy, and the occult. As
the Illuminés were utterly unscrupulous, they did not
hesitate to seek recruits in the Church of Rome itself,
of which they were the secret and deadly enemy, in
order by taking sides in the theological quarrels of the
day to increase dissensions and weaken the power of
the Pope.

However, cleverly organized though they were, the
Illuminés, composed of very young and passionate men
carefully chosen—Weishaupt himself was scarcely
twenty-eight when he founded the sect in 1776—did
not make much progress, till Baron von Knigge joined
them in 1780. He possessed the one faculty that
Weishaupt lacked—imagination. Young, monstrously
licentious, irreligious and intelligent, he was consumed
with an insatiable curiosity for fresh experiences. He
had written a number of novels which had attracted
some attention and certain pamphlets on morals that
had been put on the Index. He had been admitted
to most of the secret societies of the day, particularly
that of the Freemasons. He had experimented in
alchemy and studied every phase of occultism from the
philosophy of the Gnostics to that of Swedenborg.
Everything that savoured of the supernatural had a
profound attraction for him ; even sleight of hand
tricks, it is said, had engaged his attention. At thirty
he had seen, studied and analyzed everything, and still
his imagination remained as untired and inquisitive as
ever. An ally at once more invaluable and more
dangerous it would have been impossible for Weishaupt
to have procured.

Admitted to the confidence of Weishaupt this
young Hanoverian nobleman rapidly gained an

ascendency over him. It was owing to the advice
of Knigge that Weishaupt divided the Illuminés into
grades after the manner of the Freemasons, and
adopted the method of initiation of which the mysterious and terrifying rites were well calculated to impress
the proselyte. With a Knigge to invent and a Weishaupt to organize, the Illuminés rapidly increased their
numbers and activities. Overrunning Germany they
crossed the frontiers preaching, proselytizing, and
spreading the gospel of the Revolution everywhere.
But this rapid development was not without its dangers.
Conscious that the existence of such a society if it
became known would inevitably lead to its suppression,
Knigge, who was nothing if not resourceful, conceived
the idea of grafting it on to Freemasonry, which by
reason of its powerful connections and vast proportions
would, he trusted, give to Illuminism both protection
and the means of spreading more widely and rapidly.

The origin of this association, the oldest known to
the world, composed of men of all countries, ranks,
and creeds sworn to secrecy, bound together by
strange symbols and signs, whose real mystic meaning
has long been forgotten, and to-day devoted to the
practice of philanthropy on an extensive scale—has
been the subject of much speculation. The theory,
most generally accepted, is that which supposes it to
have been founded at the time and for the purpose of
building the Temple of Solomon. But whatever its
early history, Freemasonry in its present form first
came into prominence in the seventeenth century in
England, whence it spread to France and Germany.
It was introduced into the former country by the
Jacobites early in the eighteenth century with the

object of furthering the cause of the Stuarts. On the extinction of their hopes, however, it reverted to its original ideals of equality and fraternity, and in spite of these democratic principles obtained a strong hold upon the aristocracy. Indeed, in France it was from the first a decidedly royalist institution and this character it preserved, outwardly at least, down to the Revolution, numbering nobles and clergy alike among its members, and always having a prince of the blood as Grand Master.

In Germany, on the contrary, where since the Thirty Years' War popular aspirations and discontent had expressed themselves inarticulately in a multitude of secret societies, the principles of Freemasonry had a political rather than a social significance.

The importance it acquired from the number of its members, its international character, and its superior organization could not fail to excite the hostility of the Church of Rome, which will not tolerate within it the existence of secret and independent associations. The Jesuits had sworn allegiance to the Pope and in their ambition to control the Papacy were its staunchest defenders. But the Freemasons refused to admit the Papal authority, and treated all creeds with equal respect. War between the Church of Rome and Freemasonry was thus inevitable—a war that the Church in such a century as the eighteenth, permeated with scepticism and the desire for individual liberty, was most ill-advised to wage. For it was a war in which extermination was impossible and the victories of Rome indecisive.

Anathematized by Clement XII, persecuted in Spain by the Inquisition, penalized in Catholic

Germany by the law, and its members decreed worthy of eternal damnation by the Sorbonne in France, Freemasonry nevertheless managed to find powerful champions. Entrenched behind the thrones of Protestant Europe, particularly that of Frederick the Great, and encouraged by the philosophers who saw in it something more than a Protestant challenge to the Church of Rome, it became the rallying ground of all the forces of discontent and disaffection of the century, the arsenal of all its hopes and ideals, the nursery of the Revolution.

To render it, if possible, suspect even to its patrons Rome denied the humanity of its aims and the boasted antiquity of its origin. According to the stories circulated by the priests, which excited by their fears existed solely in their imagination, the Freemasons were the successors of the old Knights Templars sworn to avenge the abolition of that order by the bull of Pope Clement V and the death of its Grand Master, Jacques Molay, burnt alive by King Philip the Fair in the fourteenth century. But their vengeance was not to be limited to the destruction of the Papacy and the French monarchy; it included that of all altars and all thrones.[1]

This tradition, however, continually repeated and rendered more and more mysterious and alarming by rumour, merely helped to articulate the hatred of the enemies of the old *régime* who had flocked to Freemasonry as to a camp. As this association had at this period of its history no homogeneity, it was possible for

[1] One of the symbols of the Masons was a cross on which were the letters L.P.D. which were interpreted by the priests to mean *Lilia Pedibus Destrue*, Trample the Lilies under-foot.

anybody with a few followers to form a lodge, and for each lodge to be a distinct society united to Freemasonry by the community of signs and symbols. It thus became a vast confederation of independent lodges representing all sorts of opinions, often hostile to one another, and possessing each its own "rite" or constitution. Philosophy and occultism alike both found a shelter in it. Even Saint-Martin left his mystic solitude to found lodges which observed the "Swedenborg rite."

To attach themselves to the Freemasons was therefore for the Illuminés as easy as it was natural. Lodges of Illuminism were founded all over Germany. The number and variety of sects, however, that had found an asylum in Freemasonry by the diversity of their aims tended to weaken rather than strengthen the association. At length, the discovery that impostors, like Schröpfer, Rosicrucians and even Jesuits had founded lodges led to a general council of Freemasons for the purpose of giving the society the homogeneity it lacked. With this object a convention of Masons was held at Wilhelmsbad in 1782 to which deputies were sent from all parts of Europe. Knigge and Weishaupt attended and, perceiving the vast possibilities of the consolidation of the sects, they endeavoured to capture the whole machinery of the organization for the Illuminés, much as the Socialists of to-day have endeavoured to capture the Trades Unions.

The intrigue, however, not only failed, but led to a misunderstanding between the chiefs of Illuminism. Knigge definitely withdrew from the society, the existence and revolutionary aims of which were betrayed two years later, in 1784, by a member who had reached the highest grade, only to discover that the mystic secrets by which he had been attracted to the Illuminés did not exist. This information conveyed to the Bavarian government was confirmed by domiciliary visits of the police who seized many incriminating papers. Weishaupt fled to Gotha, where he found a protector in the occultist Duke, whose friendship he had nursed for years in view of just such a contingency.

But though the society he had formed was broken up, it was too late to stamp out the fire it had kindled. The subterranean rumblings of the Revolution could already be heard. Mysticism which had made use of philosophy in France to sap tyranny was in its turn in Germany turned to political account. From the seeds sown by the Illuminés sprang that amazing crop of ideals of which a few years later Napoleon was to reap the benefit.

Such, then, was the " curtain " of Cagliostro; woven, so to speak, on the loom of the love-of-the-marvellous out of mystical masonic principles and Schröpfer-Mesmer phenomena.

And now let us turn once more to the personality of the man behind it.

CHAPTER III

MASKED AND UNMASKED

I

BEFORE leaving England, during an interlude in the persecution to which he had been subjected, Cagliostro had become a Freemason. This event, innocent enough in itself, though destined years later to have such terrible consequences for him, occurred on April 12, 1777. The lodge he joined was the Esperance, which met in a room of the King's Head in Gerard Street, Soho.

According to the Editor of the *Courier de l'Europe*, who professed to have obtained the particulars of his admission and initiation from an eye-witness, the Count on this occasion described himself as "Joseph Cagliostro, Colonel of the 3rd Regiment of Brandenburg."[1] Three other members were received at the same time : Pierre Boileau, a valet ; Count Ricciarelli, "musician and alchemist, aged seventy-six" ; and the Countess Cagliostro.

There was a full attendance of members, "Brother" Hardivilliers, an upholsterer, presiding. Out of

---

[1] This statement rests solely on the word of the Editor of the *Courier de l'Europe*, who cited it as one of his reasons for identifying Cagliostro with Balsamo. The latter, it may be recalled, had passed as a colonel in the Prussian service during the time he was connected with the forger Agliata.

courtesy to her sex the Countess was received first. Her initiation consisted in taking the prescribed oath, after which "she was given a garter on which the device of the lodge, *Union, Silence, Virtue,* was embroidered, and ordered to wear it on going to bed that night."

The ceremony, however, of making the "Colonel of the 3rd Regiment of Brandenburg" a Freemason was characterized by the horseplay usual on such occasions. By means of a rope attached to the ceiling the "Colonel" was hoisted into the air, and allowed to drop suddenly to the floor—an idiotic species of buffoonery that entailed unintentionally a slight injury to his hand. His eyes were then bandaged, and a loaded pistol having been given him, he was ordered by "Brother" Hardivilliers to blow out his brains. As he not unnaturally manifested a lively repugnance to pull the trigger he was assailed with cries of "coward" by the assembly. "To give him courage" the president made him take the oath. It was as follows—

"I, Joseph Cagliostro, in presence of the great Architect of the Universe and my superiors in this respectable assembly, promise to do all that I am ordered, and bind myself under penalties known only to my superiors to obey them blindly without questioning their motives or seeking to discover the secret of the mysteries in which I shall be initiated either by word, sign, or writing."

The pistol—an unloaded one this time—was again put into his hand. Reassured, but still trembling, he placed the muzzle to his temple and pulled the trigger. At the same time he heard the report of another pistol, received a blow on the head, and tearing the bandage from his eyes found himself—a Freemason![1]

To make these perfectly harmless particulars, which were published by the Editor of the *Courier de l'Europe* with the express purpose of damaging Cagliostro, appear detrimental, their malignant author cites the menial occupations of the members of the Esperance Lodge, who were chiefly petty tradesmen and servants of foreign birth, as indicative of the low origin and questionable status of the self-styled Count. Such a reproach from its manifest absurdity is scarcely worth repeating. If any inference is to be drawn from Cagliostro's association with the hairdressers and upholsterers, the valets and shoemakers, of whom the Esperance Lodge chiefly consisted, it is to be drawn from the character of his lodge, and certainly not from the occupations of his brother masons.

The Order of Strict Observance, to which the Esperance Lodge was affiliated, was one of the many secret societies grafted on to Freemasonry in the eighteenth century. It had been founded in the middle of the century in Germany by a Baron von Hundt with the object of reviving the Order of the Knights Templar, who were regarded by the seditious as classic victims of papal and monarchical tyranny.[2] Hundt's Order of Strict Observance, however, at the beginning at any rate, was the very opposite of a

[1] His diploma, for which he paid five guineas, was formerly in the celebrated collection of autographs belonging to the Marquis de Châteaugiron.

[2] As mentioned in the previous chapter, the Order of the Knights Templar was suppressed in the fourteenth century by Pope Clement V, Jacques Molay, the Grand Master, being burnt alive by King Philip the Fair of France.

revolutionary character; though to the Church of Rome, aware that it perpetuated the tradition of the Templars, it was none the less anathema. To this fact the stories may be traced which caused Free-masonry as a whole to be suspected of conspiring to "trample the lilies under-foot."

In England the Order of Strict Observance was purely philanthropic and social, though there, as else-where, it was steeped in occultism—a fact which of itself is quite sufficient to explain why Cagliostro joined the Esperance Lodge. The importance, more-over, acquired by this masonic order, whose lodges were scattered all over Europe, also explains the comparative ease with which he afterwards exploited the curiosity his remarkable faculties aroused.

The precise manner, however, in which he laid the foundations of his fame can only be conjectured. Between November 1777, when Cagliostro left England unknown and impoverished, and March 1779, when he arrived in Courland to be received into the highest society, his movements are wrapped in mystery.

"My fifty guineas," he says, "which was all that I possessed on leaving London, took me as far as Brussels, where I found Providence waiting to replenish my purse."

As he did not deign to enlighten the public as to the guise in which Providence met him, his Inquisi-tion-biographer, who is always prejudiced and generally unreliable, was of the opinion that it was highly discreditable. This authority states that he pro-cured money from a credulous man whom he duped into believing he could predict the winning number in a

lottery, and that without waiting to learn the result
of his prediction—which, on this occasion, in spite of
his previous uniform success in London, was a failure—
fled to the Hague.

Whilst here, so it was rumoured years later, he
was admitted as a Freemason into a lodge of the
Order of Strict Observance, to the members of which
he made a speech on Egyptian Masonry. As a result
of the interest he aroused, a lodge was founded in
accordance with the Egyptian Rite, open to both
sexes, and of which the Countess was appointed
Grand Mistress.

The Inquisition-biographer professes to discover
him next in Venice, "from which he fled after swindling
a merchant out of one thousand sequins." But as he
is described as calling himself at the time Marquis
Pellegrini—one of the *aliases* under which Giuseppe
Balsamo had masqueraded some years previously, he
may be acquitted of the charge. If Cagliostro was
really Balsamo it is inconceivable that he would have
returned to Italy under a name he had rendered so
notorious. The incident, if it has any foundation in
fact, must have occurred several years before this date.
Moreover, if Cagliostro and Balsamo are the same,
Freemasonry must have wrought a most remarkable
and unprecedented spiritual reformation in the character
of the Sicilian crook, for under the name of Count
Cagliostro he most certainly ceased to descend to the
vulgar villainies formerly habitual to him.

Much more in keeping with Cagliostro's character
is the following adventure reported to have befallen
him at Nuremburg, whither rumour next traces him.
Being asked his name by a Freemason who was

staying at the same hotel, and to whom he had communicated the fact that he was also a member of the same fraternity by one of the secret signs familiar to the initiated, he replied by drawing on a sheet of paper a serpent biting its tail. This cryptic response, coupled with the air of mystery Cagliostro habitually gave to his smallest action, deeply impressed the inquisitive stranger, who with the characteristic superstition of the century at once jumped to the conclusion that he was in the presence of the chief of one of the secret societies attached to Freemasonry who, fleeing from persecution, was obliged to conceal his identity. Accordingly, with a sentimental benevolence—from which it may be inferred he was both a Mason and a German—"he drew from his hand a diamond ring, and pressing it upon Cagliostro with every mark of respect, expressed the hope that it might enable him more easily to elude his enemies."

From Nuremburg rumour follows the Count to Berlin, where the interpretation the unsentimental police of Frederick the Great put upon the mystery in which he enveloped himself was so hostile that he hastened to Leipsic. In this town, veritable home of occultism and stage on which Schröpfer a few years before had persuaded his audience to believe in him in spite of his impostures, any mysterious person was sure of a welcome. The voice of rumour, hitherto reduced to a whisper, now becomes audible. The Freemasons of the Order of Strict Observance are said to have given a banquet in Cagliostro's honour "at which three plates, three bottles, and three glasses were set before each guest in commemoration of the Holy Trinity."

Masked and Unmasked

After the repast the Count made a speech, to the eloquence of which and its effect on his hearers the mystic triad of bottles would appear to have contributed. As at the Hague, he discoursed on Egyptian Masonry; praised the superiority of its ideals and rites to those of the lodge of which he was the guest; and carried away by bibulous enthusiasm, which caused him to ignore the rules of politeness and good breeding, he turned impressively to the head of the lodge—one Scieffort—and in impassioned accents informed him that if he did not adopt the Egyptian Rite "he would feel the weight of the hand of God before the expiration of the month."

The fact that Scieffort[1] committed suicide a few days later was regarded as a fulfilment of this prophecy, which from the strange manner and appearance of the mysterious person who uttered it produced a deep impression. At once all Leipsic began to ring with the name of Count Cagliostro and his gift of prophecy. It was his first step on the road to fame. "On leaving the city," says the Inquisition-biographer, "not only did his admirers pay his hotel bill, but they presented him with a considerable sum of money."

Henceforth, wherever he went he was sure of a cordial reception in the lodges of the Order of Strict Observance. By the Freemasons of Dantzic and Königsberg he appears to have been treated as a person of great distinction. As the lodges of the

[1] Schröpfer's name is generally associated with this prediction. As he died, however, in 1774, nearly five years before—a date easily ascertainable—some idea may be gathered of the slight importance most writers on Cagliostro have attached to accuracy.

Order in these cities were wholly given up to the practice and study of occult phenomena he must, no doubt, have furnished them with some proof of his possession of "supernatural" faculties.

In this way, recommended from lodge to lodge, he reached Mittau, the capital of the Duchy of Courland, in March 1779. Here the cloud of uncertainty in which he had been enveloped since leaving England was completely dispelled.

II

Now one does not go to Courland without a reason, and a powerful one. Marshal Saxe, the only other celebrity one recalls in connection with this bleak, marshland duchy of Germanized Letts on the Baltic, was lured thither by its crown. Cagliostro too had his reason—which was not Saxe's; though the ridiculous Inquisition-biographer, remembering that the crown of Courland had been worn by more than one adventurer within the memory of the generation then living, declares that there was a project to depose the reigning duke and put Cagliostro in his place.

As a matter of fact, Cagliostro went to Courland to further his great scheme of founding the Order of Egyptian Masonry. This was the thought uppermost in his mind from the time he left England, or at least the one most frequently expressed.

The idea of Egyptian Masonry is said to have been suggested to him by some unpublished manuscripts that he purchased while in London. He himself, on the contrary, professed to have conceived it in Egypt during his travels in the East, of which he gave such an amazing account at his trial in the Diamond Necklace Affair. It is the spirit, however, in which the idea was conceived that is of chief importance, and this seems to have been wholly creditable to him.

For in spite of the vanity and ostentation he exhibited when his star was in the ascendant Cagliostro, whose "bump of benevolence" was highly developed, was inspired with a genuine enthusiasm for the cause of humanity. Egyptian Masonry had for its aim the moral regeneration of mankind. As the revelations made to men by the Creator (of whom he never failed to speak with the profoundest respect) had, in his opinion, been altered to subserve their own purposes by the prophets, apostles, and fathers of the Church, the regeneration of mankind was only to be accomplished by restoring the knowledge of God in all its purity. This Cagliostro professed was only to be effected by Egyptian Masonry, which he declared had been founded by the patriarchs, whom he regarded as the last and sole depositaries of the truth, as the means of communicating with the invisible world.

That he really believed it was his mission to re-establish this communication there can be no doubt. Even Carlyle's conception of him as a "king of liars" only serves to emphasize this. For since it is generally admitted that the habitual liar is in the end persuaded of the truth of what he says, there is no reason why the "king" of the tribe should be an exception. Had Cagliostro, therefore, *in the beginning* known that the religion he preached was a lie—of which I can find no evidence whatever—he was most certainly convinced of its truth *in the end.* In France, where his following was most numerous, the delegates of the French lodges, after hearing him, declared in their report that they had seen in him "a promise of truth which none of the great masters had so completely developed before."

If it be true that a man's works are the key to his character, nothing reveals that of Cagliostro more clearly than his system of Egyptian Masonry. Never did the welfare of humanity, sublimest of ideals, find more ridiculous expression. But to describe in detail the astonishing *galimathias* of this system for the regeneration of mankind would be as tedious as it is unnecessary, and the following rough outline must serve to illustrate the constitution and ceremonies of the Egyptian Rite.

Both sexes were alike eligible for admission to the Egyptian Rite, the sole conditions being belief in the immortality of the soul and—as regards men—previous admission to some Masonic Lodge. There were, as in ordinary Freemasonry, three grades : apprentice, companion, and master Egyptian. The master Egyptians were called by the names of the Hebrew prophets, while the women of the same grade took those of sibyls.

Cagliostro himself assumed the title of Grand Cophta, which he declared to be that of Enoch, the first Grand Master of Egyptian Masonry. His wife, as Grand Mistress, was known as the Queen of Sheba.

The initiations of the neophytes consisted of being "breathed upon" by the Grand Master or Grand Mistress, according to their sex. This proceeding was accompanied by the swinging of censers and a species of exorcism that served as a preparation for moral regeneration. The Grand Cophta then made a short speech, which he also addressed to the members on their promotion from one grade to the other, ending with the words "Helios, Mene, Tetragammaton."

Concerning the apparent gibberish of these words, the Marquis de Luchet, a clever writer of the day who never hesitated to sacrifice truth to effect, and found in Cagliostro a splendid target for his wit, pretends that "the Grand Cophta borrowed them from a conjurer, who in his turn had been taught them by a spirit, which spirit was no other than the soul of a cabalistic Jew who had murdered his own father." As a matter of fact they are often employed in Freemasonry and signify the Sun, the Moon, and the four letters by which God is designated in Hebrew.

The ceremony of initiation concluded with a sort of spiritualistic séance, for which a very young boy or girl, known respectively as a *pupille* or *colombe* was chosen as the medium, whom the Grand Cophta rendered clairvoyant by "breathing on its face from the brow to the chin."

The same rites were observed for both sexes. At the initiation of women, however, the *Veni Creator* and *Miserere mei Deus* were chanted. On these occasions the Grand Mistress drank "a draught of immortality," and "the shade of Moses was evoked." Moses, however, persistently refused to be evoked, because—so the Countess is reported to have confessed to the Inquisitors—"Cagliostro considered him a thief for having carried off the treasures of the Egyptians."

As the promise of spiritual health was not of itself

sufficient to ensure the success of Egyptian Masonry, Cagliostro in the course of time found it expedient to heighten its attraction by holding out hopes of bodily health, and infinite wealth as well. It was by his ability to cure the sick that the majority of his followers were recruited ; and as he gave to his marvellous cures the same mysterious and absurd character as he gave to all his actions, his enemies—of whom he had many—unable to explain or deny them, endeavoured to turn the "physical regeneration" that Egyptian Masonry was said to effect into ridicule.

According to a curious and satirical prospectus entitled "The Secret of Regeneration or Physical Perfection by which one can attain to the spirituality of 5557 years (Insurance Office of the Great Cagliostro)," he who aspired to such a state "must withdraw every fifty years in the month of May at the full of the moon into the country with a friend, and there shutting himself in a room conform for forty days to the most rigorous diet."

The medical treatment was no less heroic. On the seventeenth day after being bled the patient was given a phial of some "white liquid, or primitive matter, created by God to render man immortal," of which he was to take a certain number of drops up to the thirty-second day. The candidate for physical regeneration was then bled again and put to bed wrapped in a blanket, when—if he had the courage to continue with the treatment—he would "lose his hair, skin, and teeth," but would recover them and find himself in possession of youth and health on the fortieth day—"after which he need not, unless he liked, shuffle off the mortal coil for 5557 years."

Masked and Unmasked

Perhaps nothing better illustrates the boundless credulity which characterized the period immediately preceding the French Revolution than the belief that this report, intended as a *conte pour rire* by the Marquis de Luchet, its author, obtained. As Cagliostro and his followers were very likely aware that any attempt to deny such a statement would but serve to provide their enemies with fresh weapons of attack, they endured the ridicule to which this malicious invention subjected them in silence. This attitude, however, was not only misunderstood by the public, but has even misled historians of a later date, very few of whom, like Figuier in his *Histoire du Merveilleux*, have had the wit to see the humour of the lampoon which they have been too careless or too prejudiced to explain.

As a matter of fact, the mumbo-jumbo of the Egyptian Rite was no more grotesque than the Swedenborgian, Rosicrucian, or any other of the numerous rites that were grafted on to Freemasonry in the eighteenth century. If the Baron von Gleichen, whose integrity was as irreproachable as his experience was wide, is to be credited, " Cagliostro's Egyptian Masonry was worth the lot of them, for he tried to render it, not only more wonderful, but *more honourable* than any other Masonic order in Europe."

Considered as the key to Cagliostro's character, Egyptian Masonry so far fits the lock, so to speak. To turn the key, it is necessary to explain the means he employed to realize the sublime ideal he expressed so ridiculously.

It is characteristic of the tyranny of ideals to demand their realization of the enthusiast, if need be at the cost of life, honour, or happiness. All reformers magnetic enough to attract any notice have been obliged to face this lion-like temptation at some time in their careers. The perfervid ones almost always yield to it, and may count themselves lucky if the sacrifice of their happiness is all that is asked of them. The nature of the surrender is governed entirely by circumstances. Cagliostro paid for his attempt to regenerate mankind with his honour. It was an excessive price, and—considering the result obtained— useless.

As he did not hesitate to recruit his followers by imposture when without it he would have failed to attract them, many writers—and they are the most hostile—have denied that he ever had a lofty ideal at all. To them Egyptian Masonry is merely a device of Cagliostro to obtain money. Such an opinion, however, is as untenable as it is intentionally unjust.

There is not a single authenticated instance in which he derived personal profit by imposture.

Had he *succeeded*, like Swedenborg—who had a precisely similar ideal, and also had recourse to imposture when it suited his purpose—his reputation, like the Swede's, would have survived the calumny that assailed it.[1] For though Cagliostro debased his ideal to realize it, his impostures did not make him an impostor, any more than Mirabeau can be said to

---

[1] The stories told of Swedenborg are quite as fantastic as any concerning Cagliostro. "He was walking," says Brittan in *The Shekinah*, "one day along Cheapside with a friend, a person of great worth and credit (who afterwards related the incident), when he was suddenly seen to bow very low to the ground. To his companion's question as to what he was about, Swedenborg replied by asking him if he had not seen Moses pass by, and that he was bowing to him."

have been bought by the bribes he accepted from the Court.

His impostures consisted (1) in exhibiting his occult powers—which in the beginning he had not developed—on occasions and under conditions he knew to be opposed to their operation, whereby to obtain results he was obliged to forge them, and (2) in attributing to a supernatural cause *all* the wonders he performed as well as the "mysteries" of the Egyptian Rite, in which mesmerism, magnetism and ordinary conjuring tricks were undoubtedly employed.

As the establishment of Egyptian Masonry was the object he had in view, he no doubt believed with his century that the end justifies the means. But to those who shape their conduct according to this passionate maxim it becomes a two-edged sword that seldom fails to wound him who handles it. The end that is justified by the means becomes of necessity of secondary importance, and eventually, perhaps, of no importance at all. This was the case with Cagliostro's ideal. In rendering it subservient to the magic which it was originally part of its object to suppress, the latter gained and kept the upper hand. The means by which his ideal was to be realized became thus, as justifying means are capable of becoming, ignoble; and by robbing their end of its sublimity made that end appear equally questionable. That Cagliostro perceived the danger of this, and struggled hard to avert it, is abundantly proved by his conduct on numerous occasions.

At the start, indeed, imposture was the very last thing he contemplated. His strong objection to predicting winning numbers in lotteries was the cause of

all his trouble in London. From the Hague to Mittau
—wherever a glimpse of him is to be had—there is a
reference to the "eloquence with which he denounced
the magic and satanism to which the German lodges
were addicted." It was not till he arrived in Courland
that his repugnance for the *supercheries* of supernaturalism succumbed to the stronger forces of vanity and
ambition.

III

If "Providence waited for Cagliostro at Brussels,"
it was certainly Luck that met him on his arrival at
Mittau.

As hitherto the cause of Egyptian Masonry does
not appear to have derived any material benefit from
the great interest he is said to have excited in Leipsic
and other places, it seems reasonable to infer that the
lodges he frequented were composed of *bourgeois* or
uninfluential persons. At Mittau, however, the lodge
to which he was admitted, addicted like the others to
the study of the occult, consisted of people of the
highest distinction who, advised in advance of the
coming of the mysterious Count, were waiting to
receive him with open arms.

The great family of von Medem in particular
treated him with the greatest consideration, and in
them he found at once congenial and influential
friends. Marshal von Medem was the head of the
Masonic lodge in Mittau, and from boyhood had
made a special study of magic and alchemy, as had
his brother Count von Medem. This latter had
two very beautiful and accomplished daughters, the
youngest of whom was married to the reigning Duke

of Courland—a fact that could not fail to impress a
regenerator of mankind in quest of powerful disciples.

It was, however, her sister Elisa, Count von
Medem's eldest daughter, who became the *point
d'appui* of Cagliostro's hopes.

The mystical tendencies of Elisa were entirely due
to environment. She had grown up in an atmosphere
in which magic, alchemy, and the dreams of Swedenborg were the principal topics of conversation.
Familiarity, however, as the saying is, bred contempt.
In her childhood she declared that the wonders of the
supernatural which she heard continually discussed
around her, "made less impression on her than the
tale of Blue Beard, while a concert was worth all the
ghosts in the world." Nevertheless, the occult was
not without a subtle effect on her mind. As a girl she
had a decided preference for books of a mystic or
religious character, her favourites being "Young's
Night Thoughts and the works of Lavater."

Gifted with an exceptionally brilliant intellect, of
which she afterwards gave unmistakable proof, she also
possessed a most enthusiastic and affectionate nature—
qualities that her husband, a Count von der Recke,
alone appears to have neither recognized nor appreci-
ated. Their union was of short duration : after six
years of wedlock the Countess von der Recke, who
had married at seventeen to please her father, obtained
a divorce. She was amply compensated for what she
had suffered by the affection she obtained from her
family. Father, uncles, aunts, cousins seemed only to
exist to study her wishes. Her sister, the Duchess
of Courland, constantly sought her advice in political
matters, and regarded her always as her dearest friend.

But it was to her young brother to whom she was most deeply attached. Nor was he less devoted to her. Nearly of the same age, and possessing the same temperament and talents, the sympathy between them was such that "one was but the echo of the other." They differed only in one respect. Equally serious and reflective, each longed to solve the "problems of existence"; but while the Countess von der Recke was led to seek their solution in the Bible, in the gospel according to Swedenborg, or in the correspondence she formed with Lavater, her brother thought they were to be found "in Plato and Pythagoras." Death, however, prematurely interrupted his quest, carrying with him to the grave the ambition of his father and the heart of his sister.

It was at this moment, when she was overwhelmed with grief, that Count Cagliostro arrived in Mittau, with the reputation of being able to transmute metals, predict the future, and communicate with the unseen world. Might he not also evoke the spirits of the dead? In any case, such a man was not to be ignored. Mittau was a dead-and-alive place at the best of times, the broken-hearted Countess was only twenty-five, the "problems of existence" might still be solved—and workers of wonders, be they impostors or not, are not met every day. So the Countess von der Recke was determined to meet the "Spanish" Count, and—what is more to the point—to believe in him.

As usual, on his arrival in Mittau, Cagliostro had denounced the excessive rage for magic and alchemy that the Freemasons of Courland, as elsewhere, displayed. But though he found a sympathetic listener in the Countess von der Recke while he discoursed mystically on the moral regeneration of mankind and the " Eternal Source of all Good," her father and uncle, who were devoted to magic and manifestations of the occult, demanded practical proofs of the power he was said to possess. As he was relying on their powerful patronage to overcome the opposition unexpectedly raised to the foundation of an Egyptian Lodge at Mittau by some persons whose suspicions were excited by the mystery he affected, he did not dare disoblige them.

One day, after conversing on magic and necromancy with the von Medems, he gave them and a certain Herr von Howen a proof of his occult powers. Apart from his "miraculous" cures, nearly all the prodigies performed by Cagliostro were of a clairvoyant nature. As previously stated, in these exhibitions he always worked through a medium, known as a *pupille* or *colombe*, according to the sex—the *pupilles* being males and the *colombes* females. From the fact that they were invariably very young children, he probably found that they responded more readily to hypnotic suggestion than adults. Though these exhibitions were often impostures (that is, arranged beforehand with the medium) they were as often undoubtedly genuine (that is, *not* previously arranged, and baffling explanation). In every case they were accompanied by strange rites designed to startle the imagination of the onlooker and prepare it to receive a deep and durable impression of mystery.

On this occasion, according to the Countess von der Recke, Cagliostro selected as *pupille* the little son of Marshal von Medem, " a child of five." " Having anointed the head and left hand of the child with the 'oil of wisdom,' he inscribed some mystic letters on the anointed hand and bade the *pupille* to look at it steadily. Hymns and prayers then followed, till little von Medem became greatly agitated and perspired profusely. Cagliostro then inquired in a stage whisper of the Marshal what he desired his son to see. Not to frighten him, his father requested he might see his sister. Hereupon the child, still gazing steadfastly at his hand, declared he saw her.

"Questioned as to what she was doing, he described her as placing her hand on her heart, as if in pain. A moment later he exclaimed, 'now she is kissing my brother, who has just come home.' On the Marshal declaring this to be impossible, as this brother was leagues away, Cagliostro terminated the séance, and with an air of the greatest confidence ordered the doubting parent 'to verify the vision.' This the Marshal immediately proceeded to do; and learnt that his son, whom he believed so far away, had unexpectedly returned home, and that shortly before her brother's arrival his daughter had had an attack of palpitation of the heart."

After proof so conclusive Cagliostro's triumph was assured. Those who mistrusted him were completely silenced, and all further opposition to the foundation of his lodge ceased.

But the appetite of the von Medem brothers only grew by what it fed upon. They insisted on more wonders, and to oblige them "the representative of the Grand Cophta"—later he found it simpler to assume in person the title and prerogatives of the successor of Enoch—held another séance. Aware that he had to

please people over whose minds the visions of Swedenborg had gained such an ascendency that everything
that was fantastic appeared supernatural to them, he
had recourse to the cheap devices of magic and the
abracadabra of black art.

At a meeting of the lodge he declared that "he had
been informed by his chiefs of a place where most important magical manuscripts and instruments, as well
as a treasure of gold and silver, had been buried
hundreds of years before by a great wizard." Questioned as to the locality of this place, he indicated a
certain heath on the Marshal's estate at Wilzen where-
on he had been wont to play as a boy, and which—extraordinary coincidence!—he remembered the peasants of
the neighbourhood used to say contained a buried
treasure guarded by ghosts. The Marshal and his
brother were so astonished at Cagliostro's description
of a place which it seemed improbable he could have
heard of, and certainly had never seen, that they set
out at once for Wilzen with some friends and relatives
to find the treasure with the occult assistance of their
mysterious guest.

Now the Countess's interest in the occult was of
quite a different character from that of her father and
uncle. Deeply religious, she had turned in her grief
to mysticism for consolation. From the commencement
of her acquaintance with Cagliostro, she had been impressed as much by the nobility of the aims he attributed to his Egyptian Masonry, of which he spoke "in
high-flown, picturesque language," as by his miraculous
gifts. While others conversed with him on magic and
necromancy, which she regarded as "devilish," she
talked of the "union of the physical and spiritual

worlds, the power of prayer, and the miracles of the early Christians." She told him how the death of her brother had robbed her life of happiness, and that in the hope of seeing him once more she had often spent a long time in prayer and meditation beside his grave at night. And she also gave the Grand Cophta to understand that she counted on him to gratify this desire.

As to confess his utter inability to oblige her would have been to rob him at one fell swoop of the belief in his powers on which he counted to establish a lodge of Egyptian Masonry at Mittau, Cagliostro evaded the request. His great gifts, he explained, were only to be exercised for the good of the world; and if he used them merely for the gratification of idle curiosity, he ran the risk of losing them altogether, or of being destroyed by evil spirits who were on the watch to take advantage of the weakness of such as he.

But as the exhibitions he had given her father and uncle of his powers were purely for the benefit of idle curiosity, the Countess had not unnaturally reproached him with having exposed himself to the snares of the evil spirits he was so afraid of. Whereupon the unfortunate Grand Cophta, in his desire to reform Freemasonry and to spread his gospel of regeneration, having left the straight and narrow path of denunciation for the broad road of compromise, sought to avoid the quagmire to which it led by taking the by-path of double-dealing.

Conscious that his success at Mittau depended on keeping the Countess's esteem, he assumed an air of mystery and superiority when talking of the occult calculated to impress her with the utter insignificance of her views in matters of which, as she admitted, she was ignorant. Having made her feel as small as possible, he endeavoured to reconcile her to the phenomena he performed for the benefit of her relations by holding out to her a hope that by similar means it might be possible to evoke the shade of the brother she so yearned to see. When next she met him, he assured her that " Hanachiel," as he called his "chief" in the spiritual world to whom he owed his marvellous gifts, "had informed him that her intention was good in wishing to communicate with her brother, and that this was only to be accomplished by the study of the occult sciences, in which she might make rapid progress if she would follow his directions unquestioningly."

In this way, like another Jason steering his Argos-ship of Egyptian Masonry clear of the rocks and quicksands, he sought to round the cape of suspicion and come to a safe anchorage in port. But though he handled the helm with consummate skill, as the Countess herself afterwards acknowledged, it was a perilous sea on which he sailed. Unquestioning obedience, the Countess declared, she could not promise him.

" God Himself," she said, " could not induce me to act against what my conscience tells me is right and wrong."

" Then you condemn Abraham for offering up his son ? " was Cagliostro's curious rejoinder. " In his place, what would you have done ? "

" I would have said," replied the Countess : " ' O God, kill Thou my son with a flash of Thy lightning if Thou requirest his life ; but ask me not to slay my child, whom I do not think guilty of death.' "

With such a woman, what is a Cagliostro to do?

Prevented, so to speak, by this flaw in the wind from
coming to anchor in the harbour of her unquestioning
faith in him, he sought to reach port by keeping up
her hopes. To reconcile her to the magical operations
he was obliged to perform in order to retain his
influence upon the von Medems, he finally promised
her a "magic dream" in which her brother would
appear to her.

From the manner in which Cagliostro proceeded to
perform this phenomenon, one may obtain an idea of
the nature and extent of his marvellous powers. As
heretofore his effects had been produced by hypnotic
suggestion, accompanied by every accessory calculated
to assist it, so now he proceeded on similar lines.
That the thoughts of others besides himself should be
concentrated on the "magic dream," the relations of
the Countess, as well as herself, were duly agitated by
its expectation. With an air of great mystery, which
Cagliostro could make so impressive, he delivered to
Count von Medem a sealed envelope containing, he
said, a question, which he hoped by the dream to have
answered. At night, before the Countess retired, he
broke the silence which he had imposed on her and her
relations during the day to refer once more to the
dream, with the object of still further exciting the
imagination of all concerned, whose thoughts were
fixed upon the coming apparition of the dead, until
the prophecy, like many another, worked its own
fulfilment.

But this cunningly contrived artifice, familiar to
magicians in all ages, and frequently crowned with
success, was defeated on the present occasion by the
health of the Countess, whose nerves were so excited

by the glimpse she expected to have of her dearly beloved brother as to prevent her sleeping at all.

This eventuality, however—which Cagliostro had no doubt allowed for—far from complicating his difficulties, was easily turned to advantage. For, upbraiding the Countess for her weakness and lack of self-control, he declared she need not any longer count on seeing her brother. Nevertheless, he dared not deprive her of all hope. In response to her pleading, and urged by her father and uncle, he was emboldened to promise her the dream for the ensuing night, trusting that in the condition of body and mind to which he perceived she was reduced by the overwrought state of her nerves she might even *imagine* she had seen her brother.

But though the slippery road along which, impelled by vanity and ambition, he travelled was beset with danger, Cagliostro proceeded undaunted. When his second attempt to evoke the dead failed like the first, he boldly asserted that he himself had prevented the apparition, "being warned by Hanachiel that the vision of her brother would endanger the Countess's life in her excitable state." And to render this explanation the more convincing he gave the von Medems, who were plainly disappointed by the failure of the "magic dream," one of those curious exhibitions of second sight which he was in the habit of knocking off—no other word expresses it—so frequently and successfully for their benefit.

Though aware that the Countess at the moment was ill in bed, he declared that, if a messenger were sent to her house at a certain hour, he would find her seated at her writing-table in perfect health. This prediction was verified in every particular.

Such was the state of affairs when Cagliostro
accompanied the von Medems to Wilzen to prove the
existence of the buried treasure he had so craftily
located. In spite of his great confidence in himself, he
must have realized that the task he had so rashly
undertaken at Wilzen was one that would require
exceptional cunning to shirk. For the chance of
finding a treasure said to have been buried hundreds
of years before was even smaller than that on which
he counted of evoking the spirit of the Countess's
brother. But in this case, strange to say, it was not
his failure to produce the treasure, but the "magic" he
successfully employed to conceal his failure that was to
cause him the most concern.

IV

Conscious that the Countess's faith in him was
shaken by his failure to give her the consolation she so
greatly desired, Cagliostro requested they should travel
in the same carriage in order that he might have the
opportunity to clear himself of her suspicions as to his
sincerity. The very boldness of such a request was
sufficient to disarm her. She herself has confessed, in
the book from which these details have been drawn,
that "his conversation was such as to create in her
a great reverence for his moral character, whilst his
subtle observations on mankind in general astonished
her as greatly as his magical operations."

From the manner, however, in which he faced the
difficulty, he does not appear to have been in the least
apprehensive of the consequences of failing to surmount
it. The Countess was once more his ardent disciple ;

the von Medems' belief in magic was proof against unsuccessful experiments ; and Hanachiel—invaluable Hanachiel—was always on hand to explain his failures as well as his successes.

On arriving at Alt-Auz, as the von Medem estate at Wilzen was named, Cagliostro produced from his pocket "a little red book, and read aloud in an unknown tongue." The Countess, who believed him to be praying, ventured to interrupt him as they drove through the haunted forest in which the treasure was said to be buried. Hereupon he cried out in wild zeal, " Oh, Great Architect of the Universe, help me to accomplish this work." A bit of theatricality that much impressed his companion, and which was all the more effective for being natural to him.

The von Medems were eager to begin digging for the treasure as soon as they alighted. Cagliostro, however, "after withdrawing to commune in solitude with Hanachiel," declared that the treasure was guarded by very powerful demons whom it was dangerous to oppose without taking due precautions. " To prevent them from spiriting it away without his knowledge" he performed a little incantation which was supposed to bind Hanachiel to keep an eye on them. The next day, to break the fall, so to speak, of the high hopes the von Medems had built on the buried treasure, he held a séance in which the infant medium was again the chief actor. The child—"holding a large iron nail," and with only a screen between it and the other members of the party, having presumably been hypnotized[1] by Cagliostro—described

[1] The "magic" nail held by the child has a strong family resemblance to Mesmer's *baquet divinatoire*. The famous *discovery*

the site of the buried treasure, the demon that guarded it, the treasure itself, and "seven angels in long white robes who helped Hanachiel keep an eye on the guardian of the treasure." At the command of Cagliostro the child kissed, and was kissed by, these angels. And to the amazement of those in the room, with only the screen between them and the child, the sound of the kisses, says the Countess von der Recke, could be distinctly heard.

Similar séances took place every day during the eight days the von Medem party stayed at Alt-Auz. At one the Countess herself was induced to enter the "magic circle holding a magic watch in her hand," while the little medium, assisted by the representative of the Grand Cophta, in his turn assisted by Hanachiel, read her thoughts.

But, unlike her father and uncle, while the impression these phenomena made upon her mind was profound, it was also unfavourable. Though curiosity caused her to witness these séances, the Countess von der Recke strongly disapproved of them on "religious grounds." Like many another, what she could not explain, she regarded as evil. The phenomena she witnessed appeared so uncanny that she believed them to be directly inspired by the powers of darkness. At first, in her admiration of Cagliostro, she prayed that he might escape temptation and be preserved from the demons with which it was but too evident to her he was surrounded. When at last he declared that he was informed by the ever-attendant Hanachiel

of Mesmer, it is scarcely needless to say, was merely an attempt to explain scientifically powers the uses of which had been known to alchemists from time immemorial.

that the demon who guarded the buried treasure was not to be propitiated without much difficulty and delay, it did not occur to her to doubt him. The wonders he had been performing daily had convinced her, as well as the others, of his occult powers. But from regarding him with reverence, she now regarded him with dread.

Cagliostro, who never lost sight of the aims of Egyptian Masonry in the deceptions to which the desire to proselytize led him, was in the habit, " before each of his séances, of delivering lectures that were a strange mixture of sublimity and frivolity." It was by these lectures that he unconsciously lost the respect of the Countess he strove so hard to preserve. One day, while expatiating on the times when the sons of God loved the daughters of men, as described in the Bible—which, he predicted, would return when mankind was morally regenerate—carried away by his subject he declared that, " not only the demi-Gods of Greece, and Christ of Nazareth, but he himself were the fruit of such unions."

Such a statement inexpressibly shocked the Countess ; and considering that the evil spirits from whom she prayed he might be preserved had completely taken possession of him, she resolved to have no more to do with him. At her father's entreaty, however, she was persuaded to attend another séance, but as Cagliostro, not suspecting her defection, prefaced his phenomena by a discourse on " love-potions," the Countess was only confirmed in her resolution.

Nevertheless, he was not the man to lose so influential an adherent without a protest. On returning to Mittau he managed to a certain extent to regain her confidence in his sincerity. He perceived, however, that the interest he excited was on the wane, and wisely took advantage of what he knew to be the right moment to depart.

Hoping by the aristocratic connections he had made in Mittau to gain access to the highest circles in Russia, he decided to go to St. Petersburg. His intention was received with dismay by those whom his magical phenomena had so astonished. The von Medems heaped presents on him. "From one he received a gift of 800 ducats, from the other a very valuable diamond ring." Even the Countess von der Recke herself, though she made no attempt to detain him, proved that she at least believed him to be a man of honour.

A day or two before his departure, being at some Court function, "he recognized old friends in some large and fine pearls the Duchess of Courland was wearing," which, he said, reminded him of some pearls of his wife's that he had increased in size by a process known to himself and sold for the benefit of a bankrupt friend in Holland. The Countess von der Recke hereupon desired him to do the same with hers. Cagliostro, however, "refused, as he was going away, and the operation would take too long." Nor would he take them with him to Russia, as the Countess urged, and return them when the process was complete. A striking instance of his integrity, from an authentic source, that his prejudiced biographers have always seen fit to ignore.

If the above is characteristic of Cagliostro's honesty, the following episode, also related by the Countess, is equally characteristic of his vanity. Informing him once that she was writing to Lavater and wished to give him the details of a certain conversation, he objected.

"Wait twelve months," said he, "and when you write call me only Count C. Lavater will ask you, 'Is not this the Great Cagliostro?' and you will then be able to reply, 'It is.'"

As the unfavourable opinion the Countess von der Recke subsequently formed of Cagliostro, whose path never crossed hers again, has, on account of her deservedly high reputation, been largely responsible for the hostility with which history has regarded him, it is but fair to explain how she came to reverse the favourable opinion she had previously entertained.

The value of her evidence, indeed, rests not so much on her *word*, which nobody would dream of questioning, but on the *manner* in which she obtained her evidence. It was not till 1784—five years after Cagliostro had left Mittau—that the Countess von der Recke came to regard him as an impostor. To this opinion she was converted by one Bode whom she met in Weimar and who, she says, gave her "the fullest information concerning Cagliostro."

Bode was a Freemason of the Order of Strict Observance who had joined the Illuminés and was intimately acquainted with Weishaupt, the founder of the sect. As it is generally assumed that Cagliostro was also an Illuminé, Bode no doubt had excellent means of observing him. The value of his opinion, however, is considerably lowered by the fact that Cagliostro afterwards withdrew from the Illuminés when he had succeeded in turning his connection with them to the account of Egyptian Masonry. Under the circumstances Bode, who afterwards became the leader of the Illuminés, would not be likely to view Cagliostro in a favourable light.

The fact, moreover, that it took the Countess von der Recke five years to make up her mind that her "apostle of light" was an impostor, was perhaps due less to any absolute faith in Bode than to the changes that had taken place in herself during this period.

On recovering her health she became as pronounced a rationalist as she had formerly been a mystic. As this change occurred about the period of her meeting with Bode, it may possibly account for the change in her opinion of Cagliostro.

But if the manner in which the Countess came to regard Cagliostro as an impostor somewhat detracts from the importance to be attached to her opinion, the manner in which she made her opinion public was unworthy of a woman to whose character this opinion owes the importance attributed to it. For this "born fair saint" as Carlyle calls her, waited till the Diamond Necklace Affair, when Cagliostro was thoroughly discredited, before venturing to "expose" him.

V

Very curious to relate, all that is known of Cagliostro's visit to St. Petersburg is based on a few contradictory rumours of the most questionable authenticity. This is all the more remarkable considering, as the Countess von der Recke herself states, that he left Mittau in a blaze of glory, regretted, honoured, and recommended to some of the greatest personages in Russia by the flower of the nobility of Courland.[1]

According to report, Cagliostro's first act in St. Petersburg, as everywhere else he went, was to gain admission to one of the lodges of Strict Observance and endeavour to convert the members to the Egyptian Rite. As experience had taught him the futility of attempting to recruit adherents merely by expounding his lofty ideal of the regeneration of mankind, he had recourse to the methods he had adopted with such success in Mittau; but with the most humiliating result. For, being apparently unable to procure a suitable medium, he was forced to resort to an expedient which was discreditable in itself and unworthy of his remarkable faculties.

On this occasion his medium was a *colombe*, "the niece of an actress" in whose house the séance was held. There was the usual mumbo-jumbo, sword-waving passes, stamping of the feet, *et cetera*. The medium behind a screen gazed into a carafe of water and astonished the assembled company with what she saw there. But later in the evening while Cagliostro, covered with congratulations, was discoursing on the virtue of Egyptian Masonry and dreaming of fresh triumphs, the medium suddenly declared that she had seen nothing and that her rôle had been prepared beforehand by the Grand Cophta!

Cagliostro, as has been seen, was bold and

---

[1] As all the above-mentioned rumours—which, be it understood, were voiceless till the Diamond Necklace Affair—are hostile, it may be inferred that Cagliostro's visit to St. Petersburg was, to say the least, a failure. This impression is confirmed by the fact that on the publication of the Countess von der Recke's book, the Empress Catherine caused it to be translated into Russian.

resourceful when his situation seemed utterly untenable. That he would have seen his prestige destroyed in this way without attempting to save it is far from likely, and though the fact that St. Petersburg is the only city in which Cagliostro failed to establish a lodge of Egyptian Masonry may be regarded as proof of the futility of his efforts, the nature of other rumours concerning him leads one to suppose that he strove hard to regain the ground he had lost.

It was, no doubt, with this object that he turned his knowledge of medicine and chemistry to account. It is in St. Petersburg that he is heard of for the first time as a "healer." According, however, to the vague and hostile rumours purporting to emanate from Russia at the time of the Diamond Necklace Affair he was a quack devoid of knowledge or skill.

"A bald major," says the Inquisition-biographer, "entrusted his head to his care, but he could not make a single hair grow. A blind gentleman who consulted him remained blind; while a deaf Italian, into whose ears he dropped some liquid, became still more deaf."

As a few months later Cagliostro was performing the most marvellous cures at Strasburg, and was for years visited by invalids from all over Europe, may we not assume that in this instance malice only published his failures and suppressed his successes?

These rumours, however, were by no means damaging enough to please the Marquis de Luchet, who had no scruples about inventing what he considered "characteristic" anecdotes. The following story drawn from his spurious *Mémoires Authentiques* is worth repeating, less as an illustration of his inventive powers than for the sake of nailing a popular lie.

"Death," he writes, "threatened to deprive a Russian lady of an idolized infant aged two. She promised Cagliostro 5000 louis if he saved its life. He undertook to restore it to health in a week if she would suffer him to remove the babe to his house. The distressed mother joyfully accepted the proposal. On the fifth day he informed her there was a marked improvement, and at the end of the week declared that his patient was cured. Three weeks elapsed, however, before he would restore the child to its mother. All St. Petersburg rang with the news of this marvellous cure, and talked of the mysterious man who was able to cheat death of its prey. But soon it was rumoured that the child which was returned to the mother was not the one which had been taken away. The authorities looked into the matter, and Cagliostro was obliged to confess that the babe he restored was substituted for the real one, which had died. Justice demanded the body of the latter, but Cagliostro could not produce it. He had burnt it, he said, 'to test the theory of reincarnation.' Ordered to repay the 5000 louis he had received, he offered bills of exchange on a Prussian banker. As he professed to be a colonel in the service of the King of Prussia,[1] the bills were accepted, but on being presented for payment were dishonoured. The matter was therefore brought to the notice of Count von Goertz, the Prussian Envoy at St. Petersburg, who obtained an order for his arrest. This is the true explanation of his sudden departure."

[1] This seems to have been suggested to de Luchet by the *Courier de l'Europe*, which stated that Cagliostro, on becoming a Freemason, described himself as "Colonel of the Brandenburg regiment."

Rumour, however, differed widely from de Luchet. For at the same time that de Luchet declared Cagliostro to be posing as a Prussian colonel he is also said to have donned the uniform of a colonel in the Spanish service, and assumed the title of Prince de Santa Cruce. But far from being treated with the respect usually paid to any high-sounding title and uniform in Russia, this prince-colonel doctor excited the suspicions of M. de Normandez, the Spanish chargé d'affaires at the Russian Court, who demanded his passport as proof of his identity. To forge one would have been easy for Giuseppe Balsamo, who had a talent in that line, one would think. As he failed, however, to adopt this very simple expedient, M. d'Alméras, his latest and least prejudiced biographer, is forced to the conclusion that "he had long given up the profession of forger"— Freemasonry being responsible for his renunciation! The conception of Cagliostro as Balsamo reformed by Freemasonry is the most singular and unconvincing explanation ever offered of this strange man.

At any rate, the Prince de Santa Cruce could neither produce a passport nor forge one, and, hearing that a warrant was about to be issued for his arrest, he made haste to disappear. That such an adventurer was actually in St. Petersburg when Cagliostro was there is highly probable, and no doubt accounts for rumour confounding them several years later. But that Cagliostro, bearing letters of introduction from the greatest families in Courland, should have adopted any other name than that which he bore in Mittau is inconceivable.

Still more absurd is the rumour that the Empress

Catherine, jealous of the attention that her favourite the great Potemkin—"a train-oil prince," as Carlyle contemptuously styles him — paid to the Countess Cagliostro, offered her 20,000 roubles to quit the country. Catherine would certainly never have *paid* any one to leave her dominions ; she had a much rougher way of handling those whose presence offended her. The Cagliostros, moreover, who went to Warsaw from St. Petersburg, arrived there in anything but an opulent condition.

There is yet another rumour, which is at least probable, to the effect that Cagliostro was forced to leave Russia by the intrigues of Catherine's Scotch doctors, Rogerson and Mouncey, who were "so enraged that a stranger, and a pretended pupil of the school of Hermes Trismegistus to boot, should poach upon their preserves, that they contemplated a printed exposure of his quackery." It was not the last time, as will be seen, that Cagliostro excited the active hostility of the medical faculty.

Strange to say, the Countess von der Recke, who, if any one, would have known the truth concerning his visit to St. Petersburg, fails to give any particulars. Perhaps there were none, after all, to give. She merely says : "On his way from St. Petersburg to Warsaw, Cagliostro passed through Mittau, but did not stop. He was seen by a servant of Marshal von Medem, to whom he sent his greeting."

VI

In any case, the disgrace in which Cagliostro is supposed to have left St. Petersburg by no means injured him in the opinion of his former admirers in Courland, who, from their high position and close connection with the Russian official world, would have been well informed of all that befell him. For by one of them, as we are told on the best authority, he was furnished with introductions to Prince Adam Poninski and Count Moczinski, which he presented on his arrival in Warsaw.

Now Warsaw society, like that of Mittau, was on the most intimate terms with the great world of St. Petersburg. Had Cagliostro masqueraded in Russia as a bogus Prince de Santa Cruce or a swindling Prussian colonel, or had his wife excited the jealousy of the Empress Catherine, the fact would have been known in Warsaw—if not before he arrived there, certainly before he left. Of one thing we may be absolutely sure, the anonymous author of *Cagliostro démasqué à Varsovie* would not have failed to mention a scandal so much to the point. As a matter of fact, while denouncing Cagliostro as an impostor, this hostile witness even speaks of the "marvels he performed in Russia."

Nothing could have been more flattering to Cagliostro than the welcome he received on his arrival in Warsaw in May 1780. Poland, like Courland, was one of the strongholds of Freemasonry and occultism. Prince Poninski, who was as great a devotee to magic and alchemy as the von Medems, insisted on the wonder-worker and his wife staying at his house. Finding the soil so admirably adapted to the seed he had to sow, Cagliostro began at once to preach the gospel he had so much at heart. The conversion of Poninski to Egyptian Masonry was followed by that of the greater part of Polish society. Within a month of his arrival he had established at Warsaw a Masonic lodge in which the Egyptian Rite was observed.

It was not, however, by Cagliostro's ideals that Poninski and his friends were attracted, but by his power to gratify their craving for sensation. No speculations in pure mysticism *à la* Saint-Martin for them : they were occult materialists, and demanded of the supernatural practical, tangible manifestations.

As under similar circumstances at Mittau, Cagliostro had found it convenient to encourage the abuses he had professed to denounce, he had no compunction about following the same course at Warsaw. But it evidently did not come easy to him to prostitute his ideal, judging from the awkwardness with which he adapted himself to the conditions it entailed.

At first, apart from certain remarkable faculties he possessed and a sort of dilettante knowledge of magic and alchemy, he lacked both skill and experience. In Mittau, where his career as a wonder-worker may first fairly be said to begin, he failed as often as he succeeded. That the phenomena he faked were not detected at the time was due to luck, which, to judge from rumour, appears almost entirely to have deserted him in St. Petersburg.

In Warsaw, too, he was still far from expert. Here, in spite of the precautions he took, he found himself called upon to pass an examination in alchemy, a subject for which he was unprepared, and failed miserably.

In the opinion of the indignant Pole who caught him " cribbing," so to speak, "if he knew a little more of optics, acoustics, mechanics, and physics generally ;

if he had studied a little the tricks of Comus and Philadelphus, what success might he not have with his reputed skill in counterfeiting writing! It is only necessary for him to go into partnership with a ventriloquist in order to play a much more important part than he has hitherto done. He should add to the trifling secrets he possesses by reading some good book on chemistry."

But it is by failure that one gains experience. As Cagliostro was quick and intelligent, and had a "forehead of brass that nothing could abash," by the time he had reached Strasburg he was a past-master of the occult, having brought his powers to a high state of perfection, as well as being able, on occasion, to fake a phenomenon with consummate skill.

There are two accounts of his adventures in Warsaw—one favourable, the other unfavourable. The latter, it is scarcely necessary to say, is the one by which he has been judged. It dates, as usual, from the period of the Necklace Affair—that is, six years after the events it describes. It is by an anonymous writer, who obtained his information second-hand from an "eye-witness, one Count M." Even Carlyle refuses to damn his "Arch-Quack" on such evidence. This vial of vitriol, flung by an unknown and hostile hand at the Grand Cophta of Egyptian Masonry in his hour of adversity, is called *Cagliostro démasqué à Varsovie*.

Nevertheless, contemptible and questionable though it is, the *impression* it conveys, if not the actual account, is confirmed by Madame Böhmer, wife of the jeweller in the Necklace Affair. Madame Böhmer's testimony is the more valuable in that it was given *before* the anonymous writer flung his vitriol.

Masked and Unmasked

One night in "April 1785"—Cagliostro then at the height of his fame—at a dinner-party at Madame Böhmer's, the conversation turned on mesmerism. The Countess de Lamotte, who was present, declared she believed in it—an opinion that her hostess did not share.

"Such people," said Madame Böhmer, "only wish to attract attention, like Cagliostro, who has been driven out of every country in which he has tried to make gold. The last was Poland. A person who has just come from there told me that he was admitted to Court on the strength of his knowledge of the occult, particularly of the philosopher's stone. There were some, however, who were not to be convinced without actual proof. Accordingly, a day was set for the operation, and one of the incredulous courtiers, knowing that he had as an assistant a young girl, bribed her. I do not say this was the Countess Cagliostro, because I am informed that he had several [mediums] who travelled with him. 'Keep your eye,' said the girl to the courtier, 'on his thumb, which he holds in the hollow of his hand to conceal the piece of gold he will slip into the crucible.' All attention, the courtier heard the gold and, immediately seizing Cagliostro's hand, exclaimed to the King, 'Sire, didn't you hear?' The crucible was searched, and a small lump of gold was found, whereupon Cagliostro was instantly and very roughly, as I was told, flung out of the palace."

The anonymous writer's "eye-witness, Count M.," described in detail the particulars of Cagliostro's quest for the philosopher's stone. According to this authority, he made his début at Prince Poninski's with some magical séances similar to those at Mittau, adding sleight-of-hand tricks to his predictions and "divinations by *colombes*."

Unfortunately, the occultists of Warsaw were principally interested in the supernatural properties of the crucible. They were crazy on the subject of alchemy, and the pursuit of the secret of the transmutation of base metals into gold. Having bent the knee to magic, in which at least, by virtue of his own occult gifts, he could appear to advantage, Cagliostro rashly—compelled by necessity, perhaps, rather than vanity in this instance—assumed a knowledge of which he was ignorant, relying on making gold by sleight-of-hand.

Alas! "Count M." had devoted his life to the subject, of which it did not take him long to discover Cagliostro knew next to nothing. Indignant that one who had not even learnt the alphabet of alchemy should undertake to instruct him of all people, he laid the trap described by Madame Böhmer. It was not, however, at the Royal Palace that the exposure took place that caused Cagliostro to leave Poland, but at a country seat near Warsaw. Moreover, if we are to believe "Count M.," Cagliostro did not wait to be exposed, but suspecting what was a-foot, "decamped during the night."

Now, on the strength of Madame Böhmer's evidence—not given by her in person, by the way, but *quoted* by the Countess de Lamotte in her defence at the Necklace trial—while there seems to be little doubt that the statement of the anonymous "Count M." is

substantially correct, there is, nevertheless, another—
and a favourable—account of Cagliostro in Poland. It
has the advantage of being neither anonymous nor
dated, like the Countess von der Recke's book, years
after the events it relates. It is from a letter written
by Laborde, the Farmer-General, who happened to be
in Warsaw when Cagliostro was there. The letter
bears the date of 1781, which was that of the year
after the following episodes occurred.

"Cagliostro," writes Laborde, "was some time at
Warsaw, and several times had had the honour of
meeting Stanislas Augustus. One day, as this monarch
was expressing his great admiration for his powers,
which appeared to him supernatural, a young lady of the
Court who had listened attentively to him began to
laugh, declaring that Cagliostro was nothing but an
impostor. She said she was so certain of it that she
would defy him to tell her certain things that had
happened to her.

"The next day the King informed the Count of
this challenge, who replied coldly that if the lady would
meet him in the presence of His Majesty, he would
cause her the greatest surprise she had ever known in
her life. The proposal was accepted, and the Count
told the lady all that she thought it impossible for him
to know. The surprise this occasioned her caused her
to pass so rapidly from incredulity to admiration that
she had a burning desire to know what was to happen
to her in the future.

"At first he refused to tell her, but yielding to her
entreaty, and perhaps to gratify the curiosity of the
King, he said—

"You will soon make a long journey, in course of

153

which your carriage will meet with an accident, and, whilst you are waiting for the repairs to be made, the manner in which you are dressed will excite such merriment in the crowd that you will be pelted with apples. You will go from there to some famous watering-place, where you will meet a man of high birth, to whom you will shortly afterwards be wedded. There will be an attempt to prevent your marriage, which will cause you to be foolish enough to make over to him your fortune. You will be married in a city in which I shall be, and, in spite of your efforts to see me, you will not succeed. You are threatened with great misfortunes, but here is a talisman by which you may avoid them, so long as you keep it. But if you are prevented from making over your fortune to your husband in your marriage contract you will immediately lose the talisman, and, the moment you cease to have it, it will return to my pocket wherever I may be.'

"I do not know," continues Laborde, "what confidence the King and the lady placed in these predictions, but I know that they were all fulfilled. I have had this on the authority of several persons, as well as the lady herself ; also from Cagliostro, who described it in precisely the same words. I do not guarantee either its truth or its falsity, and, as I do not pretend to be an exact historian, I shall not indulge in the smallest reflection."

CHAPTER IV

THE CONQUEST OF THE CARDINAL

I

OF the difficulties that perpetually beset the biographer of Cagliostro, those caused by his frequent disappearances from sight are the most perplexing. It is possible to combat prejudice—to materialize, so to speak, rumour, to manipulate conflicting evidence, and even to throw light on that which is mysterious in his character. But when it is a question of filling up the gaps, of bridging the chasms in his career, one can only proceed by assumption.

Such a chasm, and one of the deepest, occurs between June 26, 1780, when Cagliostro suddenly fled from Warsaw, and September 19, when he arrived in Strasburg. Even rumour lost track of him during this interval. The Inquisition-biographer pretends to discover him for a moment at Frankfort-on-the-Main as a secret agent of the Illuminés, and, as an assumption, the statement is at once plausible and probable.

Cagliostro, as stated in a previous chapter, has always been supposed, on grounds that all but amount to proof, to have been at some period in his mysterious career connected with one of the revolutionary secret societies of Germany. This society has always been

155

assumed to be the Illuminés.[1]   If this assumption be true—and without it his mode of life in Strasburg is utterly inexplicable—his initiation could only have taken place at this period and, probably, at Frankfort, where Knigge, one of the leaders of the Illuminés, had his head-quarters.

As Knigge was a member of the Order of Strict Observance, in the lodges of which throughout Germany Cagliostro's reputation as a wonder-worker stood high, he had undoubtedly heard of him, if he was not personally acquainted with him.   Knigge, moreover, was just the man to appreciate the possibilities of such a reputation in obtaining recruits for Illuminism. Nothing is more reasonable, then, than to assume that certain members of the Illuminés made overtures at Frankfort to Cagliostro, who, one can imagine, would have readily accepted them as the means of recovering the influence and prestige he had lost in Poland.

His initiation, according to the Inquisition-biographer, took place in a grotto a short distance from the city.   In the centre, on a table, was an iron chest, from which Knigge or his deputy took a manuscript. On the first page Cagliostro perceived the words " *We, the Grand Masters of the Templars.*"   Then followed the formula of an oath written in blood, to which eleven signatures were appended, and which signified that Illuminism was a conspiracy against thrones.   The first blow was to be struck in France, and, after the

[1] As an agent of the Illuminés, Cagliostro would have been quite free to found lodges of Egyptian Masonry.   Many Egyptian Masons were also Illuminés, notably Sarazin of Bâle, the banker of both societies.   In joining the Illuminés, therefore, Cagliostro would not only have furthered their interests, but have received every assistance from them in return.

fall of the monarchy, Rome was to be attacked. Cagliostro, moreover, learnt that the society had ramifications everywhere, and possessed immense sums in banks in Amsterdam, Rotterdam, London, Genoa, and Venice. This money was furnished by an annual subscription of twenty-five livres paid by each member.

On taking the oath, which included a vow of secrecy, Cagliostro is presumed to have received a large sum, destined to defray the expenses of propaganda, and to have proceeded immediately, in accordance with instructions, to Strasburg, where he arrived on September 19, 1780.

II

From the nature of his entry into the capital of Alsace, it is certain that great pains had been taken in advance to excite public interest in him. The fabulous Palladium could not have been welcomed with greater demonstrations of joy. From early morning crowds of people waited on the Pont de Kœhl and on both banks of the Rhine for the arrival of a mysterious personage who was reported to go from city to city healing the sick, working miracles, and distributing alms. In the crowd speculations were rife as to his mysterious origin, his mysterious travels in strange and remote countries, and of the mysterious source of his immense wealth. Some regarded him as one inspired, a saint or a prophet possessed of the gift of miracles. To others, the cures attributed to him were the natural result of his great learning and occult powers. Yet another group saw in him an evil genius, a devil sent into the world on some diabolic mission. Among these, however—and they were not the least numerous—there were some more favourable to Cagliostro, and who, considering that after all he only did good, inferred logically that, if supernatural, he must be a good, rather than an evil, genius.

Suddenly, speculation was silenced by the approach of the being who had excited it. The rumbling of wheels, the clatter of hoofs, the cracking of whips was heard, and out of a cloud of dust appeared a carriage drawn by six horses, and accompanied by lacqueys and outriders in magnificent liveries. Within rode the Grand Cophta, the High Priest of Mystery, with his "hair in a net," and wearing a blue coat covered with gold braid and precious stones. Bizarre though he was with his circus-rider's splendour, the manner in which he acknowledged the vivats of the crowd [1] through which he passed was not without dignity. His wife, who sat beside him, sparkling with youth, beauty, and diamonds, shared the curiosity he excited. It was a veritable triumphal progress.

The advantage to which such an ovation could be turned was not to be neglected. Fond of luxury and aristocratic society though he was, Cagliostro was not the man to despise popularity in any form that it presented itself. Having lost the influence of the great, by means of whom he had counted to establish Egyptian Masonry, he was anxious to secure that of the masses. So great was the importance he attached to the interest he had aroused, he even took up his

[1] The story that it was interrupted by the sudden appearance of Marano, furiously demanding of Cagliostro the sixty ounces of gold that Giuseppe Balsamo had defrauded him of years before in Palermo, is a pure invention of the Marquis de Luchet.

abode among them, "living first over a retail tobacco-nist's named Quère, whose shop was in one of the most squalid quarters of the town, and later lodging with the caretaker of the canon of St. Pierre-le-Vieux."

According to all reports, from the very day of his arrival in Strasburg he seemed to busy himself solely in doing good, regardless of cost or personal incon-venience. No one, providing he was poor and unfor-tunate, appealed to him in vain. Hearing that an Italian was in prison for a debt of two hundred livres, Cagliostro obtained his release by paying the money for him, and clothed him into the bargain. Baron von Gleichen, who knew him well, states that he saw him, on being summoned to the bed-side of a sick person, "run through a downpour in a very fine coat without stopping to take an umbrella."

Every day he sought out the poor and infirm, whose distress he endeavoured to relieve not only with money and medicine, but "with manifestations of sympathy that went to the hearts of the sufferers, and doubled the value of the action." Though his enemies did not hesitate to charge him with the most mercenary motives in administering his charities, they were obliged to admit the fact of them. Meiners, who thoroughly disliked him and considered him both a quack and a charlatan, was honest enough to acknow-ledge that he gave his services gratis, and even refused to make a profit on the sale of his remedies.

"For some time," says this hostile witness, "it was believed that he shared with his apothecary the profits on the remedies he prescribed to his patients. But as soon as Cagliostro learnt that such suspicions were entertained, he not only changed his apothecary, but obliged the one he chose in his place, as I have been informed by several people, to sell his remedies at so low a price that the fellow made scarcely anything by the sale of them.

"He would take, moreover, neither payment nor present for his labour. If a present was offered him of a sort impossible to refuse without offence, he immediately made a counter present of equal or even of higher value. Indeed, he not only took nothing from his patients, but if they were very poor he supported them for months; at times even lodging them in his own house and feeding them from his own table."

III

At first, only the poor received attention from Cagliostro. If a rich invalid desired his attendance he referred him to the regular doctors. Though such an attitude was well calculated to attract attention, it was not, as his enemies have declared, altogether prompted by selfish considerations. In the disdain he affected for the rich there was much real resentment. Through the rich and powerful, he had gained nothing but mortification and disgrace. The circumstances under which he was forced to flee from Warsaw must have wounded to the quick a nature in which inordinate vanity and generosity were so curiously blended. Of a certainty it was not alone the hope of turning Illuminism to the advantage of Egyptian Masonry that prompted him to join the Illuminés in his hour of humiliation. In Illuminism, whose aim, revolutionary though it was, like that of Egyptian Masonry, was also inspired with the love of humanity, Cagliostro had seen both a

means of rehabilitation and revenge. Of studied vengeance, however, he was incapable; the disdain with
which he treated the rich was the extent of his revenge.
Indeed, susceptible as he was to flattery, it was not
long before his resentment was altogether appeased.
But though, in spite of his bitter experience, he was
even once more tempted to court the favour of the
great, he did so in quite a different manner. Henceforth, in pandering to their love of sensation, he took
care to give them what *he* saw fit, and not, as before,
what *they* demanded.

Particularly was this the case in the exhibitions he
gave of his occult powers. If, as on previous occasions,
he had recourse to artifice to obtain the effect he
desired, it was not detected. It is evident that his
unfortunate experiences in Warsaw had taught him the
wisdom of confining himself solely to phenomena
within his scope. No longer does one hear of séances
arranged beforehand with the medium; of failures,
exposures, and humiliations.

If from some of his prodigies the alchemists of the
period saw in him a successor of the clever ventriloquist and prestidigitator Lascaris, from many others the
mediums of the present day in Europe and America
might have recognized in him their predecessor and
even their master in table-turning, spirit-rapping, clairvoyance, and evocations. In a word, he was no longer
an apprentice in magic, but an expert.

As the manifestations of the occult of which
Cagliostro, so to speak, made a speciality were of a
clairvoyant character, some idea of the manner in
which he had developed his powers may be gathered
from the following account by a contemporary of a

séance he held in Strasburg with the customary *colombe* and carafe.

"Cagliostro," says this witness, "having announced that he was ready to answer any question put to him, a lady wished to know the age of her husband. To this the *colombe* made no reply, which elicited great applause when the lady confessed she had no husband. Another lady demanded an answer to a question written in a sealed letter she held in her hand. The medium at once read in the carafe these words : 'You shall not obtain it.' The letter was opened, the purport of the question being whether the commission in the army which the lady solicited for her son would be accorded her. As the reply was at least indicative of the question, it was received with applause.

"A judge, however, who suspected that Cagliostro's answers were the result of some trick, secretly sent his son to his house to find out what his wife was doing at the time. When he had departed the father put this question to the Grand Cophta. The medium read nothing in the carafe, but a voice announced that the lady was playing cards with two of her neighbours. This mysterious voice, which was produced by no visible organ, terrified the company ; and when the son of the judge returned and confirmed the response of the oracle, several ladies were so frightened that they withdrew."

At Strasburg he also told fortunes, and read the future as well as the past with an accuracy that astonished even the sceptical Madame d'Oberkirch. One of the most extraordinary instances he gave of his psychic power was in predicting the death of the Empress Maria Theresa.

The Conquest of the Cardinal

"He even foretold the hour at which she would expire," relates Madame d'Oberkirch. "M. de Rohan told it to me in the evening, and it was five days after that the news arrived."

IV

It was, however, as a healer of the sick that Cagliostro was chiefly known in Strasburg. Sudden cures of illnesses, thought to be mortal or incurable, carried his name from mouth to mouth. The number of his patients increased daily. On certain days it was estimated that upwards of five hundred persons besieged the house in which he lodged, pressing one another to get in. From the collection of sticks and crutches left as a mark of gratitude by those who, thanks to his skill, no longer had need of them, it seemed as if all the cripples in Strasburg had flocked to consult him.

The Farmer-General Laborde declares that Cagliostro attended over fifteen thousand [1] sick people during the three years he stayed in Strasburg, of whom only three died.

One of his most remarkable cures was that of the secretary of the Marquis de Lasalle, the Commandant of Strasburg. "He was dying," says Gleichen, "of gangrene of the leg, and had been given up by the doctors, but Cagliostro saved him."

On another occasion he procured a belated paternity for Sarazin, the banker of Bâle, who afterwards became one of his most devoted adherents. No illness

[1] Motus, another contemporary, gives the number as "over fifteen hundred."

appeared to baffle him. The graver the malady the more resourceful he became. A woman about to be confined, having been given up by the midwives, who doubted even their ability to save her child, sent for him in her extremity. He answered the summons immediately, as was his custom, and after a slight examination guaranteed her a successful *accouchement*. What is more to the point, he kept his word.

This case is worthy of note as being the only one on record concerning which Cagliostro gave an explanation of his success.

" He afterwards confessed to me," says Gleichen, "that his promise was rash. But convinced that the child was in perfect health by the pulse of the umbilical cord, and perceiving that the mother only lacked the strength requisite to bring her babe into the world, he had relied on the virtue of a singularly soothing remedy with which he was acquainted. The result, he considered, had been due to luck rather than skill."

The most famous of all his cures was that of the Prince de Soubise, a cousin of Cardinal de Rohan. In this case, however, it was the rank of the patient, even more than the illness of which he was cured, that set the seal to Cagliostro's reputation. The prince, it seems, had been ill for some weeks, and the doctors, after differing widely as to the cause of his malady, had finally pronounced his condition to be desperate. Thereupon the Cardinal, who had boundless confidence in Cagliostro's medical skill, immediately carried him off in his carriage to Paris to attend his cousin, simply stating, on arriving at the Hôtel de Soubise, that he had brought " a doctor," without mentioning his name, lest the family, influenced by the regular physicians,

who regarded him as a quack, should refuse his
services. It was, perhaps, a useless precaution, for, as
the patient had just been given up by the doctors, the
family were willing enough to suffer even a quack to
do what he could.

Cagliostro at once requested all who were in the
sick-room to leave it. What he did when he found himself alone with the prince was never known, but, after
an hour, he called the Cardinal and said to him—

"If my prescription is followed, in two days
Monseigneur will leave his bed and walk about the
room. Within a week he will be able to take a drive,
and within three to go to Court."

When one has consulted an oracle, one can do no
better than obey it. The family accordingly confided
the prince completely to the care of the unknown
doctor, who on the same day paid his patient a second
visit. On this occasion he took with him a small vial
containing a liquid, ten drops of which he administered
to the sick man.

On leaving, he said to the Cardinal : "To-morrow I
will give the prince five drops, the day after two, and
you will see that he will sit up the same evening."

The result more than fulfilled the prediction.
The second day after this visit the Prince de Soubise
was in a condition to receive some friends. In
the evening he got up and walked about the room. He
was in good spirits, and even had sufficient appetite to
ask for the wing of a chicken. But, in spite of his
insistence, it was necessary to refuse him what he so
much desired, since an absolute abstention from solid
food was one of the prescriptions of the "doctor."

On the fourth day the patient was convalescent, but

it was not till the evening of the fifth that he was permitted to have his wing of a chicken. "No one," says Figuier, "in the Hôtel de Soubise had the least idea that Cagliostro was the doctor who attended the prince. His identity was only disclosed *after* the cure, when his name, already famous, ceased to be regarded any longer as that of a charlatan."

V

The secret of these astonishing cures, by far the most wonderful of Cagliostro's prodigies, has given rise to a great deal of futile discussion. For he never cured in public, like Mesmer; nor would he consent to give any explanation of his method to the doctors and learned academicians, who treated him with contempt born of envy—as the pioneers of science, with rare exceptions, have always been treated.

From the fact that he became celebrated at about the same time as Mesmer, many have regarded them as rivals, and declared that the prestige of both is to be traced to the same source. According to this point of view, Cagliostro, being more encyclopedic than Mesmer, though less scientific in manipulating the agent common to both, had in some way generalized magnetism, so to speak. His cures, however, were far more astonishing than Mesmer's, for they were performed without passes or the use of magnets and magnetic wands. Neither did he heal merely by *touching*, like Gassner, nor by prayers, exorcisms, and the religious machinery by which faith is made active; though very probably the greater part of his success was due, like Mrs. Eddy's, to the confident tone in which he assured his patients of the certainty of their recovery.

Cagliostro's contemporaries, on the other hand, to whom the mechanism of Christian Science and the attributes of hypnotism—since so well tested by Dr. Charcot—were unknown, sought a material explanation of his cures in the quack medicines he concocted. The old popular belief in medicinal stones and magical herbs was still prevalent. One writer of the period pretended to know that Cagliostro's "Elixir Vitæ" was composed of "magical herbs and gold in solution." Another declared it to be the same as the elixir of Arnauld de Villeneuve, a famous alchemist of the Middle Ages, whose prescription consisted of "a mixture of pearls, sapphires, hyacinths, emeralds, rubies, topazes and diamonds, to which was added the scraping of the bones of a stag's heart."

Equally fantastic were the properties attributed to these panaceas by those who owed their restoration to health to Cagliostro. The following story, repeated everywhere—and believed, too, by many—gave the notoriety of a popular modern advertisement to the "Wine of Egypt."

A great lady, who was also, unfortunately for her, an old one, and was unable to resign herself to the fact, was reported to have consulted Cagliostro, who gave her a vial of the precious liquid with the strictest injunction to take two drops when the moon entered its last quarter. Whilst waiting for this period to arrive the lady who desired to be rejuvenated shut up the vial in her wardrobe, and the better to insure its preservation informed her maid that it was a remedy for the colic. Fatal precaution! By some mischance on the following night, the maid was seized with the very malady of which her mistress had spoken. Remembering the remedy so fortuitously at hand she got up, opened the wardrobe, and emptied the vial at a draught.

The next morning she went as usual to wait on her mistress, who looked at her in surprise and asked her what she wanted. Thinking the old lady had had a stroke in the night, she said—

"Ah, madame, don't you know me? I am your maid."

"My maid is a woman of fifty," was the reply, "and you——"

But she did not finish the sentence. The woman had caught a glimpse of her face in a mirror. The Wine of Egypt had rejuvenated her thirty years!

In an age unfamiliar with the cunning devices of the art of advertising and the universality of the pretensions of quack remedies, such encomiums lavished on "an extract of Saturn," a "Wine of Egypt," or an "Elixir Vitæ," were calculated to damage the reputation of their inventor in the opinion of serious people even more than the bitter denunciations to which they were exposed. One of the charges of imposture on which the case against Cagliostro rests is that of manufacturing his remedies with the object of defrauding the public by attributing to them fabulous properties which he knew they did not possess. If this be admitted, then a similar accusation must be made against every maker of patent medicines to-day, which, in view of the law of libel and the fact that many persons have been restored to health by the concoctions of quacks whom the skilled physician has been powerless to heal, would be incredibly foolish.

To regard these remedies of Cagliostro with their ridiculous names and quixotic pretensions with the old prejudice is preposterous. Judged by the number and variety of his cures—and it is the only reasonable standard to judge them by—they were, to say the least, remarkable.

In the present day, it is no longer the custom to deride the knowledge of the old alchemists. The world has come to acknowledge that, in spite of the fantastic jargon in which they expressed themselves, they fully understood the uses of the plants and minerals of which they composed their drugs. Stripped of the atmosphere of magic and mystery in which they delighted to wrap their knowledge — and which, ridiculous as it may seem to-day, had just as much effect on the imagination in their benighted age as the more scientific mode of "suggestion" employed by the doctors of our own enlightened era—the remedies of a Borri or a Paracelsus are still deserving of respect, and still employed. Cagliostro is known to have made a serious study of alchemy, and it is very probable that his magic balsams and powders were prepared after receipts he discovered in old books of alchemy. Perhaps too, like all quacks—it is impossible to accord a more dignified title to one who had not the diploma of a properly qualified practitioner—he made the most of old wives' remedies picked up haphazard in the course of his travels.

Without doubt the unparalleled credulity and superstition of the age contributed greatly to his success. Miracles can only succeed in an atmosphere favourable to the miraculous. In Europe, as the reader has seen—particularly in France—the soil had been well prepared for seed of the sort that Cagliostro sowed.

VI

The cure of the Prince de Soubise gave Cagliostro an immense prestige. " It would be impossible," says the Baroness d'Oberkirch, "to give an idea of the passion, the madness with which people pursued him. It would appear incredible to any one who had not seen it." On returning to Strasburg, "he was followed by a dozen ladies of rank and two actresses" who desired to have the benefit of his treatment. People came from far and wide to consult him ; and many out of sheer curiosity. To these, whom he regarded as spies sent by his enemies, he was either inaccessible or positively rude.

Lavater, who came from Zurich, was treated with very scant courtesy. " If," said Cagliostro, "your science [that of reading character by the features, by which he had acquired a European reputation] is greater than mine, you have no need of my acquaintance; and if mine is the greater, I have no need of yours."

Lavater, however, was not to be repulsed by the inference to be drawn from such a remark. The following day he wrote Cagliostro a long letter in which, among other things, he asked him " how he had acquired his knowledge, and in what it consisted." In reply Cagliostro limited himself to these words : *In verbis, in herbis, in lapidibus*, by which, as M. d'Alméras observes, he probably indicated correctly the nature and extent of his medical and occult lore.

The Conquest of the Cardinal

But Lavater, as credulous as he was inquisitive, impressed by the mystery in which Cagliostro enveloped his least action, read into his words quite another meaning. Believing firmly in the Devil—about whom he had written a book—the Swiss pastor returned home convinced that the Grand Cophta of Egyptian Masonry was "a supernatural being with a diabolic mission."

In nobody were the curiosity and admiration that he inspired greater than in the notorious Cardinal de Rohan. His Eminence was one of the darlings of Fortune, whose choicest favours had been showered on him with a lavish hand. Of the most illustrious birth, exceptionally handsome, enormously rich, and undeniably fascinating, no younger son ever started life under more brilliant auspices. The Church seemed to exist solely for the purpose of providing him with honours. Bishop of Strasburg, Grand Almoner of France, Cardinal, Prince of the Empire, Landgrave of Alsace—his titles were as numerous as the beads of a rosary. Nor were they merely high-sounding and empty dignities. From the Abbey of St. Waast, the richest in France, of which he was the Abbot, he drew 300,000 livres a year, and from all these various sources combined his revenue was estimated at 1,200,000 livres.

Nature had endowed him no less bounteously than Fortune. To the honours which he owed to the accident of birth, his intellect had won him another still more coveted. At twenty-seven he had been elected to the Académie Française, where, as he was particularly brilliant in conversation, it is not surprising that the Immortals should have "declared themselves charmed with his company."

Cagliostro

He possessed all the conspicuous qualities and defects which in the eighteenth century were characteristic of the aristocrat. High ecclesiastic that he was, he had nothing of the ascetic about him. Like so many of the great dignitaries of the Church under the *ancien régime*, he was worldly to the last degree. As he was not a hypocrite, he did not hesitate to live as he pleased. Appointed Ambassador to Vienna, he had scandalized the strait-laced Maria Theresa by his reckless extravagance and dissipation. The Emperor, to her disgust, "loved conversing with him to enjoy his flippant gossip and wicked stories." "Our women," she wrote to her Ambassador at Versailles, "young and old, beautiful and ugly, are bewitched by him. He is their idol."

His character was a mosaic of vice and virtue. With him manners took the place of morals. "He possessed," says Madame d'Oberkirch, "the gallantry and politeness of a grand seigneur such as I have rarely met in any one." Madame de Genlis considered that, "if he was nothing that he ought to be, he was as amiable as it was possible to be." In him vice lost all its grossness and levity acquired dignity. Anxious to please, he was also susceptible to flattery. "By my lording him," says Manuel, who disliked him, "one can get from him whatever one desires." At the same time he was obliged to confess that the Cardinal "had a really good heart."

It was to his excessive good-nature that he owed most of his misfortunes. The entire absence of intolerance in his character caused him to be regarded as an atheist, but his unbelief, like his vices, was greatly exaggerated. Men in his position never escape detraction, but in the case of the Cardinal he deliberately invited it. Gracious to all, he was generous to a fault. He dispensed favour and charity alike without discernment, giving to the poor as readily and as bountifully as to his mistresses. Of these he had had many ; the memoirs of the period contain strange, and often untranslatable, stories of his private life. For some years he was followed wherever he went by the beautiful Marquise de Marigny dressed as a page.

Besides his weakness for a pretty face, this splendid tare had a fondness amounting to passion for pomp and alchemy. "On state occasions at Versailles," says Madame d'Oberkirch, he wore an alb of lace *en point à l'aiguille* of such beauty that the assistants were almost afraid to touch it." It was embroidered with his arms and device—the famous device of the Rohans, *Roy ne puis, prince ne daigne, Rohan je suis.* It was said to be worth a million livres.

In gratifying his taste for luxury, the cost was the last thing he considered. On going to Vienna as Ambassador he took with him two gala coaches worth 40,000 livres each ; fifty horses, two equerries, two piqueurs, seven pages drawn from the nobility of Brittany and Alsace with their governors and tutors, two gentlemen-in-waiting, six footmen, whose scarlet and gold liveries cost him 4000 livres apiece, etc.

In France his style of living was still more extravagant. He spent vast sums on pictures, sculptures, and artistic treasures generally. Collecting illuminated missals was his speciality. At his episcopal palace at Saverne, near Strasburg, which he rebuilt after it was destroyed by fire in 1779 at a cost of between two and three million livres, he had a magnificent library. As printed books, according to Madame d'Oberkirch, were beneath his notice, his library was noted for its beautiful bindings, and above all for the missals ornamented with miniatures worth their weight in gold.

His principal pastime, however, was alchemy. At Saverne, besides his library, he had one of the finest laboratories in Europe. He was almost mad on the subject of the philosopher's stone. The mention of the occult sciences at once arrested his attention ; then, and only then, did the brilliant, frivolous Cardinal become serious.

Naturally, such a man could not fail to be impressed by the mysterious physician whose cures were the talk of Strasburg.

Shortly after Cagliostro's arrival, Baron de Millinens, the Cardinal's master of the hounds, called to inform him that his Eminence desired to make his acquaintance. But Cagliostro knowing, as he stated at his trial in the Necklace Affair, that the prince "only desired to see him from curiosity, refused to gratify him." The answer he returned is famous, and thoroughly characteristic of him.

" If the Cardinal is ill," he is reported to have said, "let him come to me and I will cure him ; but if he is well, he has no need of me nor I of him."

This message, far from affronting the Cardinal, only increased his curiosity. After having attempted in vain to gain admittance to the sanctuary of the new Esculapius, his Eminence had, or feigned, an attack of asthma, " of which," says Cagliostro, "he sent to inform me, whereupon I went at once to attend him."

The visit, though short, was long enough to inspire the Cardinal with a desire for a closer acquaintance.

The Conquest of the Cardinal

But Cagliostro's disdainful reserve was not easily broken down. The advances of the Cardinal, however, were none the less flattering. At last, captivated by the persistency of the fascinating prelate, he declared in his grandiose way, to Rohan's immense joy, that "the prince's soul was worthy of his, and that he would confide to him all his secrets."

The relation thus formed, whatever the motives that prompted it, soon ripened into intimacy. Needless to say, they had long, frequent, and secret confabulations in the Cardinal's well-equipped laboratory. Cagliostro, with his wife, eventually even went to live at Saverne at the Cardinal's request. He was bidden to consider the palace as his own, and the servants were ordered to announce him when he entered a room as " His Excellency M. le Comte de Cagliostro."

The Baroness d'Oberkirch, on visiting Saverne while he was there, "was stunned by the pomp with which he was treated." She was one of the few great ladies of Strasburg who refused to believe in him. To her he was merely an adventurer. On the occasions of her visit to Saverne the Cardinal, who had great respect for her, endeavoured to bring her round to his opinion. " As I resisted," she said, " he became impatient."

" Really, madame," said he, "you are hard to convince. Do you see this?"

He showed me a large diamond that he wore on his little finger, and on which the Rohan arms were engraved. This ring was worth at least twenty thousand francs.

" It is a beautiful gem, monseigneur," I said, " I have been admiring it."

Cagliostro

"Well," he exclaimed, "it is Cagliostro who made it: he made it out of nothing. I was present during the whole operation with my eyes fixed on the crucible. Is not that science, Baroness? People should not say that he is duping me, or taking advantage of me. I have had this ring valued by a jeweller and an engraver, and they have estimated it at twenty-five thousand livres. You must admit that he would be a strange kind of cheat who would make such presents."

I acknowledge I was stunned. M. de Rohan perceived it, and continued—

"This is not all—he can make gold! He has made in this very palace, in my presence, five or six thousand livres. He will make me the richest prince in Europe! These are no mere vagaries of the imagination, madame, but positive facts. Think of all his predictions that have been realized, of all the miraculous cures that he has effected! I repeat he is a most extraordinary, a most sublime man, whose knowledge is only equalled by his goodness. What alms he gives! What good he does! It exceeds all power of imagination. *I can assure you he has never asked or received anything from me.*"

But Cagliostro did not confine himself solely to seeking the philosopher's stone for the Cardinal. For the benefit of his splendid host he displayed the whole series of his magical phenomena.

One day, according to Roberson—who professed to have obtained his information from "an eye-witness very worthy of credence"—he promised to evoke for the Cardinal the shade of a woman he had loved. He had made the attempt two or three times before without success. Death seemed to hesitate to come to the

The Conquest of the Cardinal

rendez-vous. The moon, perhaps, had not been propitious, or some great crime committed at the moment of evocation may have had an unfavourable effect. But on this occasion all the conditions on which success depended were united.

"The performance," says Roberson, "took place in a small darkened room in the presence of four or five spectators who were seated far enough apart to prevent them from secretly communicating with one another. Wand in hand, Cagliostro stood in the middle of the room. The silence which he had commanded was so profound that even the hearts of those present seemed to stop beating. All at once the wand, as if drawn by a magnet, pointed to a spot on the wall where a vague, indefinite form was visible for a moment. The Cardinal uttered a cry. He had recognized—or believed he had, which amounted to the same thing—the woman he had loved."

So great was the confidence that Rohan placed in Cagliostro that he treated him as an oracle. He constantly consulted him, and suffered himself to be guided entirely by his advice. As the consequences of this infatuation were in the end disastrous, it is customary to regard the Cardinal as the dupe of Cagliostro. Many, blinded by prejudice, have supposed that Cagliostro, having previously informed himself of the tastes, character, and vast wealth of the prince, came to Strasburg for the express purpose of victimizing him. It is even asserted that the Countess had her share in the subjugation of the Cardinal, and that while Cagliostro attacked his understanding, she laid siege to his heart.

The disdainful, almost hostile, attitude that Cagliostro adopted towards his patron at the beginning of their acquaintance was so well calculated to inflame Rohan's curiosity that it is a matter of course to attribute it to design. The Abbé Georgel, who as a Jesuit thoroughly disliked the Grand Cophta of Egyptian Masonry, asserts that "he sought, without having the air of seeking it, the most intimate confidence of his Eminence and the greatest ascendency over his will."

But this very plausible statement is not only unsupported by any fact, but is actually contrary to fact. The Cardinal was *not* Cagliostro's banker, as has so often been stated. At his trial in the Necklace Affair Rohan denied this most emphatically. Moreover, it would have been utterly impossible for him, had he wished, to have supplied Cagliostro with the sums he spent so lavishly. In spite of his vast income, he had for years been head over ears in debt. If there were any benefits conferred, it was the Cardinal who received them.

"Cagliostro," says Madame d'Oberkirch, "treated him, as well as the rest of his aristocratic admirers, as if they were under infinite obligation to him and he under none to them."

This statement is the secret of the real nature of Cagliostro's so-called conquest. It was not cupidity, but colossal vanity, that lured him into the glittering friendship that ruined him. The Cardinal, with his great name and position, his influence, and his undeniable charm, dazzled Cagliostro quite as much as

The Conquest of the Cardinal

he, with his miracles, his magic, and his mystery, appealed to the imagination of the Cardinal. Each had for the other the fascination of a flame for a moth. Each fluttered round the other like a moth; and each met with the proverbial moth's fate. But the Cagliostro-flame only scorched the wings of his Eminence. It was in the flame of the Cardinal that Cagliostro perished.

CHAPTER V

CAGLIOSTRO IN PARIS

I

NOTWITHSTANDING the immense vogue that Cagliostro enjoyed throughout the three years he passed in Strasburg, his life was by no means one of unalloyed pleasure. Many a discordant note mingled in the chorus of blessing and praise that greeted his ears. In the memoir he published at the time of the Diamond Necklace Affair, he speaks vaguely of certain "persecutions" to which he was constantly subjected.

"His good fortune, or his knowledge of medicine," says Gleichen, "excited the hatred and jealousy of the doctors, who when they persecute are as dangerous as the priests. They were his implacable enemies in France, as well as in Poland and Russia."

His marvellous cures wounded the *amour propre* of the doctors as much as they damaged their reputation. Everything that malice and envy could devise was done to decry him. They accused him of treating only such persons as suffered from slight or imaginary ailments, questioned the permanency of his cures, denied that he saved lives they had given up, and attributed every death to him. He was charged with exacting in secret the fees he refused in public. His liberality to the poor was ascribed to a desire to attract attention, his philanthropy was ridiculed, and the luxury in which he lived at Cagliostrano, as he called the fine villa he rented on the outskirts of the town— attached to which was a private hospital or "nursing-home," where his poor patients were treated free of charge—was called ostentation.

Unable to penetrate the mystery in which he wrapped his origin, his fortune, and his remarkable powers, they attacked his character. As it was known that he frequently stayed at Saverne when the Cardinal was absent, attempts were made to poison the mind of the prince by informing him that his guest gave costly banquets at his expense when "Tokay flowed like water."[1] But the Cardinal only laughed.

"Indeed!" he exclaimed, when Georgel reported to him what he himself had only heard. "Well, I have given him the right to abuse my hospitality if he chooses."

As the confidence of the Cardinal in his mysterious friend was not to be shaken by the slanders of the doctors, he also was assailed. Old stories of his Eminence's private life were revived and new ones added to them. His friendship for Cagliostro was declared to be merely a cloak to hide a passion for his wife. The Countess was said, and believed by many, to be his mistress. It was consequently regarded as a

---

[1] This charge is cited by Carlyle as an instance of the baseness of Cagliostro's character. But as a matter of fact, the charge, like most of the others made against him, proves on investigation to be without any foundation. It was the Baron de Planta, one of the Cardinal's secretaries, who gave the much-talked-of midnight suppers at Saverne, "when the Tokay flowed like water." It is extremely doubtful whether Cagliostro even tasted the Tokay; his contemporaries frequently mention with ridicule his abstemiousness. Referring to his ascetic habits, Madame d'Oberkirch says contemptuously that " he slept in an arm-chair and lived on cheese."

matter of course that it was the Cardinal's money which the Count spent so lavishly.

But far from plundering the infatuated prince as his enemies asserted, Cagliostro did not so much as appeal to him for protection. Fortunately the Cardinal did not require to be reminded of the claims of friendship. Fully aware of the hostility to Cagliostro, he endeavoured to silence it by procuring for him from three members of the Government letters to the chief civil authority in which his *protégé* was recommended in the highest terms. To Cagliostro these letters, to which at any time he would have attached an exaggerated importance, had a special significance from the fact that "he neither solicited them directly nor indirectly." He counted them among his most valuable possessions.

The tranquillity, however, which they procured him was only transient. Ever employing fresh weapons and methods in attacking him, his enemies eventually found his Achilles'-heel—the impulsive sympathy of a naturally kind heart.

One day, while he was showing an important government official over his hospital, a man whom he had never seen before, and who appeared to have fallen on evil times, appealed to him for assistance. He asked to be taken into his service, and offered to wear his livery. He said that his name was Sacchi, that he came of a good family in Amsterdam, and had some knowledge of chemistry. Touched by his evident distress, Cagliostro yielded as usual to his charitable impulses. He found employment for Sacchi in his hospital, and paid him liberally.

" I was even persuaded," he said afterwards, " to

give him the receipt of certain medicaments, among others that of an elixir, which he has since sold in London as my balsam, though there is not the least resemblance between them."

A week later a man, whose wife and daughter had been cured of a dangerous illness by Cagliostro, called to inform him that Sacchi was a spy of his enemies the doctors, and that he was seeking to damage him by extorting fees from his patients. Horrified at the ingratitude and treachery of which he was the victim, Cagliostro forthwith turned "the reptile he had harboured" out of doors. Destitute of honour, rage now deprived Sacchi of common sense. Having been rash enough to threaten the life of the person who had exposed him, he was expelled from the city by the Marquis de Lasalle, the Commandant of Strasburg, who had been cured of a dangerous illness by Cagliostro.

But this action only served to increase the exasperation of the doctors, whose agent Sacchi was. Instigated by them he wrote to Cagliostro an insolent letter in which he demanded one hundred and fifty louis for the week he had passed in his service, threatening, if it were not instantly paid, to libel him. Cagliostro treated the threat with contemptuous silence, whereupon Sacchi proceeded to publish his libel, which he composed with the aid of a French lawyer who had escaped from the galleys. In it he declared the mysterious Count to be the son of a Neapolitan coachman, formerly known as Don Tiscio, a name under which he, Sacchi, had seen him exposed in the pillory at Alicante in Spain.[1]

[1] This libel attracted considerable attention, and great use was made of it in Cagliostro's lifetime by his enemies. Republished

Cagliostro

As sensitive to abuse as he was susceptible to flattery, Cagliostro was unable to endure such treatment, and convinced from his previous experience in Russia that there would be no limit to the vindictive malevolence of the doctors, he determined, he says, to leave Strasburg, where, in spite of the Cardinal's protection and his ministerial letters, he could find neither tranquillity nor security. A letter received about this time informing him that the Chevalier d'Aquino, of Naples, a friend of his mysterious past, was dangerously ill, and desired to see him, confirmed him in his resolution. Accordingly, in spite of the entreaties of the Cardinal, he shook the dust of Strasburg from his feet, and departed in all haste for Naples, where, however, he states, he arrived too late to save his friend.

II

On leaving Strasburg, as previously on leaving London and Warsaw, Cagliostro once more plunged into the obscurity in which so much of his career was passed that it might almost be described as his native element, to emerge again three months later as before on the crest of the wave of fortune in Bordeaux. As rumour, however, followed him it is possible to surmise with some degree of probability what became of him.

The imaginative Inquisition-biographer, though unable to give any account of Cagliostro's journey from Strasburg to Naples, his residence in that city,

---

during the Necklace Affair, the Parliament of Paris ordered its suppression as " injurious and calumnious." The editor of the *Courier de l'Europe* afterwards quoted it in his bitter denunciation of Cagliostro, and advanced it as proof of his identity with Giuseppe Balsamo. It has since generally been admitted to be a malicious invention.

184

or subsequent journey to Bordeaux—a singular tour!
—nevertheless unconsciously throws something like
light on the subject. He declares that the Countess
Cagliostro, who accompanied her husband, "confessed"
at her trial before the Apostolic Court in Rome that
"he left Naples owing to his failure to establish a
lodge of Egyptian Masonry." Questionable as the
source is from which this statement emanates, it is
nevertheless a clue.

Whatever difference of opinion there may be as
to the honesty of Cagliostro's motives in propagating
Egyptian Masonry, there is none as to his pertinacity.
Within three weeks of his arrival in Strasburg he had
founded a lodge for the observance of the Egyptian
Rite. The mysterious and hurried visits he paid from
time to time to Bâle, Geneva, and other places in
Switzerland during his three years' residence in Alsace
were apparently of a Masonic nature. It is, moreover,
curious to note that his hurried departure for Naples
occurred immediately after the Neapolitan government removed its ban against Freemasonry. As the
Neapolitan government would not have taken this
step had there been the least likelihood of Freemasonry obtaining a hold over the masses, it is highly
probable that Cagliostro left Naples for the reason
given by the Inquisition-biographer.

This probability is still further strengthened by his
subsequent movements, which, erratic though they may
appear, had a well-defined purpose. From the time he
left London, be it said, till his last fatal journey to
Rome, Cagliostro never went anywhere without having
a definite and preconceived purpose.

It was certainly with a very definite object that he

went to Bordeaux, where he is next heard of, and whither he travelled, as he himself says, through the cities of Southern France. Now the cities of Southern France were permeated with supernaturalism. It was at Bordeaux, that Martinez Pasqualis had held his celebrated school of magic and mystical theurgy, the most distinguished of whose pupils was Saint-Martin, the founder of the Martinists. No place was better adapted for gaining recruits to Egyptian or any other kind of Freemasonry.

It was here that Mesmer found the noisiest and most ardent of his admirers in Père Hervier, an Augustinian monk who by his eloquence had made a great reputation as a popular preacher. Summoned to Bordeaux by the municipality to preach during Lent at the Church of St. Andrew, Hervier preached not only the gospel according to Christ but that according to the Messiah of animal magnetism, with the result that he made both the clergy and the doctors his enemies.

This church, one of the finest Gothic monuments in Europe, was the stage on which he displayed his talents both as an orator and as a mesmerist. He was preaching one day on eternal damnation. His flashing eyes, commanding gestures, and alluring voice, which had from the start *prepared* the church from the holy water stoup to the candles on the altar, never once lost their hold upon the imagination. The congregation, consisting of the richest, youngest, and most frivolous women of Bordeaux, was in complete accord with the preacher. Suddenly when the monk began to picture the horrors of hell a young girl fell into a fit. Such an incident happening at such a moment

created a panic, and those in the immediate neighbourhood of the unfortunate girl fled from the spot in terror.
Suspending his sermon Père Hervier descended from
the pulpit with the sublime gravity of an apostle, and
going up to the young girl, magnetized her after the
manner of Mesmer. Immediately her convulsions
began to cease. The congregation fell on its knees.
The face of the priest seemed illumined with a divine
light. As he passed the women kissed his feet, and
were with difficulty prevented from worshipping
him.

Perceiving that the moment was, so to speak,
psychological, Père Hervier remounted the pulpit,
and taking as his text the miracle he had just performed, discoursed with all the eloquence for which he
was noted on charity and Christ healing the sick ;
finally bringing his sermon to a close with a passionate denunciation of the doctors and clergy of Bordeaux
who did not believe in magnetism and desired nothing
better than to persecute a poor monk who did.

Such a stage was too well adapted to Egyptian
Masonry not to have attracted Cagliostro. On the
night of his arrival in Bordeaux he and his wife went
to the play, and on being recognized received an
ovation. The next day the concourse of people who
flocked to consult him was so great that the magistrates
were obliged to give him a guard of soldiers to preserve
order in the street.

He had resolved, he says, on leaving Strasburg to
give up the practice of medicine in order to avoid
exposing himself again to the envy of the doctors.
However, as the number of persons of all stations who
sought his assistance was so great he was induced to

change his mind, and resume the gratuitous "miracles" which had rendered him so celebrated in Strasburg. In coming to this decision he afterwards declared that he counted on the protection of the Comte de Vergennes, Secretary of State for Foreign Affairs, and one of the three Cabinet Ministers who had previously recommended him to the Pretor of Strasburg. It was, he said, at Vergennes' special request that he returned to France. As the Comte de Vergennes failed to deny this statement, which he could easily have done when it was made by Cagliostro at his trial in the Necklace Affair, there seems no reason to doubt it.

In Bordeaux, as at Strasburg, his cures and his charities attracted general attention and procured him a large and enthusiastic following. Many of the most influential men of the city sought admittance to the lodge he founded. But, as before, Egyptian Masonry flourished at the expense of the tranquillity and security of the Grand Cophta. The influence of Vergennes and other powerful patrons was powerless to protect him from the ingenious malevolence of the envious doctors. Even Père Hervier, instead of joining forces with him, entered the lists against him. Mere "clerk of Mesmer," he had the folly to engage Cagliostro in a public discussion, in which he received so humiliating a chastisement that he was laughed out of Bordeaux. But in spite of his triumphs life was made such a burden to Cagliostro that after being continually baited for eleven months he could endure the torment no longer, and departed for Lyons.

This city was a veritable stronghold of Freemasonry. Lodges of all descriptions flourished here, notably those founded by Saint-Martin, the most mystical of occultists, in which the Swedenborgian Rite was observed. It was here that Cagliostro found his most ardent and loyal supporters. Their enthusiasm was such that they built a "temple" expressly for the observance of the Egyptian Rite. It enjoyed the dignity of being the Mother Lodge of Egyptian Masonry, the lodges at Strasburg, Bâle, Bordeaux, Paris, and other places being affiliated to it. As it was the custom for the mother lodges of every order of Freemasonry to be named after some virtue, this one received the title of *Sagesse Triomphante.* It was the only lodge specially erected by Cagliostro's followers, all the others being held in rooms rented for their needs.

It would have been well for Cagliostro had he been content to remain in Lyons. He would have enjoyed the "tranquillity and security" he so much desired ; and history, perhaps, would have forgotten him, for it is owing to his misfortunes that his achievements are chiefly remembered.

But destiny lured him to destruction and an ignominious renown. Inordinately vain and self-conscious, he was enticed to Paris by the Cardinal, who was then residing there, and with whom he had been in constant correspondence ever since he left Strasburg. So insistent was his Eminence that he sent Raymond de Carbonnières, one of his secretaries, and an enthusiastic admirer of Cagliostro, to Lyons on purpose to fetch him. Paris, too, Mecca of every celebrity, called him with no uncertain voice. Magic-struck she craved the excitement of fresh mysteries and the spell of a new idol. Mesmer's tempestuous vogue was over ; adored and ridiculed in turn he had departed with 340,000 livres, a very practical proof of his success.

So having appointed a Grand Master to represent him, and delegated his seal—a serpent pierced with an arrow—to two " venerables," Cagliostro left Lyons for Paris. If he made enemies in Lyons they did not molest him. It was the only place in which he does not complain of being persecuted.

III

On arriving in Paris, Cagliostro declares that he " took the greatest precaution to avoid causing ill-will. As the majority of contemporary documents concur in describing his life in Paris as " dignified and reserved," there is no reason to doubt the truth of his statement. But one cannot escape one's fate, and in spite of his efforts not to attract attention, he was condemned to an extraordinary notoriety.

His arrival was no sooner known than, as at Strasburg, Bordeaux, and Lyons, his house was beset with cripples and invalids of all walks of life. As usual he refused to accept payment for his services or even for his remedies.

" No one," says Grimm, " ever succeeded in making him accept the least mark of gratitude."

"What is singular about Cagliostro," says the Baron de Besenval, " is that in spite of possessing the characteristics that one associates with a charlatan, he never behaved as such all the time he was at Strasburg or at Paris. On the contrary, he never took a sou from a person, lived honourably, always paid with the greatest exactitude what he owed, and was very charitable."

Needless to say, it was not long before his name became the chief topic of conversation in the capital. In the enthusiasm his successes excited his failures were ignored. Rumour multiplied the number of his cures and magnified their importance. His fame was thus reflected on the invalids themselves. To be "healed" by the Grand Cophta became the rage. In 1785 Paris swarmed with men and women who professed to have been cured by Cagliostro.

Naturally this infatuation infuriated his inveterate enemies the doctors. It is said that they obtained an order from the King compelling him, if he wished to remain in Paris, to refrain from practising medicine. If so, they had not the courage to enforce it, for he counted among his partisans men of the very highest rank, such as the Prince de Luxembourg, who was Grand Master of the Lodge at Lyons, as well as those distinguished for their learning like the naturalist Ramon. All the same the doctors did not leave him entirely unmolested.

Urged by their masters, who from a sense of dignity or prudence dared not encounter him in person, two medical students resolved to play a practical joke upon the "healer." It was a species of amusement very popular at the period; in this instance it was regarded also as a duty. The students accordingly called on Cagliostro, and on being admitted one of them complained of a mysterious malady of which the symptoms seemed to him extraordinary. In attempting, however, to describe them, he used certain scientific terms, which at once caused Cagliostro to suspect that his visitor was an emissary of the doctors. Restraining his indignation he turned to the other and said with the greatest gravity—

"Your friend must remain here under my care for sixteen days. The treatment to which I shall subject him is very simple, but to effect his cure it will be absolutely necessary for him to eat but once a day, and then only an ounce of nourishment."

Alarmed at the prospect of so drastic a diet the mock-invalid began to protest, and asked if it was not possible to indicate exactly what it was he suffered from.

"Nothing simpler," replied Cagliostro. "Superfluity of bile in the medical faculty."

The two students, finding themselves caught in the trap they had set for him, stammered their apologies as best they could. Whereupon Cagliostro, perceiving their discomfiture, good-naturedly set them at ease and invited them to breakfast, with the result that they were converted into ardent admirers.

He did not desire, however, to be known only as a healer of the sick.

In the exhibitions he gave of his occult or psychic powers, he soon eclipsed every other contemporary celebrity from the number and variety of the phenomena he performed. Everybody wished to witness these wonders, and those who were denied the privilege were never tired of describing them in detail as if they had seen them, or of listening in turn to their recital. The memoirs of the period are filled with the marvels of his séances at which he read—by means of *colombes* and *pupilles*—the future and the past, in mirrors, carafes, and crystals ; of his predictions, his cures, and

his evocations of the dead, who appeared at his command
to rejoice or to terrify, as the case might be, those in
compliance with whose wishes he had summoned them
from the grave.

Every day some new and fantastic story was
circulated about him.

It was related, for example, that one day after a
dinner-party at Chaillot, at which the company consisted chiefly of ladies, he was asked by his hostess to
procure partners for her friends who had expressed the
desire to dance.

"M. de Cagliostro," she said half-seriously, half-
playfully, "you have only to employ your supernatural
powers to fetch us some officers from the Ecole
Militaire."

"True," he replied, going to a window from which
this institution could be seen in the distance, "it only
requires an invisible bridge between them and us."

A burst of ironical laughter greeted his words.
Indignant, he extended his arm in the direction of the
Hôtel des Invalides, which could also be seen from
the window. A few minutes later eighteen veterans
with cork-legs arrived at the house!

On another occasion it was reported that Cagliostro,
having invited six noblemen to dine with him, had the
table laid for thirteen. On the arrival of his guests he
requested them to name any illustrious shades they
desired to occupy the vacant seats. Straightway, as
their names were mentioned, the spectres of the Duc
de Choiseul, the Abbé de Voisenon, Montesquieu,
Diderot, d'Alembert, and Voltaire appeared, and
taking the places assigned them conversed with their
hosts in a manner so incredibly stupid, which had it

been characteristic of them in the flesh would have robbed them of all claim to distinction.

This anecdote, one of the gems of the Marquis de Luchet's lively imagination, who related it with much spirit, was devoid of the least particle of truth. Nevertheless the Cénacle de Treize or Banquet of the Dead, as it was called, acquired an immense notoriety. All Paris talked of it ; and even at Versailles it had the honour for some minutes of being the subject of royal conversation.

Constantly fired by such stories, the admiration and curiosity that Cagliostro aroused in all classes of society reached a degree of infatuation little short of idolatry. By his followers he was addressed as "revered father" or "august master." They spent whole hours censing him with a flattery almost profane, believing themselves purified by being near him. Some more impassioned and ridiculous than others averred that "he could tell Atheists and Blasphemers by their smell which threw him into epileptic fits."

Houdon, the most celebrated sculptor of the day, executed his bust. Replicas in bronze, marble, and plaster, bearing the words, *Le Divin Cagliostro* on the pedestal, were to be found in salons, boudoirs, and offices. Rings, brooches, fans, and snuff-boxes were adorned with his portrait. Prints of him by Bartolozzi and others were scattered broadcast over Europe, with the following flattering inscription—

De l'ami des humains reconnaissez les traits ;
Tous ses jours sont marqués par de nouveaux bienfaits,
Il prolonge la vie, il secourt l'indigence,
Le plaisir d'être utile est seul sa récompense.

Figuier's statement, however, that "bills were even

posted on the walls to the effect that Louis XVI had declared that any one who injured him was guilty of *lèse-majesté*" is extremely doubtful. He was never received at Versailles. Marie Antoinette, who had protected Mesmer, could not be induced to take the least interest in Cagliostro.

IV

The interest displayed in the prodigies he was said to perform was augmented by the profound secrecy he observed in regard to his parentage, his nationality, and his past in general. In the hectic years immediately preceding the Revolution, when credulity, curiosity, and the passion for sensation had reached a stage bordering almost on madness, it required no effort of the imagination to make this secrecy itself supernatural ; indeed, in the end the interest taken in the mystery in which Cagliostro wrapped himself surpassed that in all his wonders combined.

People speculated on the source of his wealth without being able to arrive at any conclusion. " No one," says Georgel, "could discover the nature of his resources, he had no letter of credit, and apparently no banker, nevertheless he lived in the greatest affluence, giving much to the needy, and seeking no favours whatever from the rich." In Strasburg, according to Meiners, " at the very lowest estimate his annual expenditure was not less than 20,000 livres." In Paris he was reputed to live at the rate of 100,000 livres a year. The splendid footing on which his establishment was maintained was, however, probably greatly exaggerated. He himself says that the fine house in the Rue St. Claude, which he rented from the Marquise d'Orvilliers, was "furnished by degrees."

Some, as previously stated, attributed his splendour to the Cardinal. It was attested during the Necklace Affair that proof of this was found among the Cardinal's papers. Rohan, however, at his trial denied the charge most emphatically, and Cagliostro himself declared that the Cardinal's munificence never went beyond "birthday gifts to the Countess, the whole of which consisted of a dove, his (Cagliostro's) portrait set in diamonds, with a small watch and chain also set with brilliants." [1]

Others declared that his wealth was derived from "the mines of Lima, of which his father was said to be director." By others, again, it was said that "the Jesuits supplied him with funds, or that having persuaded some Asiatic prince to send his son to travel in Europe, he had murdered the youth and taken possession of his treasures." Cagliostro himself was always very mysterious on this subject.

"But your manner of living," he was questioned at his trial in the Necklace Affair, "is expensive; you give away much, and accept of nothing in return; you pay everybody; how do you contrive to get money?"

"This question," he replied, "has no kind of relation to the case in point. What difference does

[1] To doubt these statements on the score of a popular prejudice in favour of regarding Cagliostro as a liar who never by any chance spoke the truth is quite ridiculous. Not only is there no proof on which to base this assertion, but there is not even the least suggestion that Cagliostro was ever considered a liar by his contemporaries before the Editor of the *Courier de l'Europe*—himself the biggest of liars and knaves—took advantage of the passions let loose by the Diamond Necklace Affair to brand him as such.

it make whether I am the son of a monarch or a beggar, or by what means I procure the money I want, as long as I regard religion and the laws and pay every one his due? I have always taken a pleasure in refusing to gratify the public curiosity on this score. Nevertheless I will condescend to tell you that which I have never revealed to any one before. The principal resource I have to boast of is that as soon as I set foot in any country I find there a banker who supplies me with everything I want. For instance, M. Sarazin, of Bâle, would give me up his whole fortune were I to ask it. So would M. Sancotar at Lyons."[1]

Equally various were the nationalities attributed to him. "Some thought him a Spaniard, others a Jew, an Italian, a Ragusan, or even an Arab." All attempts to discover his nationality by his language failed. Baron Grimm was "certain that he had a Spanish accent," others were equally certain that he talked "the patois of Sicily or of the lazzaroni of Naples." His enemies declared that he spoke no known language at all, but a mysterious jargon mixed with cabalistic words.

One day being pressed by the Comtesse de Brienne to explain the origin of a life so surprising and mysterious, he replied, with a laugh, that "he was born in the Red Sea and brought up in the shadow of the Pyramids by a good old man who had taken care of him when he was abandoned by his parents, and

[1] A cryptic reference to the Secret Societies, which were the real source of his wealth. The great success of Egyptian Masonry, of which the above-mentioned gentlemen were the bankers, more than compensated him for what he lost by the suppression of the Illuminés in 1784, the year before he came to Paris.

from whom he had learnt all he knew." But Mirabeau states that "M. de Nordberg, who had travelled much in the East, once addressed him some words in Arabic of which he did not understand one word."

The mystery in which he purposely enveloped himself, and which became the deeper the more it was probed, coupled with the wonders he performed, recalled the famous Count de Saint-Germain, who had created a similar sensation some twenty years before. Of the life, family or country of this mysterious individual nothing was ever known. Of many suppositions the most popular was that he was the son of a royal *femme galante*—Marie de Neubourg, widow of the last King of Spain of the House of Austria—and a Jewish banker of Bordeaux. Louis XV, who had a particular predilection for men of his stamp and was probably perfectly acquainted with his history, employed him for a time on secret diplomatic missions and gave him apartments at Chambord. His fascinating manners, good looks, lavish expenditure and mysterious antecedents attracted attention wherever he went.

In London, where he lived for a couple of years, he excited great curiosity. "He was called," says Walpole, "an Italian, a Spaniard, a Pole, a nobody that married a great fortune in Mexico and ran away with her jewels to Constantinople."

These jewels were the admiration of all who beheld them. Madame de Hausset, the companion of Madame de Pompadour, to whom he showed them once, believed them to be false. Gleichen, however, who was a connoisseur of precious stones, "could discern no reason to doubt their genuineness." Like

Cagliostro in Paris

Cagliostro, who gave a diamond valued at 20,000 livres to Cardinal de Rohan, Saint-Germain made a present of one to Louis XV worth 10,000 livres.

The secrecy he observed in regard to his origin appears in the beginning to have been due less to any intention to mystify the public than to a strong sense of humour. In an age when a supernatural significance was attached to anything that appeared mysterious, he was at once credited with occult powers which he never claimed to possess. Urged by a whim to see how far he could play upon the credulity of the public, he found the rôle of wonder-man so congenial that he never attempted to adopt another.

A particular talent for romancing, aided by a wonderful memory, enabled him to doctor up the marvellous to suit the taste of his hearers. He described people and places of the distant past with a minuteness of detail that produced the impression that he had been personally acquainted with them. As many were foolish enough to take him literally, all sorts of fabulous stories were circulated about him.

"I amuse myself," he once confessed to Gleichen, who reproved him for encouraging the belief that he had lived from time immemorial, "not by making people believe what I wish, but by letting them believe what they wish. These fools of Parisians declare that I am five hundred, and I confirm them in the idea since it pleases them."

The least credulous believed him to be at least a hundred. Madame de Pompadour said to him once that old Madame de Gergy remembered having met him fifty years before in Venice when he passed for a man of sixty.

Cagliostro

"I never like to contradict a lady," he replied, "but it is just possible that Madame de Gergy is in her dotage."

Even his valet was supposed to have discovered the secret of immortality. This fellow, a veritable Scapin, assisted him admirably in mystifying the credulous.

"Your master," said a sceptic one day, seizing him by the collar, "is a rogue who is taking us all in. Tell me, is it true that he was present at the marriage of Cana?"

"You forget, sir," was the reply, "I have only been in his service a century."

Many of the most amazing stories circulated about Cagliostro were merely a repetition of those related twenty years before of Saint-Germain. The recollection of Saint-Germain's reputed longevity led to the bestowal of a similar attribute to his successor. Thus it was reported that Cagliostro stopped one day before a "Descent from the Cross" in the Louvre and began to talk of the Crucifixion as ·if he had witnessed it. Though the story was devoid of foundation it was not without effect, and many declared, and believed too, that the Grand Cophta had lived hundreds, and even thousands of years. Cagliostro, it is but fair to add, complained bitterly of this at his trial.

On the strength of the close resemblance in the mystery and the stories concerning Saint-Germain and Cagliostro, as well as their alchemical knowledge— for Saint-Germain, needless to say, was credited with having discovered the philosopher's stone—Grimm believed Cagliostro to have been the valet alluded to above. There is, however, not the least evidence that the paths of the two men ever crossed.[1]

V

Great though the influence that an impenetrable mystery and so-called supernatural phenomena always exercise over the human mind, their appeal, even when credulity reaches the pitch it did in 1785, will never alone provoke interest so extraordinary as that taken in Cagliostro. It is only a very powerful and magnetic personality that is able to fix such curiosity and to excite such admiration. It is, moreover, equally certain, that had he been such a man as Carlyle has painted him, history would never have heard of him, much less remembered him.

Speaking of Cagliostro's physiognomy, he describes it as "a most portentous face of scoundrelism; a fat snub, abominable face; dew-lapped, flat-nosed, greasy, full of greediness, sensuality, ox-like obstinacy; the most perfect quack-face produced by the eighteenth century."

It is the *ignorance* of his subject, be it said, rather than the violence of his prejudice, which such statements as this reveal that have deprived Carlyle's opinion of Cagliostro of any value in the estimation of modern writers.[2] There is plenty of reliable information, to which Carlyle had access, to

---

[1] De Luchet's fantastic account of the visit paid by Cagliostro and his wife to Saint-Germain in Germany, and their subsequent initiation by him into the sect of the Rosicrucians, of which he was supposed to be the chief, is devoid of all authenticity.

[2] D'Alméras and Funck-Brentano—the latter extremely careless when writing of Cagliostro—never so much as mention Carlyle.

prove that Cagliostro's appearance was anything but repulsive.

Beugnot, who has described him with more mockery than any of his contemporaries, says "he was of medium height, rather stout, with an olive complexion, a short neck, round face, a broad turned-up nose, and two large eyes." From all accounts his eyes were remarkable. "I cannot describe his physiognomy," says the Marquise de Créquy, "for he had twelve or fifteen at his disposal. But no two eyes like his were ever seen; and his teeth were superb." Laborde speaks of "his eyes of fire which pierced to the bottom of the soul." Another writer declares that "his glance was like a gimlet."

All the contemporary documents that speak of him—and they are hostile with very few exceptions—refer to the powerful fascination that he exercised on all who approached him. The impression he produced upon the intellectual Countess von der Recke has already been referred to. Like her, Laborde, Motus, and others considered that his countenance "indicated genius."

Cardinal de Rohan told Georgel that on seeing him for the first time "he discovered in his physiognomy a dignity so imposing that he felt penetrated with awe."

"He was not, strictly speaking, handsome," says Madame d'Oberkirch, who certainly was not one of his admirers, "but never have I seen a more remarkable face. His glance was so penetrating that one might be almost tempted to call it supernatural. I could not describe the expression of his eyes—it was, so to speak, a mixture of flame and ice. It attracted and repelled at the same time, and inspired, whilst it terrified, an insurmountable curiosity. I cannot deny that Cagliostro possessed an almost demoniacal power, and it was with difficulty that I tore myself from a fascination I could not comprehend, but whose influence I could not deny."

Lavater, whose unfavourable opinion seems to be due to the contemptuous way in which Cagliostro received him, nevertheless thought him "a man such as few are."

Beugnot, after ridiculing him as "moulded for the express purpose of playing the part of a clown," confesses that "his face, his attire—the whole man, in fact, impressed him in spite of himself."

If, as Meiners and other hostile contemporaries assert, "he spoke badly all the languages he professed to know," there is not the least reason to infer, like Carlyle, that "he was wholly intelligible to no mortal," or that "what thought, what resemblance of thought he had, could not deliver itself, except in gasps, blustering gushes, spasmodic refluences which made bad worse."

Michelet—Carlyle's brilliant and equally learned contemporary—regarded him as "a veritable sorcerer possessed of great eloquence." Even the bitter Inquisition-biographer confessed that he was "marvellously eloquent." Motus declared that "his eloquence fascinated and subjugated one, even in the languages he spoke least well." "If gibberish can be sublime," says Beugnot, "Cagliostro was sublime. When he began any subject he seemed carried away with it, and spoke impressively in a ringing, sonorous voice."

Cagliostro

The beauty of the Countess Cagliostro was also an important element in the success of her husband. She was like a sylph with her fluffy straw-coloured hair, which she wore unpowdered, her large, deep, soft blue eyes, her small and delicately chiselled nose, her full rose-red lips, and a dazzlingly white skin.

"She is an angel in human form," said Maître Polverit, by whom she was defended when she was imprisoned in the Bastille on the charge of being implicated in the Necklace Affair, "who has been sent on earth to share and soften the days of the Man of Marvels. Beautiful with a beauty that never belonged to any woman, she cannot be called a model of tenderness, sweetness and resignation—no! for she does not even suspect the existence of any other qualities." And the judges evidently agreed, for they ordered her release without a trial.

Motus describes her as "a beautiful and modest person and as charitable as her husband." She was fond of dress, and her diamonds were the talk of Paris. The Countess de Lamotte at her trial declared that "Madame de Cagliostro's display of jewelry scandalized respectable women, as well as those who were not." It is scarcely necessary, however, to observe that Madame de Lamotte saw the Countess through her hatred of Cagliostro. To make a display of jewelry at that period did not cause the least scandal. The Countess, moreover, was a fine horsewoman, and mounted on her black mare Djèrid attracted attention quite apart from the fact that she was the wife of Cagliostro.

Uneducated—she could not write; though from mixing in the best society she had acquired the manners of a lady—she was one of those women who always remain a child. In the over-civilized, cynical, and hysterical age in which she lived, her ingenuous chatter passed for a new type of spirituality, and her ignorance for candour. That was the secret of her charm. As all the world lacked it, candour was a novelty.

"The admiration she excited," says one writer, "was most ardent among those who had never seen her. There were duels over her, duels proposed and accepted as to the colour of her eyes, which neither of the adversaries knew, or as to whether a dimple was on her right cheek or on her left."

Needless to say, scandal did not fail to attack her reputation. The enemies of Cagliostro were quick to accuse her of light conduct, and her husband of encouraging it. The Cardinal was popularly supposed to be her lover. The Countess de Lamotte asserted that she specially distinguished a Chevalier d'Oisemont among a crowd of admirers. But, as Gleichen says in reference to her supposed infidelity, "why suppose without proof?" Of Cagliostro's devotion to her at least there is no doubt. So little is known of her character that it is impossible to speak of it with any certainty; but considering the admiration that all agree she inspired and the numerous temptations she had to desert him when fortune turned against him, the fact that she stuck to him to the end is a pretty strong argument in favour of both her fidelity and affection.

Owing to her girlish appearance, the age of the lovely Countess was a subject of considerable speculation. It is said, though with what truth cannot be stated, that "she occasionally spoke of a son who was a

captain in the service of the Dutch government." As
this made her at least forty when she did not appear to
be twenty, a credulous public was ready to see in her
a living witness to the efficacy of her husband's
rejuvenating powders and elixir of life. De Luchet,
who is responsible for the story, asserts that she added
to her age expressly to advertise Cagliostro's quack-
medicines.[1]

Like Saint-Germain's valet, she was also credited
with a share of her husband's supernatural endowments.
According to certain unauthenticated information, she
was the Grand Mistress of the Isis lodge for women,
which among other conditions of membership included
a subscription of one hundred louis. This lodge is
said to have been composed of thirty-six ladies of rank,
who joined it for the purpose of being taught magic by
the wife of Cagliostro. The report widely circulated
by de Luchet, of the obscene character of the
"evocations," is devoid of the least authenticity. It is
doubtful, indeed, whether such a lodge ever existed at
all. Madame de Genlis, who figures in de Luchet's

---

[1] If it be true that the Count and Countess Cagliostro were
really Giuseppe and Lorenza Balsamo, surely the remarkable change
in the *appearance*, not to speak of the *character*, of *both*, must be
regarded as the most astonishing of all Cagliostro's prodigies. The
impression he produced from the accounts given above was totally
different from that which Balsamo was said to have produced. As
for his wife, it is preposterous to expect any one to believe that the
pretty demirep Lorenza would have looked as girlish and fresh as the
Countess Seraphina after fifteen years of the sort of life she led with
Giuseppe. As vice and hardship have never yet been regarded as
aids to beauty, those who persist in pinning their faith to the Balsamo
legend will perhaps assent to the suggestion that Cagliostro's remedies
possessed virtues hitherto denied them.

list of members, never so much as mentions the Cagliostros in her memoirs.

VI

Needless to say, Cagliostro did not fail to turn the prodigious furore he created to the account of Egyptian Masonry. Not long after his arrival in Paris a lodge was established at the residence of one of his followers in a room specially set apart for the purpose and furnished, says the Inquisition-biographer, "with unparalleled magnificence." Here from time to time the "seven angels of the Egyptian Paradise, who stand round the throne of God—Anaël, Michael, Raphael, Gabriel, Uriel, Zobriachel, and Hanachiel (with whom the Grand Cophta was a special favourite) "condescended to appear to the faithful."

Cagliostro also opened another lodge in his own house, when the angels came at the bidding of other members besides the Grand Cophta. It was not long before similar phenomena were witnessed in all the Egyptian lodges. In a remarkable letter of an adept of the lodge at Lyons found in Cagliostro's papers at the time of his arrest in Rome, the writer, in describing a ceremony held there, said that "the first philosopher of the New Testament *appeared without being called*, and gave the entire assembly, prostrate before the blue cloud in which he appeared, his blessing. Moreover" (adds the writer), "two great prophets and the legislator of Israel have given us similar convincing signs of their good-will."

It is from Cagliostro's ability "to transmit his powers," as it was termed, that the singular phenomena of modern spiritualism were developed. In reality it was nothing more or less than the discovery of the "psychic"—the word must serve for want of a better —properties latent in every human being, and which in many are capable of a very high degree of development. This discovery, till then unimagined, was the secret of the veneration in which Cagliostro was regarded by his followers.

Notwithstanding the very high development to which Cagliostro's own "psychic" powers had now attained, one gathers the impression from his own utterances that he never completely understood them. A link between the old conception of magic and the new theosophical theories, there are many indications that he regarded the phenomena he performed as direct manifestations of divine power. In an age of unbelief he always spoke of God with the greatest respect, even in circles in which it was the fashion to decry the goodness as well as the existence of the Supreme Being. Like all the mystics of the eighteenth century, he was deistic. "All duty, according to him," says Georgel, "was based on the principle: Never do to others what you would not wish them to do to you." One of the first things seen on entering his house in Paris was a slab of black marble on which was engraved in gold letters Pope's *Universal Prayer*.

Historians who have been inclined to treat him leniently as the loyal agent of a revolutionary sect are horrified that he " should have effaced the dignity of the enthusiast behind the trickeries of the necromancer." Louis Blanc, who preached a perpetual crusade against thrones and altars, and despised occultism, declares that Cagliostro's phenomena "cast suspicion on his own ideals, and were a veritable crime against the cause he proclaimed to be holy, and which there was no necessity to associate with shameful falsehoods."

The charge is a very just one. The bitterness with which Cagliostro has been regarded for a hundred years is due less to the calumnies with which he was assailed in his life—and which till the present no one has dreamt of investigating—than to the belief that he debased his ideals. As his "psychic" powers developed it cannot be denied that he attached a significance to them that, in the opinion of thoughtful people, was calculated to render his motives suspect. His real imposture was not in cheating people of their money or faking miracles, but in encouraging the belief that he was a supernatural being—" I am that I am," as he is said to have described himself profanely on one occasion. Intoxicated by his amazing success, he lost all sense of proportion. The means which he had begun to employ in Mittau to justify his end all but effaced the end itself in Paris.

To attract followers he was no longer content to gratify the passion for the marvellous, but sought to stimulate it. To enhance the effect of his phenomena he had recourse to artifices worthy of a mountebank.

The room in which his séances were held contained statuettes of Isis, Anubis, and the ox Apis. The walls were covered with hieroglyphics, and two lacqueys, "clothed like Egyptian slaves as they are represented on the monuments at Thebes," were in attendance to arrange the screen behind which the *pupilles* or *colombes* sat, the carafe or mirror into which they gazed, or to perform any other service that was required.

Cagliostro

To complete the *mise en scène*, Cagliostro wore a robe of black silk on which hieroglyphics were embroidered in red. His head was covered with an Arab turban of cloth of gold ornamented with jewels. A chain of emeralds hung *en sautoir* upon his breast, to which scarabs and cabalistic symbols of all colours in metal were attached. A sword with a handle shaped like a cross was suspended from a belt of red silk.

"In this costume," says Figuier, "the Grand Cophta looked so imposing that the whole assembly felt a sort of terror when he appeared."

The manner in which Cagliostro dressed and conducted himself in public was equally designed to attract attention, though it was scarcely of the sort he desired. A writer who saw him walking one day followed by an admiring band of street-arabs says "he was wearing a coat of blue silk braided along the seams ; his hair in powdered knots was gathered up in a net ; his shoes *à la d'Artois* were fastened with jewelled buckles, his stockings studded with gold buttons ; rubies and diamonds sparkled on his fingers, and on the frill of his shirt ; from his watch-chain hung a diamond drop, a gold key adorned with diamonds, and an agate seal —all of which, in conjunction with his flowered waistcoat and musketeer hat with a white plume, produced an instantaneous effect."

The Marquise de Créquy, Beugnot, and nearly all his contemporaries allude to the fantastic manner in which he dressed as well as to his colossal vanity, which, inflated by success, rendered him not only ridiculous to those whom he failed to fascinate, but even insufferable. Pompous in Mittau, he became arrogant, domineering, and choleric in Paris. Flattery, to which he had always been peculiarly susceptible, at last became to him like some drug by which he was enslaved. He could not tolerate criticism or contradiction. " The Chevalier de Montbruel," says Beugnot, "a veteran of the green-room, and ready to affirm anything, was always at hand to bear witness to Cagliostro's cures, offering himself as an example cured of I do not know how many maladies with names enough to frighten one."

However, Cagliostro was never so spoilt by success, never so compromised by the tricks and devices to which he stooped to perform his wonders, as to lose sight of his ideal. Had he been the vulgar cheat, the sordid impostor it is customary to depict him, he would have contented himself with the subscriptions paid by the members of the lodges he founded and have ceased to insist on the ethical character of Egyptian Masonry. In 1785 a religious element was calculated to repel rather than to attract. It was the wonder-man, and not the idealist, in whom Paris was interested. But instead of taking the line of least resistance, so to speak, Cagliostro deliberately adopted a course that could not fail to make enemies rather than friends.

Far from dropping the religious and moral character of the Egyptian Rite, he laid greater stress on it than ever, and claimed for his sect a superiority over all the others of Freemasonry, on the ground that it was based on the mysteries of Isis and Anubis which he had brought from the East. As no one ever ventured to regard him as a fool as well as a knave, it is impossible to question his sincerity in the matter. At once the seventy-two Masonic lodges of Paris rose in arms against him. He managed, however, to triumph over all opposition. At a meeting held for the purpose of expounding the dogmas of Egyptian Masonry "his eloquence was so persuasive," says Figuier, "that he completely converted to his views the large and distinguished audience he addressed."

From the respect that Cagliostro thus exacted and obtained, Egyptian Masonry acquired an importance in France not unlike that of the Illuminés in Germany. Nothing proves this so well as the Congress of Philalètes, or the Seekers of Truth.

This Masonic body was composed of members of Swedenborgian and Martinist lodges affiliated to Illuminism. Its character was at once occult and political. On the detection and suppression of the Illuminés, in 1784, the Philalètes, organized by Savalette de Langes, a revolutionary mystic, sought to finish in France the work which Weishaupt had begun in Germany. As an old Illuminé, Savalette de Langes was well acquainted with Cagliostro, and the importance he attached to him was so great that he desired to incorporate the sect of Egyptian Masonry in that of the Philalètes. He accordingly summoned a congress of Philalètes to which Cagliostro was invited to explain his doctrine.

The ambitions and aspirations of the Grand Cophta had kept pace with the steadily rising fortunes of Egyptian Masonry. He was quick to perceive the immense advantage to be derived from a union of the organization of which he was the head with that of the Philalètes, who were one of the most numerous and influential of the Masonic sects. But he had no intention of playing second fiddle to them, and in replying to their invitation he assumed that they were prepared to acknowledge the superiority of the Egyptian Rite. So with pompous condescension, which was as astute as it was bizarre, he informed them that "having deigned to extend to them his hand and consented to cast a ray of light upon the darkness of their Temple, he requested them as a sign of their submission to the truths of Egyptian Masonry to burn their archives."

Though taken aback by such an answer, the Philalètes did not abandon the hope of coming to some satisfactory arrangement. But Cagliostro proved too clever for them, and in the series of interviews and negotiations which followed they were completely over-awed and over-reached. For a moment it seemed as if Freemasonry in general was to be restored to "its original Egyptian character," and that Cagliostro would realize his sublime ideal, perform the greatest of all his prodigies, and "evoke" the Revolution, which the noblest minds in Europe had dreamt of for a hundred years.

But life has her great ironies as well as her little ones. Suddenly, to the rapt enthusiast on the Pisgah-peak of his ambition the shadow of the Revolution did indeed appear. Not the benign genius it was fondly imagined to be before 1789 : herald of freedom and the golden age ; but the monstrous demon of calumny, hatred and terror : the shadow of the Revolution as it was to be, claiming its victims in advance.

Before the Philalètes and the Egyptian Masons could effect their union, the Diamond Necklace Affair was to destroy all Cagliostro's dreams and projects.

CHAPTER VI

THE DIAMOND NECKLACE AFFAIR

I

FEW subjects have been more written about, more discussed than the Affair of the Diamond Necklace. The defences alone of those involved in this *cause célèbre* fill two big volumes. All the memoirs of the period contain more or less detailed accounts of it; in every history of France it occupies a chapter to itself; and as it suggests romance even more than history, novelists and dramatists alike have often exercised their imagination upon its entanglements.

To re-tell in detail this romance, to rehearse this drama in which the happiness and reputations of all who figure in it were destroyed, does not come within the scope of this book. For the chief interest it excites is focussed on the star—the Comtesse de Lamotte-Valois—who dominates the scene from first to last. It is only in the last act that Cagliostro appears. Nevertheless, the part he played was so important that a brief *résumé* of the action preceding his appearance is necessary to enable the reader to understand how he came to be involved in the imbroglio.

Nature had specially cast Madame de Lamotte for the part she played in this drama. Descended from the Valois through a natural son of Henry II, her family had sunk into a state of abject poverty. At her birth her father was reduced to poaching for a livelihood on his former ancestral estate. He eventually died in the Hôtel Dieu, the famous hospital for the indigent founded by Madame de Pompadour. Madame de Lamotte herself as a child was a barefoot beggar on the highway. It was in this condition that she first attracted the attention of the Marquise de Boulain-villiers, who out of pity gave her a home, educated her as well as her brother and sister, and afterwards obtained a small pension for them from Louis XVI.

Being naturally extremely precocious and intelligent, Jeanne de Saint-Remy, as she was called, did not neglect her opportunities. It was her misfortune, however, to derive but small profit from them. Having flirted with the wrong people—her bene-factress's husband and a bishop—she married the wrong man. Lamotte was good-looking, of a respectable family, and crippled with debt. Unable to support himself and his wife on his pay as a subaltern in the army, he resigned his commission, adopted the title of Count—to which he had a shadowy claim—added Valois to his name, and went to Paris to seek fortune, where the Countess made the most of her wits and her looks.

The expedient to which she most frequently resorted was to pester well-known people with petitions, in which she sought to have the claim she had set up to the lands of her ancestors recognized. As by some extraordinary coincidence the Crown had recently acquired these lands, she had, she hoped, only to find the right person to take up her cause to triumph in the end. Among those to whom she appealed was Cardinal de Rohan. His Eminence, who was both sympathetic and susceptible, manifested the greatest pity for the young and charming Countess whose condition was in such a contrast to her illustrious birth. He was amazed that the Court should so neglect a descendant of Henri II, and promised readily to support her claim. A few days later in his capacity as Grand Almoner of France, he sent his interesting *protégée* 2,400 livres as an earnest of his intention. As gratitude and necessity caused the suppliant to renew her visits frequently, the impression she produced on the Cardinal deepened. His pride as well as his sensuality urged him to protect a woman as fascinating and distinguished as she was unfortunate. He entered into her views, gave her advice ; and even confided to her his own grievances and desires.

With all his splendour his Eminence was what is known as a disappointed man. It was his ambition to play a conspicuous part in affairs of state. To flatter him the sycophants who surrounded him were in the habit of comparing his abilities to those of Richelieu, Mazarin, and Fleury, the three great Cardinals who had governed France. It was more than his right, it was his duty, they told him, to become First Minister. In reality he was utterly unfitted for such a position, though not more so than Calonne and Loménie de Brienne, the last two ministers to govern the state under the *ancien régime*. Rohan, however, intoxicated by flattery, believed what he was told ; and his desire for power developed into a passion, a fixed idea.

One obstacle alone stood between him and the pursuit of his ambition—Marie Antoinette ; a fascinating and dazzling obstacle to this consecrated voluptuary, so dazzling that it became confused in his mind with the summit from which it kept him. He did not bear the Queen the slightest resentment for her animosity to him. He was aware that it had been imparted to her by her mother Maria Theresa, at whose instance he had been recalled from Vienna twelve years before. He felt certain that if he could but meet her, get into communication with her, he could win her esteem. Unfortunately Marie Antoinette's contempt extended to Louis XVI. Versailles was thus closed to the Cardinal. He was never seen there but once a year, on Assumption Day, in his rôle of Grand Almoner, when he celebrated mass in the Royal Chapel.

The confidences of her protector gave the Countess de Lamotte more than an insight into his character. In the vanity and credulity they revealed, her alert and cunning mind saw a Golconda of possibilities which not only her necessity but her genius for intrigue urged her to exploit.[1] By circulating rumours of her friendship with the Queen, to which her frequent journeys to Versailles in search of some influential person to present her petition to the King gave weight, she had obtained credit from tradespeople. To cause this rumour to glide to the ears of his Eminence was easy. And as people generally believe what flatters them, when Madame de Lamotte spoke of the interest that the Queen took in him, an interest that circumstances compelled her

---

[1] It is the custom to brand the Countess de Lamotte as infamous, and judged by moral standards she certainly was. The amazing spirit and inventions she displayed, however, give a finish to her infamy that suggest the artist as well as the mere adventuress.

to conceal, the dissipated, amorous Cardinal, too vain to dream any one would deceive him, listened and believed all he was told.

Thus began the famous series of violet-tinted letters which during May, June, and July, 1784, passed between Marie Antoinette and Rohan. This correspondence of which the Queen, needless to say, had not the least inkling, becoming as it proceeded less and less cold and reserved, inflamed all the desires that fermented in the heart of the Cardinal. In this way it was the simplest thing in the world for the Countess de Lamotte to induce him to send the Queen through her " 60,000 livres out of the Almonry funds for a poor family in whom her Majesty was interested."

As Marie Antoinette continued to be "short of cash," Rohan, who was himself heavily in debt and had misappropriated into the bargain the funds of various institutions of which he was the trustee, was obliged to borrow the money the Queen was supposed to be in need of from the Jews. His Eminence, however, at length became restive under these incessant demands for money. He even began to suspect that the Queen might be playing him false, and in spite of all the Countess's explanations demanded some visible proof of the interest she professed to manifest in him.

It was at this juncture, when it seemed as if the game was up, that Lamotte, walking in the garden of the Palais Royal, met by accident an unfortunate female whose face bore a perfect resemblance to that of the Queen.[1] To such an *intrigante* as the Countess, this

---

[1] All contemporaries are agreed on this point. "Same figure, same complexion, same hair, a resemblance of physiognomy of the most striking kind," says Target, who defended the Cardinal at his trial.

resemblance was sufficient material out of which to forge a fresh chain for the Cardinal. On August 11, 1784, between ten and eleven at night, "the unfortunate female"—Mlle. Leguay, Baroness d'Oliva or whatever she called herself—having been carefully trained and paid to represent Marie Antoinette, gave the Cardinal,"disguised as a mousquetaire," a meeting in the park of Versailles, a meeting which the Countess de Lamotte was careful to interrupt ere it began, giving his Eminence barely time to kiss the hand of the supposed Queen, who as she was hurried away flung the kneeling prelate a rose as a token of her affection and esteem.

To Rohan that fleeting vision of the Queen of France served as the proof he had demanded. Henceforth the dream of his diseased fancy enveloped him as in a veil. Obsessed by a single idea, he became the blind instrument of the consummate enchantress by whom he was bewitched. After his romantic rendezvous in the park of Versailles, he advanced confidently and triumphantly to the abyss into which he was destined to plunge, without looking to the right or to the left, and seeing nothing but his vision of the Queen as she had dropped the rose at his feet.

So complete was his thraldom, that later in the depth of his abasement, when he lay in the terrible solitude of the Bastille, charged with swindling a jeweller of a necklace, it was with difficulty that Rohan could bring himself to believe, not that he had been basely betrayed by the Queen, but duped by Madame de Lamotte. "I was completely blinded by the immense desire I had to regain the favour of the Queen," he said at his trial, in reply to the observations of the judges how a man so cultivated, so intelligent, and even so able, as he unquestionably was—his embassy in Vienna had been a brilliant success—should have become the plaything of the Countess de Lamotte.

"His incredible credulity," says the Duc de Lévis, "was really the knot of the whole affair." However, it is not so incredible as it seems. The very fact of his intelligence partially explains it. As Suzanne says to Figaro in the *Barber of Seville,* "intellectual men are fools," particularly when there is a woman in the case, and Madame de Lamotte was clever and fascinating enough to have turned the head of the Devil himself.

As a result of this strategy the Countess managed to mulct the Cardinal of 150,000 livres. The figure that she cut on this money confirmed the rumours of her intimacy with the Queen, a circumstance she did not fail to turn to account. By paying those whom she owed she obtained from them and others still greater credit, whereby the foundations of the vast structure of deceit in which she lived were still further strengthened and extended. She had no longer to ask for credit, it was offered to her, and people even came to implore her to use her boasted influence at Court in their behalf. Some silk merchants of Lyons, who desired the patronage of the Queen, sent her a case of superb stuffs valued at 10,000 livres.

It was in this way that she became acquainted with Böhmer, the maker of the famous necklace.

Except the Cardinal, it would be impossible to imagine a more ridiculous monomaniac than this Saxon Jew. For over ten years he had locked up his whole fortune in a "matchless jewel" for which he was unable to find a purchaser. Marie Antoinette, in particular, had been pestered to buy it, till her patience being exhausted she ordered Böhmer never to mention it to her again.[1] He obeyed her, but none the less continued to hope she would change her mind. In the course of ten years this hope became a fixed idea, which he sought to realize by hook or crook. Thus hearing that Madame de Lamotte had great influence with the Queen, Böhmer came, like the silk merchants of Lyons and others, to purchase it if possible.

It did not take the wily Countess long to gauge the credulity of her visitor, or to make up her mind that it was worth her while to exploit it. Needless to say, a woman clever enough to persuade the Grand ·Almoner of France that a *fille de joie* of the Palais Royal from whom he had received a rose in the park of Versailles was Marie Antoinette, would have no difficulty in getting possession of Böhmer's necklace.

The Cardinal, who had been marking time, so to speak, at Saverne ever since his adventure, was hastily summoned to Paris to perform a service for her Majesty concerning which she enjoined the strictest secrecy. When Rohan, who had travelled post in a blizzard, discovered what the service was he was staggered. No wonder. The Queen, he was informed, wished him to be her security for the purchase of the

---

[1] Marie Antoinette is said to have told Böhmer she could not afford to buy it, but with her well-known extravagance and passion for diamonds one cannot help thinking she would have found the means had the necklace really appealed to her. The fact that Böhmer could find no purchaser suggests that he had as little taste as brains. The Cardinal, who like the Queen knew a beautiful object when he saw it, thought the necklace anything but a beautiful ornament, and when told that the Queen wanted it, wondered what she could see in it.

necklace, for which she had agreed to pay 1,600,000 livres (£64,000) in four instalments of equal amounts at intervals of six months. Madame de Lamotte, however, succeeded in persuading him to affix his signature to the necessary documents—and in due course Böhmer's "matchless jewel" was in her possession.

It did not take her long "to break it up," as Marie Antoinette had advised Böhmer to do years before. Her manner of disposing of the diamonds, which she "picked from the setting with a knife," was itself a romance. But it is impossible in so hurried a *résumé* of this imbroglio to enter into any particulars that have no connection whatever with Cagliostro.

The *dénouement* arrived six months later when the first instalment of 400,000 livres became due. Madame de Lamotte awaited it with perfect indifference. She had involved the Cardinal too deeply to have any fears for herself. The very peril to which *he* was exposed was *her* safety. At all costs Rohan would be obliged to pay for the necklace to prevent a scandal.

She made a mistake, however, in not informing him in time that the Queen was not in a position to pay the instalment, whereby as her security the liability devolved on him. For never dreaming that such a contingency was possible, he was utterly unprepared for it when it came. Crippled with debt, he was unable to put his hand on 400,000 livres at a moment's notice. The difficulty he found in raising the sum made Böhmer so nervous that he consulted Madame Campan, one of the Queen's ladies-in-waiting. She informed the jeweller that he was mad if he imagined the Queen had bought his necklace. Hereupon

The Diamond Necklace Affair

Böhmer in great agitation rushed off to Madame de Lamotte, who coolly informed him she suspected he was being victimized.

"But," she added reassuringly, "the Cardinal is, as you know, very rich; he will pay. Go to him."

This was a master-stroke; for the Countess had as much reason to believe that Böhmer would take her advice as that the Cardinal, to avoid a scandal which meant his ruin, would assume the entire responsibility of the purchase of the necklace. Unfortunately, the distracted jeweller instead of going to the Cardinal tottered off to the King!

By a dramatic coincidence it was Assumption Day, the one day in the year on which the Cardinal was entitled to appear at Versailles, when as Grand Almoner he celebrated mass to which the Royal Family always went in state. He and the Court were waiting in the Oeil-de-Boeuf for the King and Queen to appear in order to accompany them to the Chapel of St. Louis, when a door opened and a chamberlain summoned his Eminence to the sovereign. Everybody knows what followed. Böhmer, having obtained an audience of Louis XVI, had related to that amazed monarch all the details of the transaction by which the necklace had been bought for the Queen. This story, repeated in the presence of Marie Antoinette, whose honesty and virtue it alike impugned, stung her to fury. Exasperated though she was by Böhmer's assertion that she had purchased his necklace, which for ten years she had refused to do, she might nevertheless have excused him on the ground of his insanity. But when he charged her with having employed Rohan, whom she hated, to purchase the necklace through a confidante of whom she had never heard, she was transported with indignation. Forgetting that she was a Queen, which she did too often, she remembered only that she was a woman, and without thinking of the consequences, insisted that the Cardinal should be arrested and her reputation publicly vindicated. Louis XVI, whose misfortune it was to be guided by her when he shouldn't, and never when he should—a misfortune that in the end was to cost him crown and life—at once ordered the arrest of the Grand Almoner, who, attired in his pontifical robes, was carried off then and there to the Bastille like a common criminal before the eyes of the entire Court.

The arrest of the Cardinal [1] was in due course followed by that of the Countess de Lamotte, Cagliostro and his wife, the " Baroness d'Oliva," who had acted the part of the Queen in the park of Versailles, Réteaux de Vilette, who had forged the Queen's letters to Rohan, and several others on whom suspicion had fallen. " The Bastille," as Carlyle says, " opened its iron bosom to them all." [2]

Such in brief is the story of the rape of the Diamond Necklace.

The trial that followed has been justly described as the prologue of the Revolution. To the calumnies it gave birth may be traced the hatred which engendered the Reign of Terror.

[1] The Cardinal was arrested on the 15th, and Cagliostro on the 23rd August, 1785.
[2] Lamotte alone succeeded in escaping.

The Diamond Necklace Affair

"Calumny," says M. Chaix d'Est-Ange in his brilliant monograph on the Necklace Affair, "is common to all ages, but it has not always the same force and success. In times when public opinion is indifferent or feeble it is despised and powerless. At other periods more favourable to it, borne on the wings of passion it soars aloft strong, confident, and triumphant. If ever it was a power it was in the eighteenth century."

"It was everywhere," says de Goncourt, "under the roofs of courtiers and blackmailers alike, in the bureaux of the police themselves, and even at the side of the Queen."

Given such a state of society Marie Antoinette could have done nothing so calculated to injure herself as to cause the arrest of the Cardinal. If he deserved the Bastille it was not necessary to send him there. Though she may be excused for regarding him as a "vulgar swindler who stole diamonds to pay his debts," she should have remembered that he was also the head of one of the greatest houses in France. As soon as the news of his arrest was known there was but a single opinion in the *salons* of the nobility: "What, arrest the Grand Almoner of France in full pontificals before the whole Court for a bit of chiffon! Send a Rohan and the chief of the clergy to the Bastille! *C'est trop!*"

The malcontents of the Court recognized in this shameful disgrace the hand of the unpopular minister Breteuil, who was known to be the bitter enemy of the Cardinal.

"M. de Breteuil," wrote Rivarol with truth, "has taken the Cardinal from the hands of Madame de

Lamotte and crushed him on the forehead of the
Queen, which will retain the marks."

It was by his advice, indeed, that Louis XVI
had been persuaded to gratify the rage of his reckless
consort. The opportunity of ruining his enemy had
been too great for Breteuil to resist. The weakness of the King, the unpopularity of the Queen and
the faults of a blundering minister were thus alike
accentuated.

"When a king has absolute power," says Chaix
d'Est-Ange, "it is without doubt at such a time as this
that he should use it to stifle scandal." The arrest of
the Cardinal could only have been justified by his
conviction. It was a question of his honour or the
Queen's. Thirty years before it would have been an
easy matter to find him guilty, but the spirit of dis-
respect for a tyrannized and stupid authority which was
beginning to assert itself everywhere made Rohan's
conviction extremely difficult, if not altogether impossible. For Louis XVI, from a mistaken sense of equity
which was interpreted as weakness, allowed the Parliament to try him.

This was the height of folly. For sixty years
there had been war between the Court and the Parliament. In the truce which had taken place on the
accession of Louis XVI, the members had resumed
their deliberations more imbued than ever with the
spirit of resistance ; embittered by a long exile they
regarded their recall as a victory. Thus to give the
Parliament the power of determining the guilt or
innocence of the Cardinal, which was in reality that of
the Queen herself, was to take an acknowledged
enemy for a judge.

The Diamond Necklace Affair

When the news of the Cardinal's arrest reached the Parliament, one of the most popular members—he afterwards perished on the guillotine like most of them—cried out, rubbing his hands, "Grand and joyful business! A Cardinal in a swindle! The Queen implicated in a forgery! Filth on the crook and on the sceptre! What a triumph for ideas of liberty! How important for the Parliament!"

In such circumstances it is not surprising that the trial of the Cardinal and his *co-accusés* should become, as Mirabeau wrote, "the most serious affair in the kingdom."

The great family of Rohan left no stone unturned to save the honour of their name. To assist them—but inspired by quite other motives—they had all the enemies of the Queen and the Ministry, as well as the people who considered the Cardinal the victim of despotism. Women in particular were all for la Belle Eminence. It was the fashion to wear ribbons half red and half yellow, the former representing the Cardinal, the latter the straw on which he was supposed to lie in the Bastille. *Cardinal sur la paille* was the name of the ribbon, which was worn even in the palace of Versailles itself.

To save the honour of the throne the Government was obliged to descend into the arena and fight the forces arrayed against it. The attention of the civilized world was thus riveted on the trial, which lasted nine months. No detail was kept secret, accounts were published daily in which the slightest incident was recorded. France and Europe were inundated with libels and calumnies in which the reputations of all concerned were torn to shreds.

Cagliostro

Throw enough mud and some of it is sure to stick. It took more than half a century to cleanse the honour of Marie Antoinette of all suspicion of connivance in the theft of the necklace.

The mistrust that mystery and magic always inspire made Cagliostro with his fantastic personality an easy target for calumny. After having been riddled with abuse till he was unrecognizable, prejudice, the foster-child of calumny, proceeded to lynch him, so to speak. For over one hundred years his character has dangled on the gibbet of infamy, upon which the *sbirri* of tradition have inscribed a curse on any one who shall attempt to cut him down.

His fate has been his fame. He is remembered in history, not so much for anything he did, as for what was done to him. The Diamond Necklace Affair, in which the old *régime* and the new met in their duel to the death, was Cagliostro's damnation. In judging him to-day, it is absolutely essential to bear in mind the unparalleled lack of scruple with which the Government and its enemies contested this trial.

II

Implicated in her swindle by the Countess de Lamotte, to whose accusations his close intimacy with the Cardinal gave weight, Cagliostro was arrested at seven in the morning by Inspector Brugnière, accompanied by Commissary Chesnon and eight policemen.

"He desired me," says Cagliostro, who has described his arrest in detail, "to deliver up my keys, and compelled me to open my bureau, which I did. There were in it several of my remedies, amongst the rest six bottles of a precious cordial. Brugnière seized on whatever he took a fancy to, and the catchpoles he had brought with him followed his example. The only favour I asked was that I might be permitted to go in my own carriage to the place of my destination. This was refused. I then requested to be allowed the use of a cab; this also was denied. Proud of making a show of his prey to the thronging multitude, Brugnière insisted on my walking part of the way; and although I was perfectly submissive and did not make the least shadow of resistance he laid hold of me by the collar. In this way, closely surrounded by four *sbirri*, I was dragged along the Boulevards as far as the Rue Notre-Dame-de-Nazareth, where a cab appearing, I was mercifully thrust into it and driven the rest of the way to the Bastille."

The admiration amounting almost to veneration that Cagliostro inspired was shared only by his followers —of whom, however, he could count several thousands, it is said, in Paris. On the other hand, the curiosity which he had excited was general and anything but reverent. The exaggerated enthusiasm of his followers, the incredible stories related of him, and the extreme seriousness with which he took himself made him ridiculous. If he was the chief subject of conversation in all classes in Paris, it was as a subject of mirth. In the drama of the Necklace Affair it was to him that the public looked to supply the comic relief. He was by common consent the clown, the funny man of the play, so to speak. He had but to appear on the scene to raise a laugh, his slightest gesture produced a roar, when he spoke he convulsed the house.

But to Cagliostro his rôle was very far from comic. The consciousness of innocence is not necessarily a consolation in adversity. It poisons as often as it stimulates—according to the temperament. Cagliostro was utterly crushed by the blow that had fallen on him. The gloom of the Bastille, which the popular imagination haunted by old legends made deeper than it was, seemed to chill his very soul. He who had faced with "a front of brass" all the previous dangers and humiliations of his agitated existence was for the first time cowed. Illuminist, Egyptian Mason, Mystic Regenerator of Mankind—Revolutionist, in a word—he had no confidence in the justice of the power into whose hands he had fallen. He believed that he would be forgotten in his dungeon like so many others.

The severity with which he was treated was calculated to justify his fears.

"Were I left to choose," he says, "between an ignominious death, and six months in the Bastille, I would say without hesitation, 'Lead me on to the scaffold.'"

For five months he was not only in ignorance, but purposely misinformed, as to what was transpiring without his prison. During this time the beautiful Countess, less rigorously guarded, was confined near him without his knowledge. As soon as Brugnière had carried off her husband, Chesnon and the police, who had remained behind after searching for incriminating documents which they did not find, attached seals to the house and carried her off too, "half dead with fear," to the Bastille. In response to Cagliostro's repeated inquiries as to whether she shared his captivity, as he feared, his jailers "swore by their honour and God that she was not in the Bastille."

This deception was even carried to the length of permitting him to write letters to her which never reached her, and to receive replies which she never wrote, "in which she assured him that she was taking steps to restore him to freedom." As the Countess Cagliostro could not write, a friend was supposed to write the letters for her. In the same way if he wanted clothes or linen he would dispatch a line to his wife, and an official would go to his house and fetch what he required, bringing back a letter from the Countess calculated to make him believe that they had been sent by her.

At the same time the Cardinal was living in almost as much comfort as if he had been in his own palace. He occupied a spacious apartment, had three of his servants to wait on him, and saw as many people as he wished. The number of his visitors was so great that the drawbridge of the Bastille was kept lowered throughout the day. On one occasion he even "gave a dinner of twenty covers."

As money—and Cagliostro had plenty of it—like rank, was able to purchase equal consideration in the Bastille, the contrast in the treatment of the two prisoners almost warrants the supposition that the jailers derived no little amusement from making sport of the sufferings of one who was alleged to be immune from those ills to which mere clay is prone. There are many people to whom a weeping Pierrot is as funny as a laughing one.

It was not till his despondency, on discovering as he eventually did that his wife was a prisoner like himself, threatened to affect his reason that the severity of his confinement was relaxed. To prevent him from committing suicide, Thiroux de Crosne, the minister who had issued the warrant for his arrest, advised de Launay, the Governor of the Bastille, "to choose a warder, likely to be sympathetic, to sleep in his cell." He was also permitted, like the other prisoners, to have exercise and to select a lawyer to defend him.

The first use he made of this privilege was to petition the Parliament—"to release his wife from a dungeon, where a man himself had occasion for all his strength, all his fortitude, and all his resignation to struggle against despair."

The Bastille was too massive a cage for so delicate a bird. Implicated without the shadow of a reason in the Necklace Affair the Countess Cagliostro began to imagine herself ill. She pined for her fine house, her admirers, her diamonds, her black mare Djérid, and the companionship of the man to whom she owed all that spelt happiness in her inoffensive, doll-like existence. Moved to pity less by the petition of Cagliostro than by the pleading of her lawyer, Polverit, and the eloquence of d'Epremenil, the most brilliant member of the Parliament, that body was finally persuaded to set her free without a trial after having been imprisoned seven months in the Bastille.

The release of the Countess Cagliostro, to which the Court was bitterly opposed, was the first reverse of the Government in the duel to which it had so foolishly challenged public opinion.

No sooner was the news known than friends and strangers alike came to congratulate her. For more than a week nearly three hundred people came daily to inscribe their names in the visitors' book kept by the concierge.

"It is the perfection of good style," says one of the newswriters of the period, "to have made a call on the Countess Seraphina."

"Even the 'nymphs' of the Palais Royal," says d'Alméras, "discreetly manifested their sympathy with the victim of arbitrary power on recognizing her as she walked one day in the gardens."

III

Madame de Lamotte in the meantime, utterly undaunted by her imprisonment, was energetically preparing for the trial, which, in spite of all her efforts, was to end in her conviction. Her defence was a tissue of lies from beginning to end. She contradicted herself with brazen effrontery, accused Cagliostro, the Cardinal, and at last the Queen, of swindling Böhmer of the necklace. She did not hesitate to defame herself by declaring that she had been the mistress of the Cardinal—which was as false as the rest of her evidence—and, as each lie became untenable, took refuge in another, even admitting that she was lying "to shelter an exalted personage." In only one thing was she consistent; to the end she asserted her complete innocence. Her object was to confuse the issue and so wriggle herself free.

In the first of her *mémoires justificatifs*, which were printed and sold in accordance with the legal custom of the day, she boldly charged Cagliostro with the robbery of the necklace. He was represented as an impostor to make him the more easily appear a swindler. To penetrate the mystery in which he had wrapped his origin she invented for him a low and shameful past, which the editor of the *Courier de l'Europe* and the Inquisition-biographer afterwards merged into Giuseppe Balsamo's. She ridiculed his cures, and cited the Medical Faculty as witnesses of the deaths he had caused. She declared his disinterestedness and his generosity to be a fraud, and accused him of practising in private the vices he denounced in public. Having stripped him of the last stitch of respectability she proceeded to expose the woman who passed as his wife, and whose *liaisons* with the Cardinal and others she declared he encouraged. As for the wonders he was said to perform they were not even worthy of the name of tricks ; only fools were taken in by them. In fine, to Madame de Lamotte, the Grand Cophta was nothing but "an arch empiric, a mean alchemist, a dreamer on the philosopher's stone, a false prophet, and a Jew who had taken to pieces the necklace which he had beguiled the Cardinal, over whom he had gained an incredible influence, to entrust to him, in order to swell a fortune unheard of before."

This *mémoire*—the first of many which the various persons implicated in the Affair rained upon the public —was to an impatient world the signal that the battle had begun. Excitement, already at fever heat, was intensified by the boldness, directness and violence of Madame de Lamotte's denunciation. It was felt that to justify himself Cagliostro would be obliged to clear up the mystery of his past. Never before had the "Grand Coffer," as he was called by a police official who unwittingly confounded the title and the fortune of the restorer of Egyptian Masonry, roused curiosity to so high a pitch. The recollection of his reputed prodigies gave to his expected self-revelation the character of an evocation, so to speak ; and the public, as ready to mock as it had formerly been to respect him, awaited his defence as a sort of magic séance at which all the tricks of necromancy were to be explained.

Cagliostro employed to defend him Thilorier, one of the youngest and most promising advocates of the Parisian bar. Perhaps no *cause célèbre* in history has ever called forth a more brilliant display of legal talent than the Diamond Necklace Affair. Of all the *mémoires* or statements that were published by the advocates engaged in the case that of Thilorier created the greatest sensation.

Warned by the tumult occasioned by the rush of purchasers who had besieged the house of Madame de Lamotte's advocate on the publication of her *mémoire*, Thilorier took the precaution to secure eight soldiers of the watch to guard his door. Within a few hours tens of thousands of copies were scattered over Paris, and large editions were dispatched to the principal cities of Europe. It was regarded as a romance after the style of the *Arabian Nights* rather than the serious defence of a man whose liberty and very life were at stake. Everywhere people read it with a sort of amused bewilderment, and " Thilorier himself," says Beugnot, "who was a man of infinite wit, was the first to laugh at it."

As a masterpiece of irony, clearness, dignity, and wit it was equalled only by Blondel's defence of the " Baroness d'Oliva." But its chief merit lay not so much in the piquancy of its literary style as in its portrayal of Cagliostro. Those who read this fantastic document felt that they not only saw the man but could hear him speak. Thilorier had drawn his hero to the life.

Beginning with a high-flown and egotistical recapitulation of his sufferings and virtues Cagliostro proceeded to refute " those imputations (as to his origin) which in any other circumstance he would have treated with contempt " by relating " with candour " the history of his life. As a specimen of his grandiloquence it is worth quoting at some length.

" I cannot," he says, " speak positively as to the place of my nativity, nor to the parents who gave me birth. All my inquiries have ended only in giving me some great notions, it is true, but altogether vague and uncertain, concerning my family.

" I spent the years of my childhood in the city of Medina in Arabia. There I was brought up under the name of Acharat, which I preserved during my progress through Africa and Asia. I had my apartments in the palace of the Muphti Salahaym. It is needless to add that the Muphti is the chief of the Mahometan religion, and that his constant residence is at Medina.

" I recollect perfectly that I had then four persons attached to my service : a governor, between fifty-five and sixty years of age, whose name was Althotas,[1]

---

[1] The existence of Althotas is now generally conceded. A plausible attempt has been made to identify him with a certain Kölmer from whom Weishaupt received lessons in magic, and who was said to be a Jutland merchant who had lived some years in Memphis and afterwards travelled through Europe pretending to initiate adepts in the ancient Egyptian Mysteries. He was known to have visited Malta in the time of the Grand Master Pinto.

and three servants, a white one who attended me as *valet de chambre* and two blacks, one of whom was constantly about me night and day.

"My governor always told me that I had been left an orphan when only about three months old, that my parents were Christians and nobly born ; but he left me absolutely in the dark about their names and the place of my nativity. Some words, however, which he let fall by chance have induced me to suspect that I was born at Malta. Althotas, whose name I cannot speak without the tenderest emotion, treated me with great care and all the attention of a father. He thought to develop the talent I displayed for the sciences. I may truly say that he knew them all, from the most abstruse down to those of mere amusement. My greatest aptitude was for the study of botany and chemistry.

"By him I was taught to worship God, to love and assist my neighbours, and to respect everywhere religion and the laws. We both dressed like Mahometans and conformed outwardly to the worship of Islam ; but the true religion was imprinted in our hearts.

"The Muphti, who often visited me, always treated me with great goodness and seemed to entertain the highest regard for my governor. The latter instructed me in most of the Eastern languages. He would often converse with me on the pyramids of Egypt, on those vast subterraneous caves dug out by the ancient Egyptians, to be the repository of human knowledge and to shelter the precious trust from the injuries of time.

"The desire of travelling and of beholding the wonders of which he spoke grew so strong upon me, that Medina and my youthful sports there lost all the allurements I had found in them before. At last, when I was in my twelfth year, Althotas informed me one day that we were going to commence our travels. A caravan was prepared and we set out, after having taken our leave of the Muphti, who was pleased to express his concern at our departure in the most obliging manner.

"On our arrival at Mecca we alighted at the palace of the Cherif. Here Althotas provided me with sumptuous apparel and presented me to the Cherif, who honoured me with the most endearing caresses. At sight of this prince my senses experienced a sudden emotion, which it is not in the power of words to express, and my eyes dropped the most delicious tears I have ever shed in my life. His, I perceived, he could hardly contain.

"I remained at Mecca for the space of three years; not a day passed without my being admitted to the sovereign's presence, and every hour increased his attachment and added to my gratitude. I sometimes surprised his gaze riveted upon me, and turned to heaven with every expression of pity and commiseration. Thoughtful, I would go from him a prey to an ever-fruitless curiosity. I dared not question Althotas, who always rebuked me with great severity, as if it had been a crime in me to wish for some information concerning my parents and the place where I was born. I attempted in vain to get the secret from the negro who slept in my apartment. If I chanced to talk of my parents he would turn a deaf ear to my questions. But one night when I was more pressing than usual, he told me that if ever I should leave Mecca I was threatened with the greatest misfortunes, and bid me, above all, *beware of the city of Trebizond.*

"My inclination, however, got the better of his forebodings—I was tired of the uniformity of life I led at the Cherif's court. One day when I was alone the prince entered my apartment; he strained me to his bosom with more than usual tenderness, bid me never cease to adore the Almighty, and added, bedewing my cheeks with his tears: '*Nature's unfortunate child, adieu!*'

"This was our last interview. The caravan waited only for me and I set off, leaving Mecca, never to re-enter it more.

"I directed my course first to Egypt, where I inspected those celebrated pyramids which to the eye of the superficial observer only appear an enormous mass of marble and granite. I also got acquainted with the priests of the various temples, who had the complacence to introduce me into such places as no ordinary traveller ever entered before. The next three years of my progress were spent in the principal kingdoms of Africa and Asia. Accompanied by Althotas, and the three attendants who continued in my service, I arrived in 1766 at the island of Rhodes, and there embarked on a French ship bound to Malta.

"Notwithstanding the general rule by which all vessels coming from the Levant are obliged to enter quarantine, I obtained on the second day leave to go ashore. Pinto, the Grand Master of the Knights of Malta, gave us apartments in his palace, and I perfectly recollect that mine were near the laboratory.

"The first thing the Grand Master was pleased to

do, was to request the Chevalier d'Aquino, of the princely house of Caramanica, to bear me company and do me the honours of the island. It was here that I first assumed European dress and with it the name of Count Cagliostro; nor was it a small matter of surprise to me to see Althotas appear in a clerical dress with the insignia of the Order of Malta.

"I have every reason to believe that the Grand Master Pinto was acquainted with my real origin. He often spoke to me of the Cherif and mentioned the city of Trebizond, but never would consent to enter into further particulars on the subject. Meanwhile he treated me with the utmost distinction, and assured me of very rapid preferment if I would consent to take the cross. But my taste for travelling and the predominant desire of practising medicine, induced me to decline an offer that was as generous as it was honourable.

"It was in the island of Malta that I had the misfortune of losing my best friend and master, the wisest as well as the most learned of men, the venerable Althotas. Some minutes before he expired, pressing my hand, he said in a feeble voice, 'My son, keep for ever before your eyes the fear of God and the love of your fellow-creatures; you will soon be convinced by experience of what you have been taught by me.'

"The spot where I had parted for ever from the friend who had been as a father to me, soon became odious. I begged leave of the Grand Master to quit the island in order to travel over Europe; he consented reluctantly, and the Chevalier d'Aquino was so obliging as to accompany me. Our first trip was to Sicily, from thence we went to the different islands of the Greek Archipelago, and returning, arrived at Naples, the birthplace of my companion.

"The Chevalier, owing to his own private affairs, being obliged to undertake a private journey, I proceeded alone to Rome, provided with a letter of credit on the banking house of Signor Bellone. In the capital of the Christian world I resolved upon keeping the strictest *incognito*. One morning, as I was shut up in my apartment, endeavouring to improve myself in the Italian language, my *valet de chambre* introduced to my presence the secretary of Cardinal Orsini, who requested me to wait on his Eminence. I repaired at once to his palace and was received with the most flattering civility. The Cardinal often invited me to his table and procured me the acquaintance of several cardinals and Roman princes, amongst others, Cardinals York and Ganganelli, who was afterwards Pope Clement XIV. Pope Rezzonico, who then filled the papal chair, having expressed a desire of seeing me, I had the honour of frequent private interviews with his Holiness.

"I was then (1770) in my twenty-second year, when by chance I met a young lady of quality, Seraphina Feliciani, whose budding charms kindled in my bosom a flame which sixteen years of marriage have only served to strengthen. It is that unfortunate woman, whom neither her virtues, her innocence, nor her quality of stranger could save from the hardships of a captivity as cruel as it is unmerited."

From this stage of his Odyssey, beyond citing as references certain persons by whom he was known in the various countries through which he passed, Cagliostro was very reticent as to his doings. From

Cagliostro

Rome he arrived at Strasburg at a bound, whence he proceeded to his imprisonment in the Bastille with almost equal speed. His confession, rendering as it did his country and parentage more mysterious than ever, was received with derision. The credulous public, which had swallowed so easily all the extravagant stories concerning his supernatural powers refused to believe in this fantastic account of a mysterious childhood passed in Mecca and Medina, of caravans and pyramids, of tolerant Muphtis and benignant Grand Masters of Malta. It was not that the credulity of the eighteenth century had its limit but that calumny had mesmerized it, so to speak. Cagliostro's prestige had been submerged in the Necklace Affair ; the blight of the Bastille had fallen on the fame of the Grand Cophta and all his works.

As the manner in which he stated his ignorance of his birth seemed to leave it to be inferred that he knew more than he wished to say, it was determined to give him a father. While his enemies agreed with the Countess de Lamotte that he was the son of a Neapolitan coachman, his friends declared him to be the offspring of the illicit loves of the Grand Master Pinto and a princess of Trebizond. To account for the meeting of this singular pair it was gravely asserted that a Maltese galley had captured a Turkish pleasure-boat with several young ladies of distinction on board, one of whom had *exchanged hearts* with Pinto, who, prevented by his vow of celibacy from making her his wife, had sent her back to her disconsolate parents, and that to frustrate their rage at the condition in which she had returned she had caused her child as soon as it was born to be spirited away to Arabia, which accounted for the mysterious warning Acharat had received from the black slave "to beware of Trebizond."

Ridicule, however, soon disposed of this agreeable fable, and substituted instead the popular Balsamo legend in which *just as much as it has pleased subsequent biographers to accept of Cagliostro's confession* has been included. As to whether he spoke the truth wholly or partly or not at all, the present writer, confronted with his mysterious and fantastic character on the one hand and the assertions based on the prejudice of a century on the other, is unable to express any opinion. It seems, however, hard to believe that any man placed in so serious a situation as Cagliostro, and one which, moreover, had thoroughly shaken his courage, would have ventured to invent a story calculated to increase the suspicion it was his object to allay. To the present generation, accustomed by the press to infinitely greater improbabilities, Cagliostro's adventures in Mecca and Medina have at least lost the air of incredibility.

IV.

As may be surmised from the cursory account of the Diamond Necklace Affair already given, Cagliostro had no difficulty in proving his innocence. The mere comparison of the dates of the various incidents of the imbroglio with his own whereabouts at the time was sufficient to vindicate him.

Throughout the whole of 1784, while the Cardinal was corresponding, as he supposed, with the Queen, meeting her in the park of Versailles, and purchasing the necklace, Cagliostro was in Bordeaux and Lyons. He did not arrive in Paris till January 30, 1785;

it was on February 1 that the Cardinal gave the necklace to Madame de Lamotte to hand to the Queen. Accordingly, if Cagliostro had ever even seen the necklace, it could only have been between January 30 and February 1 when Böhmer had already obtained the Cardinal's guarantee in exchange for his precious jewel. This, however, he denied. " It was not," he said, "till a fortnight before the Cardinal was arrested that he informed me for the first time of the transaction about the necklace."

But Cagliostro was not content with merely establishing his innocence. Madame de Lamotte's attack on his character had deeply wounded him in his most sensitive spot—his vanity—and pride would not suffer him to ignore her gibes.

She had described him as "an arch empiric, a mean alchemist, a dreamer on the philosopher's stone, a false prophet, and a profaner of the true religion."

" Empiric," he said, refuting each epithet in turn, not without a certain dignity ; "this word I have often heard without knowing exactly what it meant. If it means one who without being a doctor has some knowledge of medicine and takes no fee, who attends to rich and poor alike and receives no money from either, then I confess I am an empiric.

" Mean alchemist. Alchemist or not, the epithet *mean* is applicable only to those who beg or cringe, and it is well known whether Count Cagliostro ever asked a favour of any one.

" Dreamer on the philosopher's stone. Whatever my opinion may be concerning the philosopher's stone, I have kept it to myself and never troubled the public with my dreams.

The Diamond Necklace Affair

"False prophet. Not always so. Had the Cardinal taken my advice he would not be in the position in which he now finds himself. I told him more than once that the Countess de Lamotte was a deceitful, intriguing woman, and to beware of her.

"Profaner of the true religion. This is more serious. I have respected religion at all times. My life and my outward conduct I freely submit to the inquiries of the law. As to what passes inwardly God alone has a·right to call me to account."

Cagliostro also took advantage of the occasion to deny the oft-repeated assertion that he was a Jew.

"My education," he said, "as I have already declared, was that of a child born of Christian parents. I never was a Jew or a Mahometan. These two religions leave on their sectaries an *outward* and *indelible* mark. The truth, therefore, of what I here advance may be ascertained; and rather than let any doubt remain on this affair, I am ready, if required, to yield to a verification more shameful for him who exacts it than for the person who submits to it."[1]

When he was confronted with Madame de Lamotte the scene in court was in the highest degree comic. The Countess, who had an unbounded contempt for the occult in general, covered the séances of Cagliostro with ridicule. She described one at which she had been present as a swindle, and reproached him with having exploited the credulity of the Cardinal by the most vulgar methods and for the most sordid motives. His Eminence, she asserted, was so bewitched that he

---

[1] Henry Swinburne, in his *Memoirs of the Courts of Europe* describing his meeting with Cagliostro, declares that there was "nothing Jewish" about him.

consulted Cagliostro on "the pricking of a thumb," which made her "regret she did not live in those blessed times when a charge of sorcery would have led him to the stake."

But while she attempted to overwhelm the unfortunate creature she had chosen to saddle with her own guilt, he dexterously turned the tables upon her. Assuming that her calumnies were inspired by the desire to clear herself rather than hatred, "he forgave her the tears of bitterness she had caused him to shed."

"Do not imagine," he said, with the air of sublime bombast that was characteristic of him, "that my moderation is a piece of mere affectation. From the bottom of the abyss into which you have plunged me I shall raise my voice to implore in your behalf the clemency of the laws; and if, after my innocence and that of my wife is acknowledged, the best of kings should think an unfortunate stranger who had settled in France on the faith of his royal word, of the laws of hospitality, and of the common rights of nations is entitled to some indemnity, the only satisfaction I shall require will be that his Majesty may be pleased, at my request, to pardon and set at liberty the unfortunate Countess de Lamotte. However guilty she may be supposed, she is already sufficiently punished. Alas! as I have been taught by sad experience, there is no crime ever so great but may be atoned for by six months in the Bastille!"

Blague or conviction, at such a moment, it would be churlish to inquire. When one is fighting for life and liberty one readily avails oneself of any weapon that comes to hand. At least so thought Madame de

The Diamond Necklace Affair

Lamotte. Failing further abuse of which she had been deprived by a *riposte* as unexpected as it was subtle, she picked up a candlestick. Hurled at the head of her adversary, it "hit him in the stomach," to the amusement of the court, the judges and Madame de Lamotte herself, who remarked to her counsel that "if he wished to render the scene still more amusing he had but to give her a broomstick."

But neither abusive epithets nor candlesticks are arguments. Finding herself on the wrong road, the Countess made haste to leave it for another. It was no longer Cagliostro who had stolen the necklace, but the Cardinal.

At last, after more than nine months, the famous affair came to an end. On May 30, 1786, all the accused were summoned before the Parliament. When Cagliostro arrived, tricked out as usual like a mountebank in a coat of green silk embroidered with gold, and his hair falling in little tails on his shoulders, the whole assemblage burst into a laugh. But to him it was anything but an occasion for merriment; he was serious to the point of solemnity.

"Who are you?" asked the president.

"An illustrious traveller," was the reply. Then with imperturbable gravity he began in his loud, metallic voice, which Madame d'Oberkirch compared to a "trumpet veiled in crape," to repeat the story of his life.

At the mention of Trebizond the laughter redoubled. This made him nervous, and either unconsciously from old habit, or in the hope of exciting an interest favourable to his cause, he related his adventures in a jargon composed, says Beugnot, "of all

known languages as well as those which never existed."
The gibberish he employed rendered him and his
story still more fantastic. The laughter in the court
was so loud that at times the voice of the speaker was
drowned. Even the judges were convulsed. At the
finish the president seemed to be on the point of
complimenting " Nature's unfortunate child." It was
evident that Cagliostro had won the sympathy of those
on whom his fate depended. Of the verdict of the
mob there was no doubt. He took the cheers with
which he was greeted on being driven back to the
Bastille as a premonition of his acquittal. One writer
says he displayed the joy he felt " by throwing his hat
into the air."

On the following day (May 31) the Parliament
pronounced the verdict. The Cardinal and Cagliostro
were unanimously acquitted—the innocence of the
latter had been acknowledged by all implicated in the
trial, even in the end by the Countess de Lamotte
herself.[1]

The verdict was immensely popular. "I don't
know what would have befallen the Parliament," said

[1] One, de Soudak, in an interesting review of M. Funck-Brentano's
L'Affaire du Collier, in the Paris *Temps*, April 1, 1902, is the only
modern writer who has ventured to question this verdict. The value
of his opinion may be judged from an article by him in the *Revue
Bleue*, 1899, in which he attempts to identify a mysterious French-
woman who died in the Crimea in 1825 with the Countess de
Lamotte, who died in London 1791, after escaping from the
Salpêtrière, to which she had been condemned for life. Her sentence—the judges were unanimous in finding her guilty—also
included being " whipped naked by the executioner, branded on the
shoulders with the letter V. (voleuse), and the confiscation of all her
property." The sentences of the others implicated in this affair need
not concern us here.

The Diamond Necklace Affair

Mirabeau, "had they pronounced otherwise." The fish-wives—the same who later were the Furies of the Revolution—forcibly embraced the judges and crowned them with flowers. In the street the name of the Cardinal was cheered to the echo. The ovation he received, however, was inspired less from any desire of the populace to acclaim him personally than to affront the Queen.

It was also to the violent hatred of the Court that Cagliostro owed the reception accorded him. His account of the scenes that took place on his deliverance from captivity would do credit to the lachrymose romances of the "age of sensibility."

"I quitted the Bastille," he says, "about half-past eleven in the evening. The night was dark, the quarter in which I resided but little frequented. What was my surprise, then, to hear myself acclaimed by eight or ten thousand persons. My door was forced open; the courtyard, the staircase, the rooms were crowded with people. I was carried straight to the arms of my wife. At such a moment my heart could not contain all the feelings which strove for mastery in it. My knees gave way beneath me. I fell on the floor unconscious. With a shriek my wife sank into a swoon. Our friends pressed around us, uncertain whether the most beautiful moment of our life would not be the last. The anxiety spread from one to the other, the noise of the drums was no longer heard. A sad silence followed the delirious joy. I recovered. A torrent of tears streamed from my eyes, and I was able at last, without dying, to press to my heart . . . I will say no more. Oh, you privileged beings to whom heaven has made the rare and fatal gift of an ardent soul and a sensitive heart, you who have experienced the delights of a first love, you alone will understand me, you alone will appreciate what after ten months of torture the first moment of bliss is like!"

Both Cagliostro and the Cardinal were obliged to show themselves at the windows of their respective houses before the crowds, which were cheering them and hissing the name of the Queen, could be induced to disperse.

To Marie Antoinette, whose popularity was for ever blasted by the trial, the verdict of the Parliament was an insult—as it was meant to be—which intolerable though it was, she would have been wise to have borne in silence. But it was her fate to the last to hold the honour of the woman higher than the majesty of the Queen. Having made the blunder of arresting the Cardinal and suffering the Parliament to try him, the King, advised by her, now committed the folly of showing his resentment of the verdict, which had after all, in the eye of the law, cleared his consort of complicity in the swindle. On June 2, the day after his release from the Bastille, Rohan was stripped of all his Court dignities and functions, and exiled to one of his abbeys in Auvergne. At the same time, Cagliostro was also ordered to leave Paris with his wife within a week, and France within three.

The news no sooner became known than an immense concourse of people flocked to manifest their disapproval in front of the house of the Grand Cophta. But if he mistook their demonstration of hatred of the Queen as a sign of sympathy for himself, popularity under such conditions was too fraught with danger for him to take any pleasure in it. Terrified lest the Government should seize the opportunity of thrusting him back into the Bastille, he came out on the balcony of his house and entreated the mob to withdraw quietly, and then hurriedly left Paris.

He went first to Passy, whither he was followed by a small band of his most faithful adherents, who during the few days he remained there mounted guard in the house in which he had taken shelter. A fortnight later he embarked from Boulogne with his wife for England. Upwards of five thousand people are said to have witnessed his departure, many of whom demanded and received his farewell blessing on their knees. France, on a page of whose history he had indelibly printed his name, never saw him more.

There is an old and uncorroborated report that he who had always been so punctilious in the discharge of his liabilities left Paris without paying his rent. It appears to have arisen from the action that he afterwards brought against the magistrate Chesnon and de Launay, the governor of the Bastille, to recover property valued at 100,000 livres which he declared had been stolen from his house during his imprisonment and for which he sought to hold them responsible. His failure to substantiate the charge gave it the appearance of having been trumped up. Whether it had any basis in fact it is impossible to say, but there can be no doubt from the manner in which the police turned his house upside down at the time he and his wife were arrested, as well as from the carelessness with which the official seals were affixed, that many valuable articles might easily have been spirited away in the confusion by unscrupulous servants and even by the police themselves.

If Cagliostro, however, failed to pay his rent the proprietor of the house certainly took the matter very lightly. " His house," says Lenôtre, " remained closed till the Revolution. In 1805 the doors were opened for the first time in eighteen years when the owner sold the Grand Cophta's furniture by auction." Surely a very long time to wait to indemnify oneself for unpaid rent?

A curious interest attaches to this house, which is still standing, though long since shorn of its splendour in the days when the Cardinal and the aristocracy of the old *régime* came to assist at Cagliostro's magic séances. Yet in the meantime it has not been without a history. In 1855 the doors of the gateway were removed during some process of repair and replaced by doors which had formerly done service at the Temple where the Royal Family were incarcerated after the fall of the monarchy. They may be still seen with their heavy bolts and huge locks.

What a fatality—the doors of Marie Antoinette's prison closing Cagliostro's house! History has her irony as well as her romance.

CHAPTER VII

CAGLIOSTRO RETURNS TO LONDON

I

IF ever a man had cause to be embittered and to nurse a grievance it was Cagliostro. He had been cast suddenly headlong, through no fault of his own, from the pinnacle of good fortune into the Bastille ; accused of another's crime ; arrested with the utmost brutality and treated with outrageous severity ; kept in uncertainty of the fate of his wife, who for six months, unknown to him, was confined within fifteen feet of him ; he had been an object of ridicule and mockery within, of calumny and detraction without his prison, of which the name alone was sufficient to reduce him to despair ; then—crowning injustice— after being acquitted on every count in a manner that could leave no doubt of his innocence, he had been arbitrarily banished within twenty-four hours of the recovery of his liberty.

Under such circumstances resentment is perfectly natural and justifiable. To " take it lying down," as the saying is, at all times a doubtful virtue, becomes frequently a downright folly.

Had Cagliostro been silent in the present instance with the protecting arm of the sea between him and a corrupt and blundering despotism he would have been utterly undeserving of pity. In " getting even," however, to his credit be it said, he did not adopt the methods of the *Rohanists*, as all the enemies of the Government were called, and launch, like Calonne, Madame de Lamotte and so many others, libel after libel at the honour of the defenceless and unpopular Queen—the low and contemptible revenge of low and contemptible natures. On the contrary, he held the Baron de Breteuil, as the head of the Government, directly responsible for his sufferings and attacked him once and once only, in his famous *Letter to the French People*.[1]

This letter, written the day after his arrival in England, to a friend in Paris, was immediately published in pamphlet form, and even translated into several languages. Scattered broadcast over Paris and all France it created an immense sensation. Directed against Breteuil, whose unpopularity, already great, it increased, it assailed more or less openly the monarchical principle itself. Of all the pamphlets which from the Necklace Affair to the fall of the Bastille attacked the royal authority none are so dignified or so eloquent. The longing for freedom, which was latent in the bosom of every man and which the philosophers and the secret societies had been doing their best to fan into a flame, was revealed in every line. It was not unreasonably regarded as the confession of faith of an Illuminé. The Inquisition-biographer declares that it was conceived in a spirit so calculated to excite a revolt that " it was with difficulty a printer could be found in England to print it."

---

[1] The *Lettre au peuple français* was dated the 20th June 1786. As stated in the previous chapter, Breteuil was the deadly enemy of Cardinal de Rohan, and encouraged Marie Antoinette in demanding his arrest of the King.

Cagliostro Returns to London

Cagliostro himself admits that it was written with "a freedom rather republican."[1]

This letter gave great offence to the French Government and particularly to the Baron de Breteuil who dominated it, and whose conduct in the Necklace Affair sufficiently proves his unfitness for the post he filled. Under ordinary circumstances he would no doubt have ignored the attack upon himself. His pride, the pride of an aristocrat—he was the personification of reaction—would have scorned to notice the insult of one so far beneath him as Cagliostro. But the prestige of the Government and the majesty of the throne damaged by the unspeakable calumnies of the Necklace Affair had to be considered. Might not the sensation caused by the inflammatory *Letter to the French People* encourage the author to follow it up by other and still more seditious pamphlets? There was but one way to prevent this contingency—*to kidnap him.* For not only would it be impossible to persuade the English Government to give him up, but futile to attempt to purchase silence from one who had a grievance and made it his boast that he never took payment for the favours he conferred.

Before the days of extradition, kidnapping was a

[1] Nearly all who have written on Cagliostro have erred in stating that the letter contained the " predictions that the Bastille would be destroyed, its site become a public promenade, and that a king would reign in France who would abolish *lettres de cachet* and convoke the States General "—all of which actually occurred three years later in 1789. The predictions are the invention of the Inquisition-biographer to whose short-comings, to put it mildly, attention has frequently been called. Cagliostro merely says that if in the future he was permitted to return to France he would only do so "*provided* the Bastille was destroyed and its site turned into a public promenade." A copy of this letter, now become very rare, is to be seen in the French National Archives.

practice more or less common to all governments. Eighteenth century history, particularly that of France, is full of such instances.[1] Breteuil was, therefore, merely following precedent when he ordered Barthélemy, the French Ambassador in London, to inform Cagliostro that "His Most Christian Majesty gave him permission to return to his dominions."

This permission, was, accordingly, duly conveyed to Cagliostro, with the request that he would call at a certain hour on the following day at the Embassy when the ambassador would give him any further information on the subject he desired. It is exceedingly unlikely that Barthélemy intended to forcibly detain him when he called, but rather to gull him by false pretences—a not difficult proceeding in the case of one so notoriously vain as Cagliostro—into returning to France. Be this as it may, on calling on the ambassador at the appointed hour he prudently invited Lord George Gordon and one Bergeret de Frouville, an admirer who had followed him from France, to accompany him. This they not only did, but insisted in being present throughout the interview.

Nettled by this veiled suggestion of treachery, Barthélemy received his visitor in a manner which served to confirm this impression. Producing a letter

---

[1] Many attempts were made at this very time to kidnap the Count de Lamotte, who alone of all "wanted" in the Necklace Affair succeeded in escaping. On one occasion his murder was even attempted. The Countess de Lamotte herself, who escaped from the Salpêtrière to London and published the vilest of all the calumnies against Marie Antoinette perished in jumping out of a window to elude capture. Numerous instances of the kidnapping of French subjects in England by the French police are cited by Brissot in his Memoirs.

from the Baron de Breteuil he informed Cagliostro that he was authorized to give him permission to return to France. But Cagliostro, having taken no steps to obtain this permission was naturally suspicious of the source from which it emanated.

"How is it possible," he asked, "that a simple letter of the Baron de Breteuil should be able to revoke the *lettre de cachet* signed by the King himself, by which I was exiled? I tell you, sir, I can recognize neither M. de Breteuil nor his orders."

He then begged Barthélemy to let him have the letter or a copy of it. The ambassador, however, for some inexplicable reason saw fit to refuse the request, whereupon the interview ended.

There was certainly nothing unreasonable in the request.

"Without having some proof of my permission to return to France," says Cagliostro in the letter he subsequently wrote to the *Public Advertiser*, "how could I have answered the Governor of Boulogne or Calais when I was asked by what authority I returned? I should at once have been made a prisoner."

The next day Lord George Gordon publicly constituted himself the champion of Cagliostro in a letter to the *Public Advertiser*, in which he made an outrageous and utterly unjustifiable attack on Marie Antoinette. No better illustration could be given of the spirit in which the established authorities sought to crush the revolutionary tendency of the times, which had begun to manifest itself, than the price that Lord George was made to pay for his libel. Exasperated by the insults and calumnies that were now continually directed against his unpopular consort,

Cagliostro

Louis XVI ordered his ambassador in London to bring an action against Gordon.

Under ordinary circumstances Gordon, relying on the resentment that England cherished against France for the part she had taken in the American War of Independence, would have had nothing to fear. But he was a rabid demagogue with a bad record. A few years before he had accepted the presidency of the Protestant Association formed to secure the repeal of the act by which the Catholic disabilities imposed in the time of William and Mary had been removed. It was this association which had fomented the famous Gordon riots, as they were called, when London had been on the point of being pillaged. Gordon, it is true, had disclaimed all responsibility for the conduct of the mob, which, however, acknowledged him as its leader, and though tried for high treason had been acquitted. But this experience had not sobered his fanaticism. He was the soul of sedition in his own country, and one of the most notorious and violent revolutionists in Europe at this period. The British Government was only too glad of the opportunity afforded it by the French to reduce him to silence.

Gordon, accordingly, fled to Holland, but learning that the Dutch Government was preparing to send him back, he returned secretly to England. Soon afterwards he was betrayed by a Jew, whose religion he had adopted and with whom he had taken shelter. The action of the French Government having in the meantime been decided against him, he was sentenced to five years imprisonment and to pay a heavy fine. This was the end of Lord George Gordon. For at the expiration of his term of confinement, being unable to pay the fine, he remained a prisoner, and eventually died in Newgate.

Compromised by the dangerous manner in which Gordon had taken up his cause, Cagliostro hastened to disclaim all connection with him. In his letter to the *Public Advertiser*, in which he described his interview with Barthélemy, he referred to the ambassador, the Baron de Breteuil, and the King of France in terms of the greatest respect. Breteuil, however, did not forget him. A month later Barthélemy called in person upon him with a warrant signed by the King's own hand, permitting him to return to France.

Cagliostro received it with profuse thanks, but he did not dare to avail himself of the privilege it accorded him.

"It is but natural," he said, "for a man who has been nine months in the Bastille without cause, and on his discharge receives for damages an order of exile, to startle at shadows and to perceive a snare in everything that surrounds him."

So suspicious did he become that when a friend, who was showing him the sights of London, suggested "an excursion down the Thames as far as Greenwich," he at once scented danger.

"I did not know who to trust," he says, "and I remembered the history of a certain Marquis de Pelleport and a certain Dame Drogard."[1]

Needless to say, he was careful not to write any more letters or pamphlets "with a freedom rather republican." Nevertheless he was a marked man, and Fate was getting ready her net to catch him.

[1] Both of whom had recently been decoyed to France, where they had at once been imprisoned.

Cagliostro

II

Had Cagliostro come to England before his fame had been tarnished by the Necklace Affair, he would in all probability have been lionized by the best society as he was in France. But the unsavoury notoriety he had acquired, the hundred and one reports that were circulated to his discredit and believed, for people always listen more readily to the evil that is said of one than to the good, closed the doors of the aristocracy to him. Instead of floating on the crest of the wave he was caught in the under-current. With few exceptions the acquaintances he made were more calculated to lower him still further in the esteem of respectable society, than to clear him of the suspicion that attached to him. The mere association of his name with Lord George Gordon's would alone have excited mistrust. But the injury he received from the questionable manner in which Gordon sought to befriend him was trifling compared with the interest that the Editor of the *Courier de l'Europe* took in him.

Theveneau de Morande, to give this individual a name, was one of the greatest blackguards of his time —the last quarter of the eighteenth century produced many who equalled him in infamy but none who surpassed him. The son of a lawyer at Arnay-le-Duc in Burgundy, where he was born in 1741, Theveneau de Morande "was," as M. Paul Robiquet truly says in his brilliant study of him, "from the day of his birth to the day of his death utterly without scruple." [1]

[1] *Theveneau de Morande: Etude sur le XVIII*ᵉᵐᵉ *Siècle* par Paul Robiquet. By his contemporaries the name of Morande was never mentioned without an abusive epithet. Brissot, meeting him for the first time in a restaurant in London, "shuddered instinctively at his approach."

Cagliostro Returns to London

When a boy he was arrested for theft in a house of ill-fame. Compelled to enlist or be sent to prison he chose the former alternative, but did not serve long. In response to his entreaties his father obtained his discharge on condition that he would reform. Instead, however, of returning home as he promised, Morande went to Paris, where his dissolute life led him to the prison of For-l'Evêque. Hereupon his father solicited the favour of a *lettre de cachet* by means of which he was confined in a convent at Armentières.

On being released two years later at the age of four-and-twenty, having been imprudent enough to lampoon one of the principal members of the Government, Morande fled the country. After tramping about Belgium he arrived in London in a condition of absolute want. But he was not long without means of subsistence. The ease with which he extorted money by threatening to inform the police of the equivocal lives of such acquaintances as chance threw in his way suggested the system of blackmail which he afterwards developed into a fine art.

Gifted with a talent for writing he ventured to attack notabilities. From fear of his mordant, cynical pen many were induced to purchase his silence. In *Le Gazetier Cuirassé, ou Anecdotes scandaleuses sur la cour de France*, all who had refused to purchase exemption had been represented by him in the worst possible light. For this work, which Brissot describes as "one of those infamous productions the very name of which one blushes to mention," he is said to have received 1,000 guineas.

Emboldened by the fright he inspired he redoubled his attacks, but they did not always meet with the same success. He thought to extort a ransom from Voltaire, but the aged philosopher of Ferney had lived through too much to be frightened for so little. He published Morande's letter, accompanied with commentaries of the sort he knew so well how to make effective. The Comte de Lauraguais replied even more effectively than Voltaire. Not only did he obstinately refuse to pay the tribute demanded of him, but, being in London at the time, gave the blackmailer a horsewhipping, and compelled him to publish an abject apology in the press into the bargain.

Morande, however, was not discouraged, and prepared to reap the most fruitful of all his harvests. For the object he had in view Madame du Barry was a gold mine. The famous favourite of Louis XV was notoriously sensitive on the subject of her reputation, and dreaded nothing so much as a libel. Morande, accordingly, wrote to inform her that he had in preparation a work in four volumes, to be entitled the *Mémoires d'une femme publique*, in which she would figure as the heroine, unless she preferred to pay a handsome sum for its suppression. To assist her to come to the latter decision a scenario of the work was sent her. "*Le Gazetier Cuirassé*," says Bachaumont, who saw it, "was rose-water in comparison with this new *chef-d'œuvre*."

Alarmed and enraged, the poor creature communicated her fears and anger to the King, who applied to George III for Morande's extradition. The attitude of the British Government was characteristic of the political morality of the age. The laws and customs of England rendering the extradition of a foreign refugee out of the question, the French Court was informed that failing an action for libel—which under the circumstances was clearly impossible—the only alternative was to kidnap the libellist. The British Government even offered its assistance, providing that Morande's "removal was done with the greatest secrecy and in such a manner as not to wound the national susceptibilities."

The French Government accordingly sent a brigade of police to London, but Morande was on the alert. Warned from Paris of his danger, he exposed the contemplated attack upon him in the Press, giving himself out as "a political exile and an avenger of public morality"—poses, needless to say, which are always applauded in England. Public sympathy was thus excited in his favour to such a pitch that the French police were obliged to return to France empty-handed, after having narrowly escaped being thrown into the Thames by an infuriated crowd.

Morande, enchanted at having got the better of the French Government, redoubled his threats. He wrote again to Madame du Barry to inform her that 6,000 copies of his scandalous work were already printed and ready for circulation. Louis XV, who had no more fear of a libel than Voltaire, would have let him do his worst, but to please his mistress he decided to come to terms. As this had now become a delicate matter, Beaumarchais was entrusted with the negotiation on account of his superior cunning. The celebrated author who had everything to gain by earning the gratitude of Madame du Barry went to London under the name of Ronac, and in a very short time succeeded in gaining the confidence of the libellist, whose silence was purchased for the sum of 32,000 livres in cash and a pension of 4,000 livres, to be paid to Morande's wife in the event of her surviving him.

It was about this time that Morande, without altogether abandoning his career of blackmail, adopted the more profitable one of spy. Instead of attacking authority, he now offered to serve it. Having been taught his value by experience, the French Government gladly accepted the offer. He began by "watching" the French colony in London, which was composed chiefly of escaped criminals and political refugees, and ended as Editor of the *Courier de l'Europe*.

This paper had been started by a refugee, Serres de Latour, with the object of instructing the French public in the internal affairs of England, particularly as regards her foreign policy. The money to finance the scheme had been supplied by a Scotchman by name of Swinton, who was granted every facility by the Comte de Vergennes, the French Minister for Foreign Affairs, that would assist the enterprise.

Thus protected, the *Courier de l'Europe* was a success from the start. In a short time it had 5,000 subscribers—an enormous number for those days—and a revenue of 25,000 livres. Brissot, the leader of the Girondins in the Revolution, who was connected with it for a time as a young man, estimated its readers at over a million. "There was not," he says, "a corner of Europe in which it was not read."

Such a widely circulated journal naturally had great influence. During the American War of Independence its ever-increasing success alarmed the English Cabinet, which, instead of suppressing it, foolishly endeavoured to circumvent the laws respecting the liberty of the Press by placing an embargo on the bales of the paper destined for export. But Swinton parried this blow by causing it to be printed simultaneously at Boulogne. "Whereupon," says Brissot, "the English Government resigned itself to the inevitable and suffered the *Courier de l'Europe* to continue to injure England under the protection of English law itself." Throughout the war which ended so humiliatingly for England, as Vergennes expressed it, "the gazette of Latour was worth a hundred spies" to France.

Under the editorship of Morande, who succeeded Serres de Latour, the journal, as may be imagined, more than maintained its reputation. "In it," says Brissot, "he tore to pieces the most estimable people, spied on all the French who lived in or visited London, and manufactured, or caused to be manufactured, articles to ruin any one he feared."

Such was the man, and such the weapon, that the Court of Versailles, which had frequently utilized both before, now employed to destroy Cagliostro.[1]

Morande, who had now become the chief of the brigade of police spies, which when he himself had been their quarry he had so loudly denounced in the English press, opened fire, in obedience to his orders, on September 1, 1786. For three months he bombarded Cagliostro unceasingly in a long series of articles that befouled, calumniated, and ridiculed him with a devilish cleverness. Like the Countess de

---

[1] Morande had one redeeming quality. Royalist to the core, he served the French Court loyally till the fall of the monarchy. Imprisoned during the Revolution, he escaped the guillotine by an accident, and having returned to his native town, retired into a respectable obscurity.

Lamotte, he did not hesitate to deny his own statements when others could be made more serviceable. Thus, after affirming " Nature's unfortunate child" to be the son of a coachman of the Neapolitan Duke of Castropignani, he declared him to be the valet of the alchemist Gracci, known as the Cosmopolite, from whom he had stolen all his secrets, which he had afterwards exploited in Spain, Italy, and Russia under various titles : sometimes a count, at others a marquis, here a Spanish colonel, there a Prussian—but always and everywhere an impostor.

In this way rambling from article to article, from calumny to calumny, without knowing where he was going, so to speak, Morande finally arrived at Giuseppe Balsamo—as described at the beginning of the book. The discovery of Balsamo was a veritable *trouvaille*. It enabled Morande to tack on to the variegated career of the Sicilian scoundrel all that he had hitherto affirmed of Cagliostro's past life without appearing to contradict himself. Once on Balsamo's track, he never lost scent of him. He ferreted out or invented all the stories concerning the Balsamos : their marriage, the manner in which they had lived, their forgeries, blackmail, poverty, licentiousness, imprisonment— everything, in fact, that could damage Cagliostro and *his* wife. He found people, moreover, to swear to the truth of all he said, or rather he asserted it, and on the strength of their accusations caused Cagliostro to be sued for debts incurred in the name of Balsamo years before. He collected all the hostile reports of the enemies the Grand Cophta had made in his travels through Europe and afterwards in the Necklace Affair, and re-edited them with the precision of an historian and the malice of a personal enemy. Then, after having done him all the injury he could and given the French Government full value for its money, Morande with brazen effrontery proposed to Cagliostro that he should purchase the silence of the *Courier*!

But Cagliostro was not the man—to his credit, be it said—to ignore the feigned indignation of the libellist who had been hired to ruin him. Aided by Thilorier,[1] his brilliant counsel in the Necklace Affair, who happened to be in England, the wonder-worker published a *Letter to the English People*, in which he flung in the face of the blackmailer all the atrocious acts of his own past. Morande, however, aware that any effort on his part to clear himself of these accusations would be useless, sought to distract attention from the subject by daring Cagliostro to disprove the charges made in the *Courier*. At the same time he thought to stab him to silence by covering with ridicule a statement which he asserted Cagliostro had made to the effect that "the lions and tigers in the forests of Medina were poisoned by the Arabians by devouring hogs fattened on arsenic for the purpose."

The laughter which this reply aroused evidently stung Cagliostro to the quick, and to refute Morande's implied accusation of charlatanism, he wrote the following letter to the *Public Advertiser*, in which, after some preliminary sarcasms, he said—

"Of all the fine stories that you have invented about me, the best is undoubtedly that of the pig fattened on arsenic which poisoned the lions, the tigers,

---

[1] Whether Thilorier had come to England at the request of Cagliostro or not is uncertain, but it is now known that he wrote Cagliostro's replies to Morande's charges.

and the leopards in the forest of Medina. I am now going, sir jester, to have a joke at your expense. In physics and chemistry, arguments avail little, persiflage nothing ; it is experiment alone that counts. Permit me, then, to propose to you a little experiment which will divert the public either at your expense or mine. I invite you to lunch with me on November 9 (1786). You shall supply the wine and all the accessories, I on the other hand will provide but a single dish—a little pig fattened according to my plan. Two hours before the lunch you shall see it alive, and healthy, and I will not come near it till it is served on the table. You shall cut it in four parts, and, having chosen the portion that you prefer, you shall give me what you think proper. The next day one of four things will occur : either we shall both be dead, or we shall neither of us be dead ; or I shall be dead and you will not ; or you will be dead and I shall not. Of these four chances I give you three, and I will bet you 5,000 guineas that the day after the lunch you are dead and that I am alive and well."

Whether or no Morande's perception had been blunted by over-taxing his imagination in the attempt to discredit his enemy, he interpreted Cagliostro's sarcasm literally. Afraid to accept the challenge, but tempted by the 5,000 guineas, he suggested "that the test should take place in public, and that some other carnivorous animal should be substituted for the pig fattened on arsenic." But this suggestion, which revealed his cowardice by reducing the culinary duel to a farce, gave his adversary an opportunity he was quick to seize.

"You refuse to come yourself to the lunch to

which I invite you," wrote Cagliostro in a letter to the *Public Advertiser* which recalls one of Voltaire's, "and suggest as a substitute some other carnivorous animal? But that was not my proposal. Such a guest would only very imperfectly represent you. Where would you find a carnivorous animal which amongst its own species is what you are amongst men? It is not your representative, but yourself, with whom I wish to treat. The custom of combat by champions has long gone out of fashion, and even if I allowed you to restore it, honour would forbid me to contend with the champion you offer. A champion should not have to be dragged into the arena, but enter it willingly; and however little you may know of animals, you must be aware that you cannot find one flesh-eating or grass-eating that would be your champion."

To this letter the unscrupulous agent of the French Court dared not reply. The man he had been hired to defame with his venomous pen had the laugh on his side. The public, moreover, were beginning to detect the mercenary hireling in the detractor, and as the gallery had ceased to be amused Morande, to avoid losing what reputation he possessed, suddenly ceased his attacks, apologizing to his readers for "having entertained them so long with so futile a subject."

Nevertheless, though the victory remained with Cagliostro, he had received a mortal wound. The poisoned pigs of the Arabians were not more destructive than the poisoned pen of Theveneau de Morande. The persistency of his attacks, the ingenuity of his detraction, were more effective than the most irrefutable proof. His articles, in spite of their too evident hostility, their contradictions, their statements either unverifiable or based on the testimony of persons whose reputations alone made it worthless, created a general feeling that the man whom they denounced was an impostor. The importance of the paper in which they appeared, quoted by other papers, all of Europe, served to confirm this impression. Thus the world, whose conclusions are formed by instinct rather than reason, forgetting that it had ridiculed as improbable Cagliostro's own story of his life, accepted the amazing and still more improbable past that Morande " unmasked " without reservation. Nor did the Court of Versailles and its friends, nor all the forces of law and order which, threatened everywhere, made common cause with the threatened French monarchy, fail to circulate and confirm by every means in their power the statements of Morande. As if the stigma which the Countess de Lamotte and the Parliament, for two totally different reasons, had cast upon the reputation of Marie Antoinette was to be obliterated by blighting Cagliostro's !

The deeper an impression, the more ineradicable it becomes. Within a quarter of a century the man whom Morande had called a cheat, an impostor, and a scoundrel had become on the page of history on which his memory is imprisoned the " Arch-quack of the eighteenth century," " a liar of the first magnitude," "an unparalleled impostor."

But in the curious mass of coincidence and circumstantial evidence on which the popular conception of Cagliostro has been based, ingenious and plausible though it is, there is one little *fact* which history has overlooked and which Morande was careful to ignore.

Cagliostro Returns to London

In turning Cagliostro into Giuseppe Balsamo, the fantastic idealist-enthusiast into the vagabond forger, "the charlatan," as Queen's friend Besenval describes him, "who never took a sou from a soul, but lived honourably and paid scrupulously what he owed," into the vulgar *souteneur*, Morande, by no trick of the imagination, with all the cunning calumnies of the French Court, and the so-called "confession" wrung from its victim by the Inquisition, to aid him, could not succeed in making the two *resemble* one another. Yet it is on the word of this journalist-bravo, hired by the French Ministry to defame an innocent man whose unanimous acquittal of a crime in which he had been unjustly implicated was believed by Marie Antoinette to be tantamount to her own conviction, that Cagliostro has been branded as one of the most contemptible blackguards in history.

Surely it is time to challenge an opinion so fraudulently supported and so arbitrarily expressed? The age of calumny is past. The frenzied hatreds and passions that, like monstrous maggots, so to speak, infested the dying carcass of the old *régime* are extinct, or at least have lost their force. We can understand the emotions they once stirred so powerfully without feeling them. In taking the sting from the old hate Time has given new scales to justice. We no longer weigh reputations by the *effects* of detraction, but by its *cause*.

The evidence on which Morande's diabolically ingenious theories are based has already been examined in the early chapters of this book. It requires no effort of the imagination to surmise what the effect would be on a jury to-day if their decision depended upon the

271

evidence of a witness who, as Brissot says, "regarded calumny as a trade, and moral assassination as a sport."

III

The campaign against Cagliostro was by no means confined to defamation. Morande assailed not only his character, but his person.

On the first shot fired by the *Courier de l'Europe*, as if it were the signal for a preconcerted attack, a swarm of blackmailers, decoys, and spurious creditors descended upon the unfortunate Grand Cophta. Warned by the noise that the daring, but unsuccessful, attempts of the secret agents of the French police to kidnap the Count de Lamotte had created, Morande adopted methods less likely to scandalize the British public in his efforts to trepan Cagliostro. While apparently confining himself to the congenial task of "unmasking" his victim daily in the columns of his widely-read journal, he was a party to, if he did not actually organize, the series of persecutions that embittered the existence of the now broken and discredited wonder-worker.

If, as he declared, in his efforts to convince the public that Cagliostro was Giuseppe Balsamo, the perjured Aylett and the restaurant-keeper Pergolezzi were prepared to corroborate his statement, then given his notorious character, unconcealed motive, and the money with which he was supplied by the French Government, the presumption that these questionable witnesses were bought is at least well founded. In the *Letter to the English People* in which Cagliostro, with the aid of Thilorier, sought to defend himself from the charges of the *Courier de l'Europe*, he states, as "a fact well known in London," that Morande went about purse in hand, purchasing the information, witnesses, and accomplices he required.

He offered one hundred guineas to O'Reilly, to whose good offices Cagliostro owed his release from the King's Bench jail in 1777, to swear that he had left England without paying his debts. But though O'Reilly refused to be bought, Swinton, Morande's intimate friend and the proprietor of the *Courier de l'Europe*, proceeding on different lines, succeeded in making mischief between O'Reilly and Cagliostro, by which the latter was deprived of a valuable friend when he had most need of him.

According to Brissot, who knew him thoroughly, and whose testimony is above dispute, Swinton was every bit as unprincipled as his editor. A Scotchman by birth, he had lived the greater part of his life, married, and made his fortune in France. On settling in London he had drifted naturally into the French colony, in which, by reason of his sympathies, connections and interests he had acquired great influence, which he turned to account on every possible occasion. One of his many profitable enterprises was a "home" for young Frenchmen employed in London. "He also ran a druggist's shop," says Brissot, "in the name of one of his clerks, and a restaurant in the name of another." [1] And when Cagliostro arrived in London with a letter of introduction to him, Swinton, who was as full of schemes as he was devoid of principle, thought to run him, too, for his own profit. The

[1] Perhaps Pergolezzi?

273

wonder-worker with his elixirs, his balsams, and his magical phenomena was, if properly handled, a mine of gold.

Taking advantage of Cagliostro's ignorance of the language and customs of the country in which he had sought refuge, Swinton, who was assiduous in his attentions, rented him a house in Sloane Street, for which he desired a tenant, induced him to pay the cost of repairing it, and provided him with the furniture he needed at double its value. To prevent any one else from interfering with the agreeable task of plucking so fat a bird, and at the same time the better to conceal his duplicity, Swinton endeavoured to preclude all approach to his prey. It was to this end that he made trouble between Cagliostro and O'Reilly. Having succeeded thus far in his design he redoubled his attentions, and urged Cagliostro to give a public exhibition of his healing powers, as he had done at Strasburg. But warned by previous experience of the danger of exciting afresh the hostility of the doctors, Cagliostro firmly refused. Swinton then proposed to become his apothecary, and to push the sale of the Grand Cophta's various medicaments, of which his druggist's shop should have the monopoly, in the *Courier de l'Europe*.

To this, however, Cagliostro also objected, preferring, apparently, not to disclose the secret of their preparation—if not to share with the apothecary, as Morande afterwards declared, the exorbitant profit to be derived from their sale. Perceiving that he was not to be persuaded by fair means, Swinton injudiciously tried to put on the screw. But his threats, far from accomplishing their purpose, only served to betray his designs, and so disgusted Cagliostro that he ceased to have any further communication with him. Swinton, however, was not to be got rid of in any such fashion. Living next door to his enemy, his house became the rendezvous of the various bailiffs and decoys hired by Morande to seize or waylay his unfortunate adversary.

Among numerous schemes of Swinton and Morande to capture Cagliostro were two attempts to obtain his arrest by inducing persons to take out writs against him for imaginary debts—a proceeding which the custom of merely swearing to a debt to procure a writ rendered easy. In this way Priddle, who had behaved so scurvily in Cagliostro's arbitration suit with Miss Fry in 1777, was induced to take out a writ for sixty pounds, due, as he pretended, for legal business transacted nine years before. Warned, however, that the bailiffs were hiding in Swinton's house to serve the writ the moment he should appear, Cagliostro was able to defeat their intention by procuring bail before they could accomplish their purpose. In the end it was Priddle who went to Newgate. But instead of the former demand for sixty pounds, Cagliostro, by means of one of the various legal subterfuges in the practice of which the eighteenth century lawyer excelled, was obliged to pay one hundred and eighty pounds and costs.

Immediately after this dearly-bought victory, the baited victim of ministerial tyranny and corruption was similarly attacked from another quarter in a manner which proves how great was the exasperation of his enemies. Sacchi, the blackmailer, who had published a libellous pamphlet against Cagliostro—quoted by

Madame de Lamotte at her trial, when it was generally regarded as worthless, and its suppression ordered by the Parliament of Paris—appeared in London and obtained a writ for one hundred and fifty pounds, which, he claimed, Cagliostro owed him for the week passed in his service in Strasburg in 1781. The impudence of this claim on examination was, of course, sufficient to disprove it ; but Morande, who had brought Sacchi to England and assisted him to procure the writ, all but succeeded in having Cagliostro igno-miniously dragged to Newgate on the strength of it. The proximity, however, of Swinton's house—in which the bailiffs had secreted themselves pending an oppor-tunity of seizing their prey, as on the former occasion—helped to betray their presence, and once again Cagliostro managed to forestall them by giving the necessary bail in due time.

Such an existence was enough to give the most fearless nature cause for alarm, and the Bastille had effectually damped the courage of the Grand Cophta. " Startling at shadows " the pertinacity of his enemies left him not a moment's peace. The fate of Lord George Gordon was ever in his thoughts. If the French Government was powerful enough to effect the imprisonment of an Englishman who had offended it in his own country, what chance had he of escaping ?

His Masonic experiences in England, moreover, were not of a nature to encourage the hopes he had entertained of making converts to the sect he had founded. At first it seemed as if Egyptian Masonry might prosper on English soil. Assisted by a number of adepts from Paris and Lyons, whose zeal had induced them to follow their master to London,

Cagliostro Returns to London

Cagliostro had sought to found a lodge for the observance of the Egyptian Rite. To this end he had held séances which many people of distinction attended. These were so successful that to encourage some of the more promising of his clientele he "transmitted to them, as a mark of exceptional favour, the power to obtain manifestations in his absence." Unfortunately, instead of the angels they expected to evoke, devils appeared.[1] The effect produced upon these inexperienced occultists was deplorable ; combined with the attacks of the *Courier de l'Europe* it effectually killed Egyptian Masonry in England.

The Freemasons, who had welcomed him to their lodges with open arms, as the victim of a degenerate and despicable despotism, influenced by the scathing attacks of Morande, who was himself a Mason, now gave him the cold shoulder. At a convivial gathering at the Lodge of Antiquity which he attended about this time, instead of the sympathy he expected he was so ridiculed by one " Brother Mash, an optician," who gave a burlesque imitation of the Grand Cophta of Egyptian Masonry as a quack-doctor vending a spurious balsam to cure every malady, that the victim of his ridicule was compelled to withdraw.

The mortification which this incident occasioned

[1] Cagliostro's pretended transmission of his supernatural powers, as previously stated, was nothing more than the discovery that the so-called " psychic " faculty, instead of being confined to a few exceptional people, as was till then generally believed, existed in a more or less developed state in everybody. Before his time, and in fact till many years after, the "psychic" faculty was so little understood that the above phenomenon, familiar enough to spirit-rappers and planchette-writers of the present day, was believed to be the work of the powers of darkness whose manifestations inspired terror, of which familiarity has apparently robbed them now-a-days.

Cagliostro

Cagliostro was further intensified by the wide notoriety that it was given by Gillray in a caricature entitled "A Masonic Anecdote," to which the following lines were attached in English and French :—

"EXTRACT OF THE ARABIAN COUNT'S MEMOIRS

"Born, God knows where, supported, God knows how,
From whom descended—difficult to know;
Lord Crop adopts him as a bosom friend,
And madly dares his character defend.
This self-dubb'd Count some few years since became
A Brother Mason in a borrow'd name;
For names like Semple numerous he bears,
And Proteus-like in fifty forms appears.
'Behold in me (he says) Dame Nature's child
Of Soul benevolent and Manners mild,
In me the guiltless Acharat behold,
Who knows the mystery of making Gold;
A feeling heart I boast, a conscience pure,
I boast a Balsam every ill to cure,
My Pills and Powders all disease remove,
Renew your vigour and your health improve.'
This cunning part the arch-impostor acts
And thus the weak and credulous attracts.
But now his history is render'd clear
The arrant hypocrite and knave appear;
First as Balsamo he to paint essay'd,
But only daubing he renounc'd the trade;
Then as a Mountebank abroad he stroll'd;
And many a name on Death's black list enroll'd.
Three times he visited the British shore,
And ev'ry time a different name he bore;
The brave Alsatians he with ease cajol'd
By boasting of Egyptian forms of old.
The self-same trick he practis'd at Bourdeaux,
At Strasburg, Lyons and at Paris too.
But fate for Brother Mash reserv'd the task
To strip the vile impostor of his mask.
May all true Masons his plain tale attend!
And Satire's laugh to fraud shall put an end."

To recover the prestige he had lost in the Masonic world Cagliostro seems for a moment to have sought affiliation with the Swedenborgians, whose extravagant form of spiritualism was not unlike that of the Egyptian Rite. It was undoubtedly with this object in view that he inserted a notice in the *Morning Herald* in which he invited "all true Masons in the name of Jehovah to assemble at O'Reilly's Hotel to form a plan for the reconstruction of the New Temple of Jerusalem." The Swedenborgians, however, failed to respond to the invitation.

Smitten thus hip and thigh, England became impossible to Cagliostro; and having made the necessary preparations he set out with great secrecy and alone for Switzerland some time in May 1787. But Morande even now did not cease persecuting him. Not content with boasting that " he had succeeded in hunting his dear Don Joseph out of England," he circulated the report that " the charlatan had gone off with the diamonds of his wife, who in revenge now admitted that her husband was indeed Giuseppe Balsamo and that all the *Courier de l'Europe* had written about him was true."

This report is another instance of the vindictive rumours on which so much of the prejudice against Cagliostro is based. It was devoid of the least particle of truth, and was deliberately fabricated and circulated solely for the purpose of injuring the man it slandered.

As a matter of fact, in travelling without his wife for the first and only time in his career, Cagliostro did so from necessity. Beset with spies who, as he was informed, suspecting his intention of leaving England had planned to capture him *en route*,[1] he had need of

---

[1] One of his followers, de Vismes, was induced to come to London from Paris on purpose to act as a decoy.

observing the greatest caution in his movements. The Countess Cagliostro, far from being left in "great distress," as Morande asserted, had ample means at her disposal as well as valuable friends in the Royal Academician de Loutherbourg and his wife, with whom she lived till her own departure for Switzerland.

Philip James de Loutherbourg was a painter of considerable note in his day. An Alsatian by birth, he had studied art under Vanloo in Paris, but meeting with little success in France, migrated to England, where fortune proved more propitious. His battle-pieces and landscapes in the Salvator Rosa style were very popular with the great public of his day. Engaged by Garrick to paint scenery for Drury Lane Theatre, the innovations that he introduced completely revolutionized the mounting of the stage. He was also the originator of the panorama. His "Eidophusicon," as he called it, in which, by the aid of mechanical contrivances, painted scenes acquired the appearance of reality, when exhibited in London excited the unbounded admiration of Gainsborough.

Of a decidedly visionary temperament, de Loutherbourg "went in" for alchemy, till his wife, who was equally visionary and more spiritually inclined, smashed his crucible in a fit of religious exaltation. Converted in this violent fashion to a less material though no less absurd form of supernaturalism, the popular Royal Academician, whose pictures at least had nothing mystical about them, became assiduous in attending Baptist chapels, revivalist meetings, and Swedenborgian services. After associating with the enthusiast Brothers, who called himself "the nephew of the Almighty" and was more fitted for a lunatic asylum than the prison to which his antics led him, de Loutherbourg turned faith-healer. At the same time his wife also acquired the power to heal.

Beside the cures the de Loutherbourgs are reported to have performed those of Cagliostro pale into insignificance. Even Mrs. Eddy, of Christian science fame, with her "absent treatment," has only imitated them. Unlike her, the de Loutherbourgs healed free of charge.

Sometimes the sufferer they treated would be in another room or even in another house. On one occasion, if "A Lover of the Lamb of God" is to be believed, they cured "a boy suffering from scrofula who had been discharged from St. Bart's as incurable in five days without seeing him."

Naturally their fame soon spread, and as they professed to be able to cure all diseases, people suffering from all sorts of infirmities flocked to consult them. Horace Walpole declares that de Loutherbourg had as many as three thousand patients. Certain days in each week were appointed for their treatment, which were regularly advertised. On one occasion all the three thousand, apparently owing to some error in the announcement, are said to have surrounded the house at once, so that it was with the greatest difficulty one could either enter or leave it.

"A Lover of the Lamb of God" was so impressed by the miracles the de Loutherbourgs performed as to call upon the Archbishop of Canterbury "to compile a form of prayer to be used in all churches and chapels that nothing may impede their inestimable gift having free course." Their practice, however, was brought to an abrupt close by some indignant patients whom they had failed to cure, and who, accompanied by a mob, attacked the house and very nearly lynched the faith-healers.

De Loutherbourg's mystical tendencies, however, do not appear to have injured him in the least in the opinion of the general public. On resuming his career as painter he found the same encouragement as before, and was highly respected by all who knew him. As contrasted with the enmity of so notorious a black-guard as Morande, the friendship of so estimable a man as de Loutherbourg speaks volumes for Cagliostro's own probity.

The charity of the de Loutherbourgs, on which Morande, Swinton and Company declared that the Countess Cagliostro lived after her husband's escape from their clutches, consisted entirely in defeating their attempts to take advantage of her defenceless state. Receiving information that a writ was to be issued by which Cagliostro's furniture was to be seized, de Loutherbourg advised the Countess to sell it and take up her abode in his house until her husband sent for her, when to ensure her travelling without molest-ation he and Mrs. de Loutherbourg accompanied her to Switzerland.

The first thing that she did on arriving at Bienne was to go before a magistrate and make an affidavit to the effect that her reported corroboration of the charges made against her husband in the *Courier de l'Europe* was a lie. The fact that the Countess Cagliostro did this with the knowledge of the de Loutherbourgs is sufficient to prove the truth of her words.

CHAPTER VIII

"NATURE'S UNFORTUNATE CHILD"

I

On leaving England in 1787 Cagliostro was doomed to resume the vagabond existence of his earlier years; with the difference, however, that whereas previously his star, though often obscured by clouds, was constantly rising, it was now steadily on the decline.

At first its descent was so imperceptible as to appear to have been checked. After the manner in which he had been harried in London the tranquillity and admiration he found in Bâle must have been balm to his tortured spirit. At Bâle he had followers who were still loyal, particularly the rich banker Sarazin, on whom he had " conferred the blessing of a belated paternity," and whose devotion to him, as Cagliostro declared in his extravagant way at his trial in Paris, was so great that "he would give him the whole of his fortune were he to ask for it."

It was at Bâle, moreover, that the dying flame of Egyptian Masonry flickered up for the last before expiring altogether. Under the auspices of Sarazin a lodge was founded on which the Grand Cophta conferred the high-sounding dignity of the "Mother Lodge of the Helvetic States." The funds, however, did not run to a "temple" as at Lyons, but the room in which the faithful met was arranged to resemble as closely as possible the interior of that edifice. Both sexes were admitted to this lodge, and Cagliostro again transmitted his powers to certain of the members who, having been selected for the favour apparently with more care on this occasion than in London, performed with the greatest success.

It was, however, in the little town of Bienne that Cagliostro seems to have resided chiefly while in Switzerland. According to rumours that reached London and Paris "he lived there for several months on a pension allowed him by Sarazin." Why he left this quiet retreat, or when, is unknown. He is next heard of vaguely at Aix-les-Bains, where the Countess is said to have taken the cure. Rumour follows him thence to Turin, "but," says the Inquisition-biographer, "he had no sooner set foot in the town than he was ordered to leave it instantly."

Henceforth fortune definitely deserted him. Against the poison in which Morande had dipped his barbed pen there was no antidote. It destroyed him by slow degrees, drying up the springs of his fabulous fortune, exhausting the resources of his fertile brain, withering his confidence, his ambition, and his heart. But though the game was played, he still struggled desperately to recover all he had lost, till he went to Rome, into which he crawled like a beast wounded to the death that has just enough strength to reach its lair.

The luxury and flattery so dear to him were gone for ever. His journeys from place to place were no longer triumphal processions but flights. Dishonoured, discredited, disillusioned, the once superb High Priest of the Egyptian Mysteries, the "divine Cagliostro," accustomed to be courted by the greatest personages, acclaimed by the crowd, and worshipped by his adherents, was now shadowed by the police, shunned wherever he was recognized, hunted from pillar to post. All towns in which he was likely to be known were carefully avoided ; into such as seemed to offer a chance of concealment he crept stealthily. He dared not show his face anywhere, it was as if the whole world, so to speak, had been turned by some accident of his magic into the Trebizond that the black slave of the Arabian days had warned him to beware of.

If this existence was terrible to him, it was equally so to his delicate wife. The poverty and hardship through which Lorenza Balsamo passed so carelessly, left their mark on the Countess Seraphina. Under the pinch of want her charms and her jewels began alike to vanish. At Vicenza necessity "obliged her to pawn a diamond of some value."

Rumour, following in their track, mumbles vaguely of petty impostures, small sums gulled from the credulous, and of shady devices to make two ends meet, but gives no details, makes no definite charge. If the rumour be true, it is not surprising that one so bankrupt in reputation, in purse, and in friends as Cagliostro had now become, should have lost his self-respect. In the pursuit of his ideal, having formed the habit of regarding the means as justifying the end, what wonder when the end had changed to hunger that any means of satisfying it should have appeared to him justifiable?

At Rovoredo, an obscure little town in the Austrian Tyrol, where he found a temporary refuge, he did not scruple to make capital out of his knowledge of both magic and medicine. Here he managed to interest several persons in the mysteries of Egyptian Masonry to the extent of being invited to give an exhibition of his powers. He even succeeded in founding a lodge at Rovoredo, which he affiliated with the lodge at Lyons, the members of which still believed in him. At the same time, followers being few and subscriptions small, he resumed the practice of medicine, making a moderate charge for his attendance and his medicaments.

But in spite of all his precautions to avoid exciting ill-will or curiosity, it was not long before his identity was discovered. Some one, perhaps the author of a stinging satire [1] which from its biblical style was known as the "Gospel according to St. Cagliostro," notified the authorities. The "quack" was obliged to discontinue the exercise of his medical knowledge in any shape or form ; and the matter coming to the ears of the Emperor Joseph II, that sovereign signed an order expelling him from the town altogether.

Cagliostro then went to Trent, where there reigned a prince-bishop as devoted to alchemy and magic as Rohan himself. This little potentate was no sooner informed of the arrival of the pariah than instead of following the example of his Imperial suzerain, he invited him to the episcopal palace. It was an invitation, needless to say, that was gladly accepted ; for a moment, protected by his new friend, it seemed as if he might succeed in mending his broken fortunes. But while the prince-bishop was willing enough to turn his guest's occult knowledge to account he was not inclined to countenance Egyptian or any other form of Freemasonry.

---

[1] *Liber memorialis de Caleostro dum esset Roberetti* contains an account of Cagliostro's doings in Rovoredo.

Accordingly to allay suspicion Cagliostro foreswore his faith in Masonic observances, sought a confessor to whom he declared that he repented of his connection with Freemasonry, and manifested a desire to be received back into the bosom of the Church.

The prince-bishop, in his turn, pretended to believe in this feigned repentance, boasted of the convert he had made, and, assisted by the reformed wonder-worker, resumed his quest of the philosopher's stone and any other secret his crucible might be induced to divulge. The little world of Trent, however, which had palpitated like the rest of Europe over the revelations of the Diamond Necklace Affair and Morande, was profoundly scandalized. Certain persons felt it their duty to inform the Emperor how the prince-bishop was behaving. The free-thinking, liberty-affecting Joseph II could be arbitrary enough when he chose. Severely reprimanding his episcopal vassal for harbouring so infamous an impostor, he commanded him to banish the wretch instantly from his estates.

Judging from the itinerary of his wanderings in northern Italy and the Tyrol, Cagliostro seems to have intended to go to Germany, hoping, no doubt, to find an asylum, like Saint-Germain, Weishaupt, Knigge and many other, at the Court of some Protestant prince, most of whom were Rosicrucians, alchemists, Freemasons, and revolutionary enthusiasts. But whatever hopes he may have had in this direction were effectually dashed by the hostility of the Emperor. Expelled from Trent in such a fashion he dared not enter Germany.

To turn back was equally perilous. In Italy,

where the Church, brutalized out of all semblance to Christianity by centuries of undisputed authority, regarded the least attempt to investigate the secrets of nature as a reflection on its own ignorance, a certain and terrible doom awaited any one who excited its suspicions. But to Cagliostro, with fate's blood-hounds on his track, an Imperial dungeon seemed a more present danger than an Inquisition torture-chamber. It was no "Count Front of Brass," as Carlyle jeeringly stigmatized him, that was brought to bay at Trent. His courage was completely broken. Spent in this struggle against destiny, he was no longer able to devise new schemes and contrivances as of old. Retracing his steps with a sort of defiant despair, as if driven by some irresistible force to his doom, he took the road to Rome, where he and his wife arrived at the end of May 1789.

According to the Inquisition-biographer it was to please his wife, who desired to be reconciled to her parents, that Cagliostro went to Rome. If, indeed, the parents of the Countess Seraphina, or Lorenza Balsamo, as you will, were still living or even resident in Rome, they were apparently unwilling or afraid to recognize the relationship, for nothing further is heard of them. It is much more likely that Cagliostro chose Rome on account of its size, as being the one place in Italy which offered him the most likely chance of escaping observation. In so large a city his poverty was itself a safe-guard.

Cagliostro's first efforts to drive the wolf from the door were confined to the surreptitious practice of medicine. On such patients as he managed to procure he enjoined the strictest silence. But in

losing his confidence in himself he had lost the art
of healing. The Inquisition-biographer cites several
instances of his failure to effect the cures he attempted
to perform. After "undertaking to cure a foreign
lady of an ulcer in her leg by applying a plaster that
very nearly brought on gangrene," he had the prudence
to abandon altogether a practice that exposed him to
so much danger.

The risk he ran in exploiting his psychic gifts in
Rome was even greater than the peril connected with
the illicit practice of medicine. On leaving Trent
he seems to have resolved to renounce Egyptian
Masonry altogether, and he wrote to such of his
followers as he still corresponded with, imploring
them to avoid all reference to it in their letters
to him. But the occult was now his only resource,
and whether he wished it or not, he was obliged to
turn to it for a living.

In spite of all the efforts of the Church to stamp
out Freemasonry in Italy it still beat a feeble wing.
For two years the Lodge of the Vrais Amis had existed
in secret in the heart of Rome itself. This lodge,
which had received its patent from the Grand Orient
in Paris and was in correspondence with all the principal lodges in France, was really a revolutionary club
of foreign origin. It had been founded by "five
Frenchmen, one Pole, and one American," who, to
judge from the character of the ceremonies they
observed at the initiation of a member, were Illuminés.
As a Freemason and an Illuminé himself Cagliostro
must have known of the existence of this lodge
before coming to Rome.

His fear of the Inquisition was so great that before

making himself known to the Vrais Amis he contemplated leaving Rome altogether. The fall of the Bastille, which occurred about this time, having inaugurated the Revolution in France, he petitioned the States General for permission to return there, as "one who had taken so great an interest in liberty." At the same time not being in the position to take advantage of the privilege were it granted, he wrote urgent appeals for money to former friends in Paris. But in the rapidity with which the Revolution marched, Cagliostro had ceased to have the least importance, even as a missile to hurl at the hated Queen. Whether the petition or the letters ever reached their destination is unknown ; in neither case, however, did he obtain a reply.[1]

With all hope of retreat cut off and starvation staring him in the face, the wretched man timorously proceeded to seek the acquaintance of the Vrais Amis. The difficulties and dangers they encountered in obtaining recruits won for the discredited Grand Cophta a cordial welcome. Notwithstanding, he refused to seek admission to their lodge, and contented himself with begging a meal or a small loan of the members with whom he fraternized.

Even Morande, who had himself experienced the horrors of abject poverty in his early struggle for existence in London, must have pitied the victim of his remorseless persecution had he seen him now. In his miserable lodging near the Piazza Farnese everything—save such furniture as was the property of the landlord—on which he could raise the least money had

---

[1] The *Moniteur*, however, was subsequently informed by its Roman correspondent that he had received bills of exchange from both London and Paris.

been pawned. Not a stone of the diamonds that had so dazzled, or scandalized, as Madame de Lamotte maliciously declared, the high-born ladies of Paris and Strasburg, was left his once lovely, and stilled loved, Countess. Faded, pinched with hunger, she still clung to this man, himself now broken and aged by so many calumnies, persecutions and misfortunes, whose enemies had falsely accused him of treating her brutally, as she had clung to him for fifteen years—the first and the last of his countless admirers and followers.

To one of his vain and grandiose temperament the abasement of his soul must have been terrible as he who had been as good as master of the splendid palace of Saverne cowered day after day in that bare attic with hunger and terror, like sullen lacqueys in constant attendance, and thought of all the past—of the fascinating Cardinal whose friendship had brought him to this pass and who had now forsaken him; of Sarazin, the rich banker " who would give me the whole of his fortune were I to ask for it," dead now, or as good as dead ; of de Loutherbourg, the Good Samaritan ; of the reverent disciples to whom he had been the *père adoré*, the " master "; of the Croesus' fortune which he had lavished so ostentatiously and generously ; of the *gaudeamus* with which the sympathetic crowds had greeted him on his release from the Bastille ; of the miracles of which he had lost the trick ; and last but not least of his fantastic scheme for the regeneration of mankind which he had promulgated with such enthusiasm and success.

One day at a dinner to which some of his Masonic acquaintances invited him when the memory of the past was perhaps more vivid, more insistent than usual, influenced by the festal atmosphere of the occasion, Cagliostro was persuaded to discourse on Egyptian Masonry. But alas! instead of exciting interest as in former times his eloquence was without effect. The ice, however, was broken, and necessity becoming stronger than his fears he endeavoured to procure recruits in the hope of maintaining himself and his wife on their subscriptions.

According to the Inquisition-biographer two men whom he approached resolved to have a practical joke at his expense. They manifested a lively desire to be instructed in the Egyptian Rite, and Cagliostro, deceived into the belief that he had to do with men of means, "by a false diamond, which he took to be real, on the hand of one," decided to gratify them. After having explained to them the aims and character of Egyptian Masonry he proceeded to initiate them in conformity with the usual ridiculous rites, passing them, as Grand Master, by the wave of a sword through the three Masonic grades of apprentice, companion and master at once. But to his mingled terror and mortification when it came to the payment of the fifty crowns that he demanded as their subscription fees, they excused themselves in a manner which showed him only too plainly he was their dupe.

Alarmed lest they intended to inform against him, he thought to avoid the consequences of detection by confessing to a priest as he had done at Trent. It was the last effort of a beast at bay. In accordance with the monstrous principle that the means justify the end confessors have been known on occasion to betray the secrets confided to them in the confessional. In this instance, however, there is no proof that the

Church profaned the sanctity of the sacrament to which it attaches so much importance. It is much more likely that the Inquisition had discovered Cagliostro's presence in Rome, and that the men by whom he had been duped were spies of the Holy Office. On the evening of December 27, 1789, he and his wife were arrested by the Papal police and imprisoned in the Castle of St. Angelo.

Cagliostro, it is said, had been warned of his danger anonymously by some unknown well-wisher. But where could he flee without money? The consolations of the confessional, moreover, seemed to have allayed his fears to such an extent that he did not even take the precaution to destroy any letters or documents that might compromise him.

On the same day that Cagliostro was seized the *sbirri* of the Inquisition made a raid on the Lodge of the Vrais Amis. But the members, who had also received warning, better advised or better supplied with funds than the ex-Grand Cophta, had taken time by the forelock and fled.

II

The manner in which the Papal government tried those accused of heresy and sedition is too notorious to require explanation. In all countries, in all languages, the very name of the Inquisition has become a by-word for religious tyranny of the cruelest and most despicable description. If ever this terrible stigma was justified it was in the eighteenth century, particularly in the Church's struggle with the Revolution for which clerical intolerance was more directly responsible than any other factor of inhumanity and stupidity that led to the overthrow of the *ancien régime.*

In the case of Cagliostro, who was one of the last to be tried by the Apostolic Court, the Inquisition lived up to its reputation. Threatened and execrated everywhere by the invincible spirit of freedom which the fall of the Bastille had released, the Jesuits, who controlled the machinery of the Papal government,[1] strove without scruple to crush the enemies which their arrogant intrigues had created for the Church. To them Freemasonry was a comprehensive name for everything and everybody opposed to them and their pretensions. In a certain sense they were right, and in France at any rate where the lodges and secret societies no longer took the trouble to conceal their aims there was no mistaking the revolutionary character of the Freemasons. So great, therefore, was the fear and hatred that Freemasonry inspired in the Church that in seizing Cagliostro the Inquisition never dreamt of charging him with any other crime. Beside it his occult practices or the crimes of which, on the assumption that he was Giuseppe Balsamo he might have been condemned, paled into insignificance.

The fact that the Inquisition-biographer seeks to excuse the Apostolic Court for its failure to charge him with these offences, on the ground that "all who could testify against him were dead" proves how slight was the importance his judges attached to them. Had they desired to bring him to the gallows for the forgeries of Balsamo, the judges of the Inquisition

[1] The abolition of their Order was but temporary. It had been forced upon the Pope by sovereigns whose power in an atheistical age had increased as his declined. The Jesuits continued to exist in secret, and to inspire and control the Papacy.

would have found the necessary witnesses. As a matter of fact they never so much as attempted to identify him with Balsamo, as they could easily have done by bringing some of the relations of the latter from Palermo.[1]

The news that Cagliostro had been arrested as a revolutionary agent caused great excitement. As the Papal government took care to foster the belief that he was connected with all the events that were occurring in France, the unfortunate Grand Cophta of Egyptian Masonry suddenly acquired a political importance he had never possessed. " Arrested," says the *Moniteur*, " he evoked as much interest in Rome as he had formerly done in Paris." In all classes of society he became once more the chief topic of conversation.

It was reported that before his arrest he had written a circular letter to his followers, of whom he was popularly supposed to have many in Rome itself, calling upon them to succour him in case he should fall into the hands of the Inquisition, and if necessary to set fire to the Castle of St. Angelo or any other prison in which he might be confined. Even from his dungeon, " which was the same as the one that the alchemist Borri had died in a century earlier," he was said to have found the means to communicate with his accomplices without. According to the *Moniteur* " a letter from him to a priest had been intercepted which had led to the detection of a conspiracy to overthrow the Papal monarchy."

[1] To justify the attitude they adopted the Inquisition-biographer was accordingly obliged to blacken the character of Cagliostro by *attributing* to him the infamous reputation of Balsamo as a means of emphasizing the odious lives of Freemasons in general.

Cagliostro

Whether the report was true or not, the Papal government, which had probably circulated it, made it the excuse to arrest numerous persons it suspected. These mysterious arrests caused a general feeling of uneasiness, which was increased by rumours of more to follow. Fearing, or affecting to fear, a rising the Papal government doubled the guards at the Vatican, closed the Arsenal, which was usually open to the public, and surrounded St. Angelo with troops. There was even talk of exiling all the French in Rome.

It required no gift of prophecy to foretell the fate of the unhappy creature who was the cause of all this excitement. From the first it was recognized that he had not the ghost of a chance. Two papal bulls decreed that Freemasonry was a crime punishable by death. To convict him, moreover, the Inquisition had no lack of proof. Laubardemont, Cardinal Richelieu's famous police-spy, deemed a single compromising line sufficient to hang a man. In Cagliostro's case, thanks to his singular lack of prudence in not destroying his papers, the documents seized on his arrest were a formidable *dossier*. Nevertheless, before dispatching their luckless victim the " Holy " Inquisition played with him, like a cat with a mouse, for over a year.

As usual at all Inquisition trials the *forms* of justice were observed. Permission was granted Cagliostro to choose two lawyers to defend him. This privilege, however, was a mockery, for his choice was in reality limited to certain officials especially appointed by the Apostolic Court to take charge of such cases as his. They were not free to acquit; at most their defence could only be a plea for mercy. In the present instance, if not actually prejudiced against their client, they certainly took no interest whatever in him. Aware that he was utterly incapable of paying them for their services, they grudged the time they were obliged to devote to him. Their defence consisted in advising him to acknowledge his guilt and throw himself on the mercy of his judges.

Nor were the witnesses he was likewise permitted to summon in his defence to be depended on. At Inquisition trials all witnesses, fearing lest they should themselves be transformed into prisoners, turned accusers. Before the terrible judges of the Holy Office, whose court resembled a torture-chamber rather than a court of justice, even his wife testified against him.[1] But though surrounded with indifference, contempt or hate, and threatened with death, Cagliostro did not abandon hope. His spirit was not yet wholly broken. The terror in which he had lived so long gave place to rage. Caught in the gin of the Inquisition he defended himself with the fury born of despair, and something of his old cunning.

According to the Inquisition-biographer, when he was examined for the first time four months after his arrest " he burst into invectives against the Court of France to which he attributed all the misfortunes he had experienced since the Bastille." He accused the witnesses of being his enemies, and on being told that his wife had "confessed" he denounced her as a traitress. But the next moment, as if realizing what she must have been made to suffer, "he burst into tears, testified the liveliest tenderness for her, and implored

---

[1] The Roman correspondent of the *Moniteur* states that at each examination of Cagliostro and his wife, the rack was displayed.

the favour of having her as a companion in his cell."

"One may well imagine," reports the Inquisition-biographer, "that this request was not granted." One may indeed! According to the *Moniteur* he also asked to be bled, placed in a larger cell, allowed fresh linen,[1] a fire and a blanket. The first and the last alone were granted him, for the Inquisition had no desire to have him die before they had finished trying him. As, however, his judges professed to be deeply concerned for the health of his soul, when to the above request, he added one for "some good book," no objection was made to satisfy him. He was, therefore, given three folio volumes on "the defence of the Roman Pontificate and the Catholic Church."[2]

Cagliostro took the cynical hint, and after reading the book manifested the deepest contrition, admitted that Freemasonry was a veritable crime, and the Egyptian Rite contrary to the Catholic religion. "No one, however," says the Inquisition-biographer, "believed him, and if he flattered himself on recovering his liberty by this means he was mistaken." Perceiving that this act of repentance, far from being of any avail, only served to furnish his enemies with fresh weapons, he declared that "everything he had done in his life had been done with the consent of the Almighty, and that he had always been faithful to the Pope and the Church."

Unhappily for him, however, he had to deal with

---

[1] In the Bastille he also asked for fresh linen, which was given him. If he dressed like a mountebank, he was at least always scrupulously clean.

[2] *Difesa del Pontificato romano e della Chiesa catholica*, by P. N. M. Pallavicino, Rome 1686.

men of a very different type to those who composed the Parliament of Paris. Nothing he could say would satisfy them. "I will confess whatever you wish me to," he said. Told that the Inquisition only desired the "truth," he declared that all he had said was true. He demanded to be brought before the Pope himself. "If his Holiness would but hear me," he said, "I prophesy I should be set at liberty this very night!"

And who shall gainsay him? With Cardinals and Prince-Bishops steeped in alchemy and the occult, perhaps even the Pope might have been tempted to exploit the extraordinary knowledge and faculties of his famous, mysterious prisoner. It would not have been the first time that the philosopher's stone and the elixir of life had been sought by a Papal sovereign. At any rate Cagliostro's request to be brought before Pius VI was not granted. The judges of the Inquisition were taking no risks calculated to cheat them of their prey.

But to give all the details of this trial as related by the Inquisition-biographer, who was evidently himself one of the judges, would be tedious. Suffice it to say, Cagliostro "confessed," retracted, and "confessed" again, "drowning the truth in a flood of words." One day he would acknowledge that Egyptian Masonry was a huge system of imposture which had as its object the destruction of throne and altar. The next he declared that it was a means of spreading the Catholic religion, and as such had been recognized and encouraged by Cardinal de Rohan, the head of the Church in France.

As regards his own religious convictions, which, by catechizing him on the cardinal virtues and the difference between venial and mortal sins, the Inquisition-biographer asserts to be the chief object of the trial, they were those of the enlightened men of his century. "Questioned," he declared he believed all religions to be equal, and that "providing one believed in the existence of a Creator and the immortality of the soul, it mattered not whether one was Catholic, Lutheran, Calvinist, or Jew." As to his political opinions, he confessed to a "hatred of tyranny, especially of all forms of religious intolerance."

At length, on March 21, 1791, the Inquisition judges brought their gloomy farce to an end. As an instance of the hatred of the Papal government for secret societies and especially for Freemasonry, Cagliostro's sentence is worth quoting in full—

"Giuseppe Balsamo, attainted and convicted of many crimes, and of having incurred the censures and penalties pronounced against heretics, dogmatics, heresiarchs, and propagators of magic and superstition, has been found guilty and condemned to the said censures and penalties as decreed by the Apostolic laws of Clement XII and Benedict XIV, against all persons who in any manner whatever favour or form societies and conventicles of Freemasonry, as well as by the edict of the Council of State against all persons convicted of this crime in Rome or in any other place in the dominions of the Pope.

"Notwithstanding, by special grace and favour, the sentence of death by which this crime is expiated is hereby commuted into perpetual imprisonment in a fortress, where the culprit is to be strictly guarded without any hope of pardon whatever. Furthermore, after he shall have abjured his offences as a heretic in the place of his imprisonment he shall receive absolution, and certain salutary penances will then be prescribed for him to which he is hereby ordered to submit.

" Likewise, the manuscript book which has for its title *Egyptian Masonry* is solemnly condemned as containing rites, propositions, doctrines, and a system which being superstitious, impious, heretical, and altogether blasphemous, open a road to sedition and the destruction of the Christian religion. This book, therefore, shall be burnt by the executioner, together with all the other documents relating to this sect.

" By a new Apostolic law we shall confirm and renew not only the laws of the preceding pontiffs which prohibit the societies and conventicles of Freemasonry, making particular mention of the Egyptian sect and of another vulgarly known as the Illuminés, and we shall decree that the most *grievous corporal punishments* reserved for heretics shall be inflicted on all who shall associate, hold communion with, or protect these societies."

Throughout Europe, which was everywhere impregnated with the doctrines of the Revolution, such a sentence for such a crime at such a time created a revulsion of feeling in Cagliostro's favour. His fate, however, evoked less sympathy for him than indignation against Rome. An article in the *Feuille Villageoise* best expresses the general opinion.

" The Pope," says the writer, " ought to have abandoned Cagliostro to the effects of his bad reputation. Instead he has had him shut up and tried by charlatans far more dangerous to society than himself. His sentence is cruel and ridiculous.

If all who make dupes of the crowd were punished in this fashion, precedence on the scaffold should certainly be granted to the Roman Inquisitors."

That the trial of Cagliostro was really intended by the Papal government as a proof of its determination to show no quarter in its war against the Freemasons may be gathered from the Inquisition-biographer's *Vie de Joseph Balsamo*, which is less a life of Balsamo or Cagliostro, as it purports to be, than a furious attack on Freemasonry, which is depicted in the blackest and most odious colours. Its publication exasperated the secret societies in Lombardy and they were emboldened by the progress of the Revolution to publish a reply. "This pamphlet," says the *Moniteur*, "appeared under the auspices of the Swiss government and produced such a sensation throughout Italy, and particularly in Rome, that the Conclave, terrified at the revolutionary fury it had awakened, instructed its agents to buy up every copy they could find."

The Conclave would have been better advised to suppress the work of the Inquisition-biographer. The account it contains of Cagliostro's trial completely justifies the popular belief in the bigotry, cruelty, tyranny, and total lack of the Christian spirit that characterized the proceedings of the Holy Inquisition.

III

For some time after his trial the public continued to manifest great interest in Cagliostro. The recollection of his extraordinary career gave to his sentence a dramatic character, which made a deep impression on the imagination. Speculation was rife as to his fate, which the Papal government foolishly saw fit to shroud in mystery that only served to keep his memory alive.

All sorts of rumours were current about him. One day it would be said that he had attempted to commit suicide; the next that he was chained to his cell a raving maniac. Again it was rumoured that he had predicted the fall of the Papacy and was impatiently awaiting the Roman populace to march on St. Angelo and deliver him. The *Moniteur's* correspondent relates that in a terrific storm " in which Rome was stricken with a great fear as if the end of the world was at hand, Cagliostro mistook the thunder for the cannon of the insurgents and was heard shouting in his dungeon, *Me voici! à moi! me voici!* "

Knowing, as he did from his Masonic connection, how widespread was the revolutionary movement, and what hopes were raised in Italy by the stirring march of events in France, it is not unlikely that he may have counted on some popular rising to set him free. That he despaired of such a deliverance, however, and contemplated recovering his liberty by his own efforts seems much more probable.

According to Prince Bernard of Saxe-Weimar who guaranteed the accuracy of the story, Cagliostro did, indeed, make a bold attempt to escape from St. Angelo. " Manifesting deep contrition," says the Prince, " he demanded penance for his sins and a confessor. A Capucin was sent him. After his confession, Cagliostro entreated the priest to give him the ' discipline ' with the cord he wore as a belt, to which the latter willingly consented. But scarcely had he received the first blow when he seized the cord, flung himself on the Capucin, and did his best to strangle him. His intention was to escape in the priest's cloak, and had he been in his vigour and his opponent a weak man he might have succeeded. But Cagliostro was lean and wasted from long imprisonment and the Capucin was strong and muscular. In the struggle with his penitent he had time to call for help."

What followed on the arrival of the jailers is not known, but it is not likely that the prisoner was handled with gloves.

As a sequel to that frantic struggle for life and liberty, Cagliostro was secretly sent "in the middle of the night" to the Castle of San Leo, near Montefeltro. The situation of this stronghold is one of the most singular in Europe. The enormous rock, whose summit it crowns, rising on three sides precipitously from an almost desert plain, is like a monument commemorative of some primeval convulsion of nature. In early times it had been the site of a temple of Jupiter, the ruins of which after its destruction by the barbarians became the abode of a Christian hermit, whose ascetic virtues were canonized, and who bequeathed his name to it. In the Middle Ages the holy ruins gave place to an almost impregnable fortress, which at a still later period was converted into a Papal prison, compared to which the Bastille was a paradise.[1]

In the eighteenth century the condition of the surroundings rendered it well-nigh inaccessible. The roads leading to San Leo were only practicable for horses in fine weather; in winter it was only approached on foot. To accentuate still further this isolation, the

[1] San Leo is now a well-conducted Italian state prison.

' Nature's Unfortunate Child '

Papal government had taken care that those convicted of sedition or heretical doctrines, should find there an everlasting seclusion. An official, commissioned by Napoleon to visit and examine the Italian prisons, gives an account of the cells, which were partly in the old castle of San Leo itself and partly excavated out of the rock on which it stands.

" The galleries," he reports, " which have been cut out of the solid rock, were divided into cells, and old dried-up cisterns had been converted into dungeons for the worst criminals, and further surrounded by high walls, so that the only possible egress, if escape was attempted, would be by a staircase cut in the rock and guarded night and day by sentinels.

" It was in one of these cisterns that the celebrated Cagliostro was interred in 1791. In recommending the Pope to commute the sentence of death, which the Inquisition had passed upon him, into perpetual imprisonment, the Holy Tribunal took care that the commutation should be equivalent to the death penalty. His only communication with mankind was when his jailers raised the trap to let food down to him. Here he languished for three years without air, movement, or intercourse with his fellow-creatures. During the last months of his life his condition excited the pity of the governor, who had him removed from this dungeon to a cell on the level with the ground, where the curious, who obtain permission to visit the prison, may read on the walls various inscriptions and sentences traced there by the unhappy alchemist. The last bears the date of the 6th of March, 1795." [1]

[1] " These facts," says Schlosser in his *History of the Eighteenth Century*, "were unknown to Goethe." The same statement may also be applied to Carlyle.

Cagliostro

This is the last definite trace of Cagliostro.

On the 6th October, 1795, the *Moniteur* states "it is reported in Rome that the famous Cagliostro is dead." But when he died, or how, is absolutely unknown. "That his end was tragic," says d'Alméras, "one can well suppose, and his jailers, to make sure that he should not escape, may have put him out of his misery." The *Moniteur* speaks of the probability of such an end as being a topic of conversation in Rome. In any case, it seems impossible to believe that he could long have survived so terrible a doom, which, whatever his offence, was utterly disgraceful to the government that pronounced it.

This mysterious end, so in keeping with Cagliostro's mysterious origin and personality, appeals to the imagination. Nothing excites curiosity like a mystery. Since his death there have been as many attempts to lift the veil in which his end is shrouded as were made in his lifetime to discover the secret of his birth. Of these specimens of sheer futility, Madame Blavatsky's is the most interesting, the most unlikely, and the most popular among the believers in the supernatural who have allowed their imaginations to run riot on Cagliostro generally.

According to the equally extraordinary High Priestess of the Theosophists, Cagliostro escaped from San Leo, and long after his supposed death in 1795 was met by various people in Russia, even residing for some time in the house of Madame Blavatsky's father, where "in the midst of winter he produced by magical power a plate full of fresh strawberries for a sick person who was craving it."

Had Cagliostro survived his terrible sufferings in

San Leo till 1797, when the French invaded the
Papal States, he certainly would have been set at
liberty. San Leo, to which the Pope's troops had
retired, was taken by the famous Polish legion under
General Dombrowski. The first thing the officers did
on entering the fortress was to inquire anxiously if
Cagliostro, whom they regarded as a martyr in the
cause of freedom, was living.

"They thought to rescue him," says Figuier, "and
perhaps even to give him an ovation similar to that
which he had received in Paris after his acquittal by
the Parliament. But they arrived too late. Cagliostro,
they were told, had just died."

According to another version, they demanded to
be shown his grave, and having opened it, filled the
skull with wine, which they drank to the honour of
the Revolution!

The fate of the inoffensive and colourless Countess
Cagliostro was quite as mysterious, though less cruel,
perhaps, than her husband's. The Inquisition sentenced
her, too, to imprisonment for life. She was confined
in the convent of St. Appolonia, a penitentiary for
women in Rome, where it was rumoured she had died
in 1794.

INDEX

Index

Index

Index